The Trekker's Guide to Voyager®

COMPLETE, UNAUTHORIZED, AND UNCENSORED

Hal Schuster

Prima Publishing

Star Trek, Star Trek: The Next Generation, Star Trek: Deep Space Nine, and *Star Trek: Voyager* are registered trademarks of Paramount Pictures Corporation.

This book was not prepared, approved, licensed, or endorsed by any entity involved in creating or producing the *Star Trek* television series or films.

PRIMA PUBLISHING and its colophon are registered trademarks of Prima Communications, Inc.

Library of Congress Cataloging-in-Publication Data

Schuster, Hal.
The Trekker's guide to Voyager: complete, unauthorized, and uncensored/
Hal Schuster.
p.   cm.
Includes bibliographical references
ISBN 0-7615-0572-5
1. Star trek, voyager (television program) I. Title.
PN1992.77.S73S38 1996
791.45'72—dc20   96-8195
                                  CIP

96 97 98 99 GG 10 9 8 7 6 5 4 3 2 1
Printed in the United States of America

How to Order
Single copies may be ordered from Prima Publishing, P.O. Box 1260BK, Rocklin, CA 95677; telephone (916) 632-4400. Quantity discounts are also available. On your letterhead, include information concerning the intended use of the books and the number of books you wish to purchase.

Visit us online at http://www.primapublishing.com

Contents

Preface

Star Trek: Voyager plays with several motifs basic to the human psyche: the stranger in a strange land, the explorer on the new frontier, the camaraderie of shared adventure. Each character is a cliché: the Amerindian on a spiritual quest, the American-born Chinese from San Francisco, the captain, the half-breed suffering inner conflict, the Vulcan, and, in some ways the most familiar cliché of all, the expat ex-aviator who can never return home.

You see, I've met Tom Paris. I've met him in Taipei and Shanghai among the ex-Flying Tigers who fought through World War II. He lives on Sukhumvit Road, just a ride down Ratchadapisek from my home in Bangkok. He worked for Air America, then stayed on when everyone else packed their bags and headed back for America after the Vietnam War. He's been here ever since.

Living in a place where the language, religion, culture, and daily way of life are not your own offers a challenge to a certain kind of restless soul. It offers opportunities not only to learn the new and different but also to rediscover that which is familiar. Most people spend their lives doing the routine, often having accepted choices without conscious thought, not even knowing an alternative existed. Full immersion in a new world changes that.

Voyager is on a similar voyage. Use of cliché characters offers a touch of the familiar in a distant space quadrant to which viewers have never been before. They offer a touchstone. The creators' choice works if the characters grow beyond clichés.

I will try to tell you the story I found when I went in search of *Voyager*, about the creation of the series, the plotting of the continuing adventures, and the decisions of the future. We will also meet the actors, creators, and characters along the way. Side explorations of the 24th century offer diversion on our voyage. Have fun!

Hal Schuster
Bangkok, 1996

Acknowledgments

There are numerous people I would like to thank for granting me permission to use their work. For season one episode deconstructions in Chapter 10, special thanks to Daniel "Admiral Wombat" Feit (df003d@uhura.cc.rochester.edu). Additional thanks to Steve Dinn, Robert Levandowski, Dianne Parry, Timothy Breuning, Tom Thatcher, Ceth Eslick, Cantabile, and Elizabeth Newell.

For the sidebar "52 Reasons Why Janeway Is Better than Picard," thanks to Gerard Monsen. If you have any suggestions, please e-mail them to him at gmonsen@hou.lbl.gov. The master list is held at http://hou.lbl.gov/~gmonsen/janeway.html. Additional thanks to Karyn Lou, Richard Hanson, Davide Hawkins, Dee Elling, Jeffrey K. Stier, Hemi and the Frakmaster, Patrick Stewart Estrogen Brigade (I didn't make this up), Admiral Wombat, Matthew Carlton, Randy Patton, Terry Arzola, Seth Dilday, Mikael G. Haxby, James Railton, and Merv Sutai-Jare'achan.

Additional thanks to Joseph Creighton, Roger Stewart, Jennifer Fox, and, of course, my wife Sirinan, and our understanding nephews, Gop and Dtye.

CHAPTER ONE

Launching Star Trek: Voyager

Star Trek: Voyager came to life when Paramount feared they were putting their biggest cash cow at risk. Sometimes marvelous creations begin from very mercenary motives. Paramount needed a new Star Trek series faithful to tradition that still discovered new directions, since they had decided to cancel Star Trek: The Next Generation while it stood at the peak of its popularity, the most-watched dramatic series in syndication. Star Trek: Deep Space Nine, the only remaining Trek series offering new episodes, had failed to capture a large enough audience.

Gene Roddenberry's brilliantly constructed Trek universe had already supported three television series, one animated series, six movies, hundreds of books, and mountains of merchandise. Clothes, amusement parks, bedding, and even a space shuttle and the Smithsonian Institute bore the mark of Roddenberry's brainchild. But this kind of support depended on the world's continuing love affair with the Star Trek characters and universe, and, perhaps, on the weekly doses of new stories.

The Mission: Recapture the Magic

Paramount knew that the heroes and stories of Star Trek: Deep Space Nine never fully captivated audiences in the same way as the original series and Star Trek: The Next Generation had. DS9's ratings have been anemic compared to its older siblings, and Paramount feared Trekkers might desert

the franchise if all they had was Star Trek: Deep Space Nine. But more than the future of the Trek franchise was at stake—the newly launched United Paramount Network (UPN) would rise or fall on the success of the newest Star Trek series, Voyager. Paramount planned to follow in the footsteps of the successful Fox Network, stepping out of syndication to compete directly with ABC, CBS, and NBC. While Star Trek: Deep Space Nine remained in syndication, Star Trek: Voyager would be the flagship show of UPN, whose executives were banking that the popularity of both the classic Star Trek and The Next Generation would carry over to Paramount's newest Trek. Paramount might not have sold Platypus Man and Pig Sty without

> "For all the new challenges and all the new things fans will see, at the core, Voyager will still very much be Gene's universe."

Star Trek: Voyager. Kerry McCluggage, president of Paramount Television, clearly understood the importance of Star Trek: Voyager when he said, "When you're trying to start a new network, you have to get distribution, and you have to get people to actively make a decision to tune to another channel that they may or may not be used to tuning into on a regular basis. When you're asking stations to make that kind of commitment, and you're asking the viewing public to change their habits, you have to give them a strong reason to do that. *Star Trek* is a powerful motivator."

Star Trek: Voyager's executive producer Jeri Taylor told *Entertainment Weekly*, "There's a great deal of pressure on us. Affiliates were drawn into the fold by the prospect of getting *Voyager*. We know the expectations are inordinately high." They knew their ratings wouldn't equal those of *Star Trek: The Next Generation*, though. *Star Trek: Voyager*'s executive producer Michael Piller told *Entertainment Weekly*, "*Voyager* will not have the same ratings that *The Next Generation* had. It just won't. I don't think even the studio expects that."

Paramount understood its mission. They needed the first Star Trek series created after the death of its creator to recapture the magic of the original. With the added pressure of launching a new network, they needed it to be good, hoping to lure advertisers and television stations with viewers hungry for more Trek. However, they could no longer turn to Gene Roddenberry for help in guiding the expanding Trek universe.

Star Trek After Roddenberry

No one knew for certain if there could be Star Trek after Roddenberry. But perhaps Paramount remembered, even as others had forgotten, that there already was Star Trek without Roddenberry. Eric Stillwell, the script coordinator of *Star Trek: The Next Generation*, has said that Gene Roddenberry was only heavily involved in the first three seasons of *The Next Generation*, and that by seasons four and five, before Gene's death, the show had already effectively become Trek without Gene. Ominously, he also said that the writers and producers did not agree with Gene's "perfect world, people, and relations," that they deemed it "boring." Roddenberry had little part in creating *Star Trek: Deep Space Nine*, which abandoned his bright vision and suffered in its audience ratings. And yet, if *The Next Generation* now belongs more truthfully to Rick Berman, Michael Piller, and Jeri Taylor than to Gene Roddenberry, Roddenberry still supplied the pioneering vision.

Paramount knew the answer lay in returning to the roots of Roddenberry's creation and extending them in new directions. Pilot director Winrich Kolbe told *Cinescape*, "Rick Berman and Michael Piller may create new series, but they never forget who started this whole thing. Ultimately, as long as it's Star Trek, it will be Gene Roddenberry's. It's all a matter of where you start from." Taylor was very open about their debt to Roddenberry's vision, telling *Orbit*, "*Voyager* has a high action and adventure quotient. It has a fascinating blend of characters that are everything we've come to expect from our characters. For all the new challenges and all the new things fans will see, at the core, *Voyager* will still very much be Gene's universe."

Michael Piller underlined the same point when he said to *Entertainment Weekly*, "You go back to the original show in the '60s and the spirit of that was: one ship with a bunch of people, out there alone, exploring the unknown, never sure what they were going to find around any corner. That's what we wanted, so that *Voyager* wouldn't be just a pale imitation of *The Next Generation*."

A Vision of the Future

Plans for the new series began before many knew that *The Next Generation* would end only a year and a half after *Deep Space Nine* premiered. Paramount publicly denied plans for ending the series, although, a half decade before, Majel Barrett had announced that Paramount would run the series for six years. It ran a season longer than intended.

Finding a hit replacement series for their new network would not be easy. How could they restore the Trek franchise to full glory, keeping the keystones of the original series, without repeating themselves? Had the final frontier been completely explored?

For *Voyager*, Berman, Piller, and Taylor, the series cocreators, imagined a small spaceship that would bring its crew together as a family and stories that would deliver exciting action as well as messages relevant to both eternal issues and the problems confronting humankind in the '90s. They wanted to force their characters into a new place, out of easy, frequent contact with the rest of Starfleet. They wanted to explore new worlds, encounter new civilizations, and meet new alien races. If one space quadrant

had now been trod too often to offer surprises, they would lose the new ship in an unexplored quadrant far from home.

Creating the new series, Taylor said to the *L.A. Times,* "was a very daunting experience, because between the original series, *The Next Generation*, and *Deep Space Nine*, so much territory had been covered with storytelling and characters. Every direction we went, it seemed like we were repeating ourselves." While speaking at a *Star Trek* convention, she said, "The Alpha Quadrant was getting to be a little bit like *Mr. Roger's Neighborhood*. It was very cozy, very comfortable, you knew everybody. That sense of the unknown, of the wonder, the excitement, was not necessarily there. So we feel it is our responsibility to populate the Delta Quadrant with fascinating new aliens, which will be just as interesting to the audience eventually as the Klingons are to them now." Further amplifying her point, Taylor told *Entertainment Weekly*, "We are cutting our ties with a part of the universe that our audience is very comfortable with. No more Klingons, or Romulans, or Cardassians. The Federa-

> *Everything that we've known during the last twenty-five years of Star Trek is somewhere else, and we are going to face all new challenges, all new aliens.*

tion is seventy thousand light-years away. We are taking all of that away and starting from scratch."

Piller added, "When we created this show, we basically said to ourselves, 'Based on our current place in history, where does Star Trek fit in? We find ourselves today as a society, here in America, with a lot of problems that cannot be easily and quickly solved. We're working on solving problems for our children. The *Voyager* is on the same journey.'

"Jeri, Rick, and I realized, when we started this process, that what we were coming up with must be similar to what Gene Roddenberry faced when he created the original *Star Trek* because we have taken our ship to the edge of the galaxy. We don't know anybody who's there; we don't know the aliens, we don't know the politics, we have no contact with home. Everything that we've known during the last twenty-five years of Star Trek is somewhere else, and we are going to face all new challenges, all new aliens. Of course, we have the advantage of having the Starfleet language and tradition that Gene gave us. It's a very exciting and somewhat intimidating circumstance we've put ourselves in as writers."

General concepts crystallized into specific plans. Berman outlined the details of the new series for *Orbit*: "There is a ship that a Starfleet vessel is following. One of these vessels is the *Voyager*, the other is inhabited by a small number of Maquis renegades. Renegades may be too strong of a word, but they're ex-Starfleet officers who have taken on a certain vigilante-type activity near their home planets. Both this ship and the *Voyager*, through a series of circumstances I don't want to give away, find themselves at the very end of the galaxy, seventy-five years from Earth, even if traveling at top warp speed."

The series creators also wanted to recapture the feel of the original triangle of characters—Kirk, Spock, and McCoy. However, this time the hard-driving captain would be female, the powerful first officer an American Indian, and the crusty doctor a hologram. A Vulcan would again walk the bridge, but this time he would be black.

Newer elements also appeared, such as the Maquis. These rebel freedom fighters, at odds with the Federation but still part of it, were introduced on *The Next Generation* and *Deep Space Nine*, but on *Voyager*, half the crew would be Maquis rebels and half would be Federation Starfleet officers, creating the potential for new dramatic conflict aboard the starship. Kolbe loved the idea, telling *Cinescape*, "Right now I'm very high on *Voyager*. I think we have an excellent opportunity to just take off and break new ground. We're pushing the envelope here. I want to keep on pushing."

Choosing a Captain

As *Voyager* was being put together, the Trekker grapevine roared with rumors. One rumor reported that the studio opposed having a female captain as the series lead. The rumor had the ring of truth because a studio (Desilu, before Paramount bought it), and the NBC network, had once before stood squarely in the path of placing a woman in a key power role in a Trek series. For the original *Star Trek,* Roddenberry had wanted to cast a woman, Majel Barrett (whom he later married), as first officer aboard the *Enterprise,* but the studio balked at the idea. Leonard Nimoy, who played Star Trek's original Vulcan, Spock, recalled the story in his book *I Am Spock* (Hyperion, 1995). Nimoy wrote, "Gene was fond of telling the story this way: 'NBC finally said that either the woman or the Martian—meaning Spock—had to go. So I kept the Vulcan and married the woman, because, obviously, I couldn't have done it the other way around.'" Nimoy may have expressed relief upon hearing Roddenberry's decision. Perhaps Nimoy's wife, the former Sandi Zober, did so as well.

Berman insisted there was no truth to the rumor, telling *Entertainment Weekly,* "I told them, 'I want to do this with a woman,' and they were very supportive. They just said, 'Let's not close the door to men. Look at men as well.' But being opposed to hiring a woman—that's nonsense. They just weren't 100 percent sure we would find the right woman."

Men and women tested for the part. Kolbe told *Cinescape,* "We did make some attempts to look at male actors for the part when time was running out, and it seemed that we might have a problem, but every time a male read for Janeway, I couldn't quite get my head into it. There is a difference a woman would bring that we all felt was important."

Still, Piller told *TV Guide,* "Early on [in the talent hunt], we had two female candidates that we felt quite good about but the studio didn't." In August, with shooting scheduled to begin in a month, Robert Picardo, the actor who portrays *Voyager's* Holodoc, told a Chicago Star Trek convention audience that the plan for a female captain had been abandoned. Despite Berman's statements to the contrary, many still believed that the studio feared male fans would reject a female commander. Taylor told the *L.A. Times,* "One of the dangers in choosing a woman with a show that has a high male demographic is that the men in the audience would not accept her as a commander. So we knew that we needed to find someone who would be convincing; who had a sense of authority."

They made contingency plans. If the captain became a man, the Amerind first officer and Asian ensign would be recast as women. When this became known, the Internet and other electronic bulletin boards came alive with rapid fire exchanges of heated protest. For the first time, the world's electronic highway played a role in creating a television series, providing fans with inexpensive, effective, and instant mass communication. Both male and female fans drowned Paramount in a torrent of faxes and letters supporting the producers' original plan for a female captain at the center of a Trek series.

With this ammunition in hand, the producers stuck to their guns, despite time strictures and studio pressures. Berman said, "We thought it was time to put a woman at the helm and to create a character who was not just a captain who happened to be a woman but a captain who was different in ways that women can be different than men."

Actor Nigel Havers, best known for his role in *Chariots of Fire*, almost got the part. Then someone suggested Genevieve Bujold, and everyone liked the idea. They cast her without a screen test, which later led to problems. Kolbe later told *Cinescape*, "I told Rick, 'This will either be a total disaster or a total triumph.' At that point I didn't know which it was going to be. At that particular moment, I guess there was a little panic to get somebody so we could get going. Some of us were very high on Genevieve, so we hired her."

After an apparently successful search for their captain, an optimistic Jeri Taylor told *TV Guide*, "It's been hard casting the captain regardless of gender—because whoever we picked would be in the bright, blinding light of Patrick Stewart." She still didn't know how difficult it would prove to be.

Although Genevieve Bujold carried an impressive résumé, she lasted only two days on the job. She arrived on the set on September 7, and by the end of the day on September 8, she had turned in her Starfleet pips. Paramount announced that Bujold left because of the demands of a weekly television series. The studio paid off her contract, reportedly around $300,000, and said nothing negative about the actress. But rumor reported she had problems with her wardrobe, her hairstyle, and even the notoriously difficult Trek technical dialogue. *Parade Magazine* said, "It has been reported that she didn't like the script, the costumes, and—according to at least one account—a request that she pad her bra. But the major factor

was the hectic production schedule." Tim Russ, *Voyager*'s Tuvok, later told *Entertainment Weekly*, "There was this feeling of unease when we were working with her. I wrote it off to her getting started, but as it turns out, it probably would have been fairly consistent." Robert Duncan McNeill, the actor who portrays Paris, agreed, adding, "She just didn't fit. It was clear to everybody."

Series pilot director Winrich Kolbe told *Cinescape* it was more than just the hectic TV schedule, which the movie actress didn't fully appreciate at first, that discouraged her. "Her concept of the show was completely her own. I do not understand why she took the show in the first place. It turned out that her idea of the captain was that she wasn't really a captain. She wanted to be Genevieve Bujold, not Captain Janeway. She didn't want to run the ship. We shot for a day and a half, we did a lot of things, and she was pretty much involved in everything. I tried to get her to give us the authority that I wanted from the character, and that never came through. We had a chat about it, and I said, 'Why can't you give it to me?' She said to me, 'I don't want to be Janeway, I want to be me.'

"We started shooting her on Monday, working hard to get going, and on Tuesday afternoon we were just about ready to break

> If the captain became a man, the Amerind first officer and Asian ensign would be recast as women.

for lunch when she said, in front of every-one, 'It's just not working out too well. I don't think I'm right for the part.' To which I said, a little bit angry, 'Don't ever say that!' Not because I wanted to lecture her or be-cause she was wrong but because she shouldn't have said this in front of the crew. It creates a psychological problem. The cap-tain of the ship is supposed to be the cap-tain of our crew, of us. The star of a show is not just an actor or an actress. He or she defines how a unit works. Patrick Stewart did it his way; Avery Brooks does it his way.

"At that moment I got together with her; we had a chat about the situation. I called the producers, and about half an hour later it was decided to cancel her re-lationship with the show. It wasn't that Paramount or anyone fired her, she just decided to pull out."

Bujold appears to have no intention of telling her side of the story. Her publicist only told *Parade*, "She realized it wasn't for her, and she wanted to let people know sooner rather than later."

All this served to heighten tensions on an already strained set. Most new television se-ries suffer from behind the scenes birth pains. *The Next Generation* kept its out of the public eye. *Star Trek: Voyager* had worse luck. It became common knowledge that Bujold had walked off the set in front of the whole crew. The fledgling show's morale began to dip. Bujold's interpretation of Cap-tain Janeway had pleased no one. An un-named source told *TV Guide*, "Midway through her second day, she walked off the set and no one went running after her." The producers hurried to recast the role, consid-ering Kate Mulgrew, Linda Hamilton, Lind-say Wagner, and Joanna Cassidy, among many others.

Meanwhile, new rumors spread that *Star Trek: Voyager* had fallen disastrously behind schedule and that Berman was spread too thin with obligations to three television se-ries to do his job properly. Berman, show-ing visible signs of strain, told *TV Guide*, "People don't realize we had a big buffer zone in our production schedule, which al-lowed us to take our sweet time to find the right captain. We were—and remain—completely within our time and budgetary parameters. I'm spread no thinner than I have been for the last three years. *Next Gen-eration* wrapped six months ago. For the last three months, my involvement with the movie has been minimal. [The insinuations] are just not valid. The whole situation has gotten out of hand. All we really want to do is make good television. People have pur-posely been looking for things to bitch about; they're grabbing onto ridiculous, completely false information. It's annoying. It's insulting. It's hurtful."

Kate Takes the Helm

Kate Mulgrew disliked her original video-taped audition for Captain Janeway. She had gone to the studio to do a second audi-tion on the day Paramount signed Genevieve Bujold to the part. That second audition now helped her land the role. On September 16, one week after Bujold quit, the producers announced Mulgrew as the new captain, and the crew applauded her when she arrived on the set the first day. Russ said, "It was an absolute relief. When Kate came in during her first scene, she marched in, said her lines, and we were ready to go. It was definitely the captain on the bridge at that point. It was a major and welcome difference."

At the time, Mulgrew observed, "In the wake of what happened with Genevieve, I feel both a great responsibility and great expectation. I've set some pretty high standards for myself because I feel what I absolutely have to do here on *Voyager* is what no woman has done before. We do not want a butch, screaming, tough broad. We want an excellent human being running this ship, one who's sexy, alive, and who is completely in control of what she's doing on that ship."

> When Kate came in during her first scene, she marched in, said her lines, and we were ready to go.

Berman later said, "We look at Kate and can't even imagine anyone else sitting in that captain's chair. The Genevieve Bujold incident was a blessing. It was a marriage that wasn't meant to be—and, luckily, we found that out before there were any children."

Mulgrew quickly learned that her new role required long hours of work. She now refers to her trailer on the lot not as her home away from home but *as* her home. Then there's the notorious Star Trek technobabble. She compares that challenge to learning medical terminology when she played a doctor on the short-lived 1988 TV series *Heartbeat*. She said, "The same kind of fidelity applies here. We're in the operating room. Just because you and I don't really understand it doesn't take me off the hook. I have to endow the words. I have to know what they mean. Or I have to make it up in my brain so that I understand it, and then it has to be like water off a duck's back."

At first it appeared that *Star Trek: Voyager* would enter the history books as the first television series to put a woman at the helm of a starship as the lead. Then Steven Spielberg's *Earth 2* beat *Voyager* to America's living rooms. It featured a female commanding officer. That ended Star Trek's chances of breaking that particular gender barrier—even though, three decades earlier, Majel Barrett had played the first officer in the original, unaired pilot of the classic *Star Trek*, only to be removed from the series by the network and studio.

Choosing the Crew

Then another rumor spread. *The Next Generation*'s seventh season episode "Lower Decks" focused on a new group of crewpeople, including a Vulcan, and word had it that these characters would be the new *Star Trek: Voyager* cast. While that rumor proved false, strong similarities exist.

Chakotay, the Amerind first officer, and Tuvok, the full-blooded Vulcan security chief, proved difficult to cast. There are few

Amerinds in the Screen Actors Guild, and Kolbe told *Cinescape*, "You're probably talking about two handfuls of actors who are well known enough to ask to be considered. We had another actor in mind, but there were pros and cons. Ultimately it came down to two actors." They finally chose Robert Beltran, one of the pair, for the role of Chakotay, the Maquis captain who becomes Captain Janeway's first officer aboard the *Voyager*. Beltran, a veteran television, film, and theater star, said of his role, "Chakotay is a man deeply committed to his people, the Maquis. While he is passionate about the Maquis cause, he understands the discipline necessary to run the starship *Voyager*. As a result, he is often in conflict between two worlds."

The first series bible caused problems casting Tuvok. He was originally 160 years old. Kolbe told *Cinescape*, "When we were looking for established, older actors to play the part of Tuvok, we had some damn good actors come in and read for us, but we couldn't quite agree. So we started scaling down the age." They finally chose Tim Russ. The actor had almost been cast as Lieutenant Commander Geordi La Forge in *The Next Generation*. His strong showing led to guest appearances as a terrorist on *The Next Generation*, as a Klingon on *Deep Space Nine*, and as a lieutenant in the film *Star Trek: Generations*. Russ told *Sci-Fi Entertainment*, "I think our show is a throwback to the original series as far as the type of characters we have. We have a variety of cultures and races on the ship. Also, we're able to fly through uncharted space, so by virtue of circumstance, we're doing the same kind of

things they did on the original series. I feel we also have some of the same qualities of *The Next Generation* in terms of the production value, dialogue, and style."

After Harry Kim (Garrett Wang), B'Elanna Torres (Roxann Biggs-Dawson), the Doctor (Robert Picardo), Tom Paris (Robert Duncan McNeill), Kes (Jennifer Lien), and Neelix (Ethan Phillips) had been cast, the crew stood ready to fly the starship *Voyager*.

Starship Voyager

The new ship's name has precedent. Two real-world, NASA deep-space satellites launched in the early 1970s bore the name *Voyager*, and a *Voyager VI* satellite returned to Earth in the twenty-third century, under the name "V'ger," in *Star Trek: The Motion Picture*.

The *Star Trek: Voyager Writers'-Directors' Guide, First Season Version*, produced by Paramount, reported that the *Voyager* "is smaller, sleeker, and more advanced than the *Enterprise*." It holds a crew of some 125, elsewhere reported as 140, "and does not have families on board." By comparison, the *Enterprise-D*, seen on *The Next Generation*, a Galaxy-class Cruiser, would run the length of the entire Paramount Studios lot and carries a thousand-plus people, but it can accommodate fifteen thousand in an emergency.

The *Guide* continued, "The ship is outfitted with many of the same facilities as the

Enterprise: bridge, engineering, briefing room, captain's ready room, crew's quarters, transporter room, cargo bay, holodecks, and a general eating-gathering room called the officer's mess. One of the technological improvements is the inclusion of bio-neural circuitry [combining electronic and organic components].

Voyager has the capacity to land on a planet and to take off again. Its nacelles are articulated and move into an 'up' position when jumping to warp speed. This is part of a new technology which allows the ship to fly at warp speed without damaging the fabric of space."

Both starships carry bridge plaques bearing a legend. While the *Enterprise-D* plaque reads, "To boldly go where no one has gone before," *Voyager* carries the words of the poet Alfred Lord Tennyson, "For I dipped into the future, far as the human eye could see, saw the vision of the world, and all the wonder that would be."

Voyager weapons include hand phasers and a "Compression Phaser Rifle." The series uses both the regular tricorder and a medical tricorder, which includes a detachable scanning mechanism.

The new ship design created a number of story possibilities. The smaller complement allowed for more of a feeling of family aboard ship. The bio-neural circuitry suffers from the many maladies that afflict organic beings, including infection, addiction, hallucination, starvation, and, possibly, even madness.

Shooting Begins

Television production schedules require multiple episodes to share production at any given time. The studio films one episode while another is in editing and postproduction and a third is in preproduction. They often build sets and write scripts several weeks in advance. They take costume measurements on Monday, do fittings on Tuesday, and film with the actors on Wednesday.

The staff at Paramount creates motion-control photography using a computer-controlled camera. Specialists build models and paint mattes. Dick Bromfield works on pyrotechnic effects, such as miniature explosions. He worked on the very first *Star Trek* pilot, "The Cage," which starred Jeffrey Hunter. Bromfield said the technology today is "just astounding." Sophisticated electronics have replaced much of the primitive methods used on the original show, which used "hoses and moving things, and a lot of puppeteering work."

The *Voyager* model surpasses previous ship models in detail. Slides contained in

> **The bio-neural circuitry suffers from the many maladies that afflict organic beings, including infection, addiction, hallucination, starvation, and, possibly, even madness.**

windows correspond to that part of the vessel, allowing viewers to look inside the ship. Today's sophisticated special effects help make the characters and their ship "real" to viewers. David Stipes heads a special effects company that works on *Voyager*. He elaborated on a point mentioned in *The Guide*, saying, "One of the features that's going to be very unique on this craft, as opposed to the *Enterprise*, will be that the wings [nacelles] will raise up for the warp functions, so we will see the ship come flying along. The wings will raise up, and we'll have a nice blue warp engine flash, and then it will streak off into warp."

The studio shot parts of the premiere episode, "Caretaker," on location, such as at the El Mirage dry lake bed in Southern California, which was the surface of a desert planet. Kolbe, who directed the episode, explained, "This has been an especially difficult shoot because we have so many extras who require extensive prosthetic makeup." Applying hair and makeup took several hours each morning before transporting the extras to the desert locale.

The Voyage Ahead

Devoted fans as well as the general public anticipated an exciting new Star Trek even before they had seen the first episode. They surprised the cast of *Star Trek: Voyager* with their unbridled enthusiasm. Ethan Phillips, who plays Neelix, told *TV Guide*, "I'm getting fan mail, and we haven't even finished shooting the first episode. If it all goes right

and they keep me, it's a security you don't often get as an actor."

An equally surprised Robert Picardo, the actor who portrays the series's holographic doctor, told *Entertainment Weekly*, "Does the prognosis look good to me? Yes, it does. I am definitely looking forward to the possibility that these characters could go beyond television. As an actor, I've never had a job like this, where you think in terms of something lasting that long."

Perhaps Beltran summed up their attitude best when he told *Entertainment Weekly*, "We're going to really have to suck to fail." Ratings for the *Star Trek: Voyager* premiere episode "Caretaker" hit big, racking up spectacular audiences in every major market, seeming to justify Beltran's confidence in the new series. In twenty-nine metered markets, the show averaged a 14.5 rating/20 share at 8–10 P.M., according to Nielsen overnight numbers supplied by UPN. Fox finished second to UPN, followed by CBS, NBC, and ABC. In Sacramento the premiere pulled in a whopping 25/34 for the two hours. By comparison, the station's average rating and share for the month before *Voyager* pre-

> "We wanted to return to the original series' sense of being out in the unknown, to that sense of adventure that you're going out there where no one has gone before."

miered was a 2.9/4. *Voyager* was nearly as dominant in the larger markets. In Los Angeles, it averaged a 20.7/27 and was number one in the time period for every half hour between 8 and 10 P.M. The 20.7 rating beat any two of the Big Three networks' ratings combined.

The premiere attracted an enthusiastic audience, but it remains to be seen if the series will hold viewers for an extended run, creating interesting characters and involving stories. *Star Trek: Voyager* began with many strengths but perhaps a few unexpected weaknesses as well.

The Creators

Gene Roddenberry created the Trek universe. D. C. Fontana, Samuel Peeples, Gene L. Coon, and others helped him populate the Alpha Quadrant (though we didn't know it by that name at the time) with Vulcans, Klingons, Romulans, and myriad other races. Later, other creative minds helped Roddenberry add a "next generation," including Cardassians, Bajorans, Dominion, Borg, Ferengi, and many more races to that now familiar space quadrant. Now, after Roddenberry's death, Rick Berman, Jeri Taylor, and Michael Piller have extended that universe, adding a new Delta Quadrant, complete with new races and unexplored worlds. The three creator/producers have crafted the first addition to the Trek universe built completely without Roddenberry.

Taylor admitted to a convention audience, "Most of us are not that familiar with the original series. As I think you all know, there are only so many stories in the universe, and what's important is the way they're told. We wanted to return to the original series's sense of being out in the unknown, to that sense of adventure that you're going out there where no one has gone before. That's the reason we put them in the Delta Quadrant, to get away from the familiarity."

Piller said, "It's a litmus test that we put through every idea in the room: What does this touch that we've done before? How do we make it different if it's in a, you know, certain genre—time travel—or whatever it is? How do we get away from what we've done before and do something fresh and new?"

Berman said that breaking away from what has already appeared is difficult. "There have been over 350 hours of *Star Trek* produced, and I would challenge anybody to come up with a story that would not relate in some way to one of those 350 stories. There's always going to be comparisons and similarities between stories about a group of people on a space ship that lasts approximately forty-five minutes. So we try—we try very hard. We've had stories pitched that we all like, and someone says, 'That's Episode 24 of the original series, called "The Blossoms of Katiria 3,"' and none of us ever saw it. The potential of similarity is always there when you have so many episodes."

Berman added, "I think it's also important to note that when you're doing Star Trek, anything can happen, really. So we have wormholes and we have alternate realities and parallel universes."

Taylor noted that while they will make additions to the Star Trek universe, they do intend to keep the familiar, popular elements. "We'd like to keep the franchise of the show, which is we're out there in the unknown, we don't know what's coming around the next star or the next nebula. There will be monsters out there, and some of those bigger action, shoot-'em-up kinds of adventures will appear throughout the season. There was a conscious attempt to rekindle that sense of adventure. But in terms of storylines, of course not, we try to tell fresh stories as uniquely as we can."

Most fans are familiar with the story of the fighter pilot turned L.A. cop turned television producer, Gene Roddenberry. Fewer know the backgrounds of the new heads of the Star Trek universe, Rick Berman, Michael Piller, and Jeri Taylor.

Rick Berman

Berman served as producer and cowriter of the feature film *Star Trek: Generations*, executive producer of *Star Trek: The Next Generation*, and creator/executive producer of *Deep Space Nine* before coming to *Voyager*. He began his service as executive producer on *The Next Generation* at its inception in 1987. Under Berman and creator/executive producer Michael Piller, the series became the first syndicated show in this decade to be nominated for an Emmy Award for Outstanding Drama. With fifty-five Emmy nominations, the series remains one of the

most nominated dramatic series on television. With Berman and Piller at the helm of the series, *Star Trek: Deep Space Nine* has consistently ranked among the top ten hour-long series on television and soared to the number-one position among new hour-long series on television among eighteen- to forty-nine-year-old men.

Berman first came to Paramount in 1984 as director of current programming, overseeing *Cheers*, *Family Ties*, and *Webster*. A year later, he moved over to executive director of dramatic programming, to head up the miniseries *Space*, *Wallenberg: A Hero's Story*, and ABC's top-rated series *MacGyver*. He received a promotion in May 1986 to vice president of longform and special projects for UPN. His new responsibilities included the development of telefilms, miniseries, and specials.

> There will be monsters out there, and some of those bigger action, shoot-'em-up kinds of adventures will appear throughout the season.

Before coming to Paramount, Berman served as director of dramatic development for Warner Brothers Television and as an independent producer on numerous projects from 1982 through 1984, including *What on Earth*, an informational series for HBO and *The Primal Mind*, a one-hour award-winning special for PBS. From 1977 through 1982, Berman acted as senior producer of *The Big Blue Marble*, for which he won an Emmy Award for Outstanding Children's Series.

Michael Piller

Cocreator/executive producer Michael Piller has an equally impressive background. Before coming to *Star Trek: Voyager*, he served the same role for *Deep Space Nine*, and since 1989, he has acted as executive producer of *Star Trek: The Next Generation*. *Star Trek: Deep Space Nine* set ratings history when it aired as the highest-rated series premiere in syndication history, since only bested by the premiere of *Star Trek: Voyager*.

Piller graduated from the University of North Carolina at Chapel Hill. He began his Emmy Award–winning broadcasting career with CBS News in New York, then served as managing editor of the WBTV-TV News in Charlotte, North Carolina, and as senior news producer at WBBM-TV, the CBS affiliate in Chicago. His first job in entertainment television was as a censor in the CBS docudrama unit. Piller later spent two years as a programming executive before leaving CBS to write full-time. He left freelance journalism to join the Paramount staff.

Piller's credits as a writer-producer include the series *Simon & Simon, Cagney & Lacey, Miami Vice, Probe,* and *Hard Time on Planet Earth*. In addition, he cocreated and executive-produced the syndicated series *Group One Medical*.

Jeri Taylor

Jeri Taylor served as the third member of the team until she left the show after the second season. Her talents include experience as a writer, director, and producer. As cocreator/executive producer of *Star Trek: Voyager*, she also worked on a *Star Trek: Voyager* hardback novel featuring Captain Janeway.

Taylor previously served as an executive producer of *Star Trek: The Next Generation* for the 1993–94 season. In 1992, she was coexecutive producer of the series. The Emmy Award–nominated writer joined *Star Trek: The Next Generation* in 1990 as supervising producer for the fifth season.

Taylor's prior credits as a producer include work for the series *Quincy, M.E.,* for which she also directed episodes, *Blue Thunder, Magnum, P. I., In the Heat of the Night,* and *Jake and the Fatman*. She also cowrote and produced the CBS television film *A Place to Call Home,* starring Linda Lavin. Taylor wrote two ABC After School Specials, *But It Wasn't My Fault* and *Please Don't Hit Me, Mom,* for which she earned Writer's Guild and Emmy Award nominations, and she wrote for the television series *Little House on the Prairie, The Incredible Hulk,* and *Cliffhangers*.

Taylor graduated from Indiana University with a bachelor's degree in English, and she received her master's degree in English from California State University at Northridge.

CHAPTER TWO

Creating the Continuing Saga

Audiences expected a lot from the newest Trek. They tuned in to see what *Star Trek: Voyager* had to offer, and they stayed for the season. *Star Trek: Voyager* ranked ninety-fifth for the 1994–95 TV season, which is not bad considering it had been on for only about half the year. The series received nine Emmy nominations and won two for 1994–95, although, notably, none for acting, writing, or directing (see sidebars).

The First Reviews

The heavily watched premiere established the characters, setting, and general tone of what would follow. *SFX*, a British science fiction media publication, graded it a B+, noting, "Technically, *Voyager* features some superb special effects—the pilot culminates in one of the best space battles ever created for a TV science fiction show." However, it said, "Old problems rear their heads in new ways with the latest Star Trek spin-off."

SFX concluded, "After its first match of the season, how does the new Trek team shape up? Overall, it's a strong performance, with some classy teamwork and great attacking moves, but strategy definitely needs some work—there's far too much emphasis here on tried-and-tested maneuvers."

USA Today proved more enthusiastic, saying, "Though lost in space, 70,000 light-years from home, the crew of the starship *Voyager* (NCC-74656) will surely find a place in the video log of all but the most persnickety Trekkers. The smashing two-hour pilot is better already than *Deep Space Nine*, and lets the mediocre *Generations* movie recede even further into disappointed memory. It's no classic *Trek*, or even *Next Generation*. Those days are over. But this looks terrific, with an unusually well-cast ensemble of showy characters." The newspaper awarded the pilot with 3.5 stars out of a possible 4.

Though casting the series lead wasn't easy, reviewers appreciated the result. *USA Today* said, "Trek's first female captain, Kathryn Janeway, played by raspy-throated Kate Mulgrew is a spitfire of hands-on-hips, lockjawed authority. She's tough and cool." While the reviewer at *SFX* wrote, "The cast impresses immediately. Coming on like Katherine Hepburn playing the headmistress of St. Trinians, Kate Mulgrew is superb as Captain Janeway. She oozes authority, but always remains more approachable and ready to muck in than Picard."

The fans also liked the premiere. One unnamed fan offered an opinion over the Internet, writing, "'Caretaker' serves as a solid introductory episode, although subsequent entries would show this to be a typical first season series as it tries to find its creative center and proves to be inconsistent in quality as a result. But the pre-

> **Voyager Emmy Awards, 1994–95**
> Voyager was nominated for nine Emmy Awards and won two for 1994–95.

miere episode does solidly demonstrate what is possible."

Another fan, Tim Lynch, wrote, "Writing: A nice introduction. The plot was a bit thin owing to the necessities of the pilot, but there really doesn't seem to be much in the way of plot holes or character idiocies, which is a good way to start. Directing: Sharp. The show kept moving; that's all one needs to say. Acting: A little stiff out of the starting gate for a few people, but everything seems pretty promising. Tim Russ in particular is off to a terrific start. Overall: Call it an 8."

The Captain and Her Crew

Although the *Star Trek: Voyager* premiere got things off to a good start, not everyone would always be as happy with the series. The first season started with several very specific goals already obvious in the series premiere. First among these was defining Captain Kathryn Janeway. As the year progressed, Mulgrew believed they made considerable progress in establishing Trek's first female captain as a series lead, telling the *Houston Chronicle*, "We've come a long way, and what's marvelous about it is, on no level is this woman a victim. She's the person she is because of her own development and her own passions."

Mulgrew didn't consider the job yet completed at the end of the first season. She told *The Official* Star Trek: Voyager *Magazine*, "I feel very good about what we did our first year, but I think I have a long way to go. Let

me make that perfectly clear. As a matter of fact, I reviewed a few episodes the other night, just to see what I felt about my progress, and I think I was motivated by fear at first. I was shot out of a cannon, so I didn't have much time to think about Janeway's development until February. Then I began to take note of certain things that I wanted to work on, like her scenes on the bridge."

The actress told *Sci-Fi Entertainment*, "I would like to explore more of Janeway this year. I would like to be on more away missions if possible because that leads directly into personal confrontation. And then you could really see the emotional complexity of the character."

Mulgrew described how she felt at the beginning of the second season when she spoke to *The Official* Star Trek: Voyager *Magazine*, saying, "Usually after a season like last year, there would be a little bit of burnout, but there was none. I'm challenged by [Janeway] every day. I do think Janeway is much more relaxed as a person. Kate Mulgrew is more relaxed as an actress playing this role, and, as a result, Janeway has relaxed a little. But I'm still trying to use every tool I have to bring a fluency, an energy, and, for lack of a better word, a beauty to her scenes."

Mulgrew believed it was time to concentrate on Janeway's crewmates aboard the starship *Voyager*. One weakness during the first season was the lack of proper development of the other characters. Mulgrew thought they could rectify this problem during the second season with episodes showcasing her costars. Unlike some series hams—including, purportedly, the original *Star Trek*'s own series star, William Shatner—

Mulgrew was happy her costars would get their chance in the spotlight.

Tim Russ, who plays the Vulcan Tuvok, agreed, telling *The Official* Star Trek: Voyager *Magazine*, "All of these relationships will build one on another because Tuvok is so different from Torres, and Torres is so different from Captain Janeway, who is so different from Paris and the others. All of those parts should balance out and build upon one another as time goes on."

Cocreator and executive producer Jeri Taylor also acknowledged that the series failed to develop many of its characters during the first season. She told a convention audience, "We feel that we left some of the characters undeveloped toward the latter part of the first season, one of those being Chakotay, and for that reason a very early episode this season will be one that features Chakotay in a wonderful, really rip-roaring yarn that's full of action and adventure and pathos.

"Tom Paris is another one that we wanted to do something with early on, and we're going to start shooting next week on a wonderful kind of two-person charming story between Tom Paris and Neelix. And beyond that, we've got lots of things that will keep people interested."

> ### Emmy Award Won, 1994–95
>
> Outstanding Individual Achievement in Special Visual Effects ("Caretaker"): *Dan Curry, Visual Effects Producer; David Stipes, Visual Effects Supervisor; Michael Backauskas, Visual Effects; Joe Bauer, Visual Effects Coordinator; Edward L. Williams, Visual Effects Coordinator; Scott Rader, Visual Effects Compositing Editor; Don R. Greenburg, Visual Effects Compositing Editor; Adam Howard, Visual Effects Animator; Don Lee, Digital Colorist and Compositor; Robert Stromberg, Matte Artist; John Parentau, Computer Animation; Joshua Rose, Computer Animation; Joshua Cushner, Motion Control Camera*

A More Complex Second Season

Chakotay, Tuvok, Paris, Kim, Neelix, Kes, and the Holodoc did indeed get their moments in the sun as promised. Most second-season stories focused on the *Voyager* crew rather than its captain, revealing more about their characters and more about Janeway through her relationships with them. Not only individual episodes but continuing subplots expanded on the crew's conflicts and tensions, which usually resolved themselves in a climactic episode. However, some viewers complained that it sometimes took too long for these story threads to resolve.

For example, the triangular relationship between Neelix, Kes, and Paris appeared to be a figment of Neelix's insecure imagination for more than a season. Neelix clearly suspected every innocent word. Then, in "Parturition," the subplot finally resolved when Paris realized he actually did love Kes, but that he couldn't, and wouldn't, pursue her because of Neelix. By the end of the episode, Neelix and Paris had linked arms as buddies, and Paris had reassured the insecure Talaxan of Kes's faithful love. After that, Neelix became Paris's biggest booster, as demonstrated in "Investigations."

That episode brought another long story thread to a conclusion. Paris was a two-time loser until Captain Janeway took him out of prison and ultimately gave him a chance at redemption. He appeared to rise to the opportunity throughout the first season.

Then, in the second season, his performance took a bad term. Paris rarely showed up for his shift on time, engaged in frequent holodeck gambling, became a disruptive influence with the crew, and repeatedly needled Chakotay. When he landed in the brig for altercating with Chakotay on the bridge, he asked Janeway to find him other work. Paris then transferred to a Talaxan merchant vessel, and he ultimately became part of a Kazon ship's crew alongside Seska, all in a plot to oust a traitor aboard *Voyager*, Michael Jonas. By the end of the episode, Paris's image had been redeemed by public revelation of the ploy.

This led into another potential continuing story thread, one earlier hinted at by Mulgrew. News of the plot by Janeway, Tuvok, and Paris irritated *Voyager* second-in-command Chakotay, who had not been informed of the plan even though he bore the brunt of Paris's antics. He asked, "And why wasn't I let in on this?" Because, said Tuvok, it was believed the traitor was one of the Maquis crew, and they didn't want to put Chakotay in an awkward position. "In other words you didn't trust me," Chakotay replied, clearly upset.

> **Emmy Award Won, 1994–95**
> Outstanding Individual Achievement in Main Title Theme Music: *Jerry Goldsmith, Composer*

In "Alliances," Chakotay took issue with Starfleet rules, telling Janeway, "I don't think we can afford to keep on doing business as usual." He urged Janeway to cast aside strict adherence to Starfleet protocol and to cut a deal with the alien Kazon. Clearly ground is being laid for future conflict between *Voyager* captain Janeway and former Maquis captain Chakotay, and possibly also between ex-Maquis and ex-Federation crew members as they are forced to take sides.

Chakotay resolved another ongoing conflict, the one with Tuvok, the officer pushed aside when Chakotay took his position as second-in-command aboard *Voyager*. Chakotay acknowledged that it must have been difficult for Tuvok to have been passed over in the chain of command, and Tuvok admitted that he had resented it and made things rough in their relationship.

In a busy season, Chakotay also had an interesting visit with the Kazon ("Initiations"), made love to Torres ("Persistence of Vision"), and, in "Tattoo," came to terms with both his deceased father and the heritage of his people after meeting the aliens his tribe traditionally called "the Sky Spirits." The Doctor had his programming warped and temporarily couldn't choose reality between two conflicting visions of himself—human Dr. Lewis Zimmerman, dying of radiation poisoning in a simulation on Jupiter or a holographic creation—in "Projections." He also fell in love with a Vidiian converted into a holo-gram in "Lifesigns," and he acted as Kes's father in the ritual of "Elogium." Kes be-gan learning medicine from the Doctor and shuttle piloting from Paris.

Harry Kim entered an alternate reality when a freak series of occurrences yanked him into a "time stream" in "Non Sequitor," while Paris passed warp 10 and became one with the universe in "Threshold." Both Paris (also in "Threshold") and Kim (in "Dead-lock") died, al-though Paris came back and Kim was replaced with an exact duplicate. Torres played god to a race of robots ("Prototype") and confronted her own obsessed "Fran-kenstein" creation ("Dreadnought"). Tuvok descended into violence and inves-tigated the nature of Vulcan mind melds in "Meld" and revealed that he misses his favorite strumming guitar in "Persistence of Vision." And Neelix proved to be an idiot-savant, assisting the experts with homespun wisdom in "Prototype" and "Threshold."

Janeway was further defined by her inter-actions with her crew, acting as Kes's par-ent-figure and telling protégé Kim he routinely exceeded her expectations. After producing strange sluglike offspring with a mutated Paris in "Threshold," Janeway ad-mitted, "I've thought about having children, but I never thought I'd have them with you." Flustered, Paris stumbled an apology

and swore he recalled nothing, only to have her reply, "What makes you think it was your idea?"

Janeway will not engage in an ongoing sexual or romantic relationship, though. As Mulgrew told *TV Guide*, "We can't have Janeway doing what everyone else on board does—have sex and stuff like that. That is a line I personally don't want [the writers] to cross."

Piller, Taylor, and Berman be-lieve that rela-tionships between characters can't be forced. That makes them very difficult to plan ahead. Taylor told a convention audience, "I think that's still unfolding. We don't plan ahead for a reason. If you set a goal and try to reach it, then all you can do is get to your precon-ceived notion. So we never say, 'You know, I think it'll be cool if we had a relationship between B'Elanna and Tuvok.' If you try to force something like that, then it just doesn't work as well as if you let the stories unfold and sometimes you get on to some-thing. One scene can then become an arc between two people that will play out for a season or even more."

Piller added, "I think the Kes-Doctor re-lationship is an example. When we started, we sort of looked at each other and said, 'What are we going to do with these charac-ters, and you know, where are the stories going to come from?' And yet, I think that the relationship between those two, and the growth of both of them into the medical

> **Emmy Award Nomination, 1994–95**
> Outstanding Individual Achievement in Music Composition for a Series (Dramatic Underscore): *Jay Chataway ("Caretaker")*

situation and supporting one another in a personal way, has really reaped terrific rewards. And it seems very popular from the feedback we're getting."

Each cast member is working to get a better understanding of the character they portray. Tim Russ, *Star Trek: Voyager*'s new Vulcan, told *Sci-Fi Entertainment*, "The believability is there that he is a Vulcan. The fans are very critical about the details and consistency. There are rules you have to follow that have been established by the previous series."

Roxann Biggs-Dawson has begun to better understand her half-Klingon, half-human character, B'Elanna Torres. She told *Starlog*, "I've created all these different reasons in my head about why she hates her Klingon half so much. B'Elanna is a character that you can look forward to watching as she grows and progresses. The more conflict, the better, as far as I'm concerned."

Robert Picardo, the actor who brings the ship's holographic doctor to life, thinks that his character will finally get off *Voyager*. He told a convention audience, "I think that that's something we can look forward to in the holographic doctor's future. However, I'd like to point out that some of the most interesting things about the character are his limi-

> **Emmy Award Nomination, 1994–95**
> Outstanding Individual Achievement in Music Composition for a Series (Dramatic Underscore): *Dennis McCarthy ("Heroes and Demons")*

> **Emmy Award Nomination, 1994–95**
> Outstanding Individual Achievement in Cinematography for a Series: *Marvin Rush, ASC, Cinematographer ("Heroes and Demons")*

tations. And if we solve them all too quickly, well, then I'll have nothing left to do. So I think I'm going to get to an M-class planet sooner or later." (Although to date, the doctor still hasn't gotten off *Voyager*, he did enjoy both an interesting Away Team mission in "Heroes and Demons" and a date with a lady hologram on the holodeck in "Lifesigns.")

Several *Star Trek: Voyager* cast members feel a special duty to their characters because they act as symbols for specific groups. Mulgrew knew that many, including possibly Paramount, questioned the decision of having a woman as captain of *Voyager*.

Robert Beltran, who portrays Chakotay, knows he has a special obligation because his screen character is an Amerindian. He told *Daily News L.A. Life*, "I take that responsibility very seriously because I take my own indigenous roots very seriously. I think that even full-blooded Native Americans can see this actor portray Chakotay and know that I don't have to reach very far to find the reality of it because it's in me."

Garrett Wang, the son of Chinese American immigrants, portrays Asian crew member Harry Kim. Wang told *A Magazine*, "I believe that I now have a huge responsibility in being one of a very small number of Asian

Americans appearing on television regularly. My goal now is to do the best job possible playing Harry Kim and to begin repaying my parents for the unaccountable financial support they have given me throughout the years."

Mulgrew believes that one key to the success of *Star Trek: Voyager* thus far is the chemistry between the members of the cast. Jennifer Lien, the actress who portrays the Ocampan Kes, agrees, believing it is the key to the future success of the series.

Trekking Forward

Mulgrew sees many new story ideas naturally arising out of elements already established in the series. Giving one example, she told *The Official* Star Trek: Voyager *Magazine*, "We have to start thinking about families on board the ship. If in fact we want to get back to Earth, and if in fact it's going to take seventy-five years, we're going to have to perpetuate the race, aren't we? All of these terribly difficult, almost epic questions. But there's not a person in the world who I think can't understand them at least on some level." (When Ensign Wildman gave birth on *Voyager* to a half-human/half-Katarian, Janeway said she didn't know whether to welcome the first baby born on board or apologize to it.)

Piller believes there are many exciting possibilities ahead for his new series. He told a convention audience, "That's a commitment we've made for this season, to really open up and meet the aliens and the canvas of this quadrant. We met the Kazon last year, and we have been formulating quite a deep investigation of their culture that will turn them, I think, into perhaps one of the top five adversarial alien races in Star Trek history."

Taylor felt fans would accept such changes to the Star Trek universe, saying, "We knew that one of the risks that we took when we developed this show was in cutting off the audience from everything that was familiar. But we felt that that was a good thing to do. It challenged us creatively."

For the second season, the series creators knew they wanted more action in *Voyager* than they had in most of their first season. Taylor told a convention audience, "In terms of upcoming stories, one of the things that we want to do . . . is to parcel out our big action-adventure shows over the course of the season. Last year we kind of front-loaded and then evolved into a series of smaller interior shows."

They were still deciding whether Q would appear on the series before the second season began. Taylor told a convention audience, "We've given it a great deal of thought and tried to figure out if that is appropriate or not. There are serious questions as to whether it is, even though he is acknowledged as a very popular character. First of all you ask the question, 'Why would Q ap-

> **Emmy Award Nomination, 1994–95**
> Outstanding Individual Achievement in Costume Design for a Series: *Robert Blackman, Costume Designer ("Caretaker")*

pear on *Voyager*? Does he only go to starships that have their own series?' And beyond that, what more could we do with Q? It would not be enough creatively to have him repeat the same kind of relationship with Captain Janeway and the crew of *Voyager* as he did with Picard on the *Enterprise*. If he just drops in to bedevil humans, I think that's an arc we've played out. So, if we come up with a wonderful story or a wonderful reason to bring Q in, if there's a good creative reason, if we can develop a relationship that would seem appropriate, and not just fall back on the same kind of thing just because he's there, then of course we'll do it."

Berman explained their concerns to *TV Guide*, "As much as we've wanted Q on *Voyager*, getting him here has been tricky. The *Voyager* crew is lost in space and Q has the power to bring them home. Obviously we can't let him do that or we wouldn't have a series. Nor did we need yet another oh-here's-Q-being-a-pain-in-the-neck story. We needed to move into new Q territory."

Mulgrew told *TV Guide*, "I have campaigned very hard to get him on *Voyager*. Rick Berman was very concerned about how to get Q into the Delta Quadrant. I even threw a dinner party with the Bermans and the de Lancies and we talked all night long. I said, 'You've got to find a way.'"

Mulgrew had many reasons for wanting Q to board *Voyager*. One was her personal re-

---

Emmy Award Nomination, 1994–95

Outstanding Individual Achievement in Graphic Design and Title Sequences: *Dan Curry, Title Designer; John Grower, Effects and Animation Supervisor; Eric Tiemens, Storyboard/Design; Eric Guaglione, Animation Supervisor*

---

lationship with the actor who portrays Q. *TV Guide* reported, "Mulgrew and John de Lancie have enjoyed a riotous off-camera friendship for fifteen years—part Nick and Nora Charles, part Ralph and Alice Kramden—but until now, they've never worked together on-screen." When the leading TV magazine asked how they met, Mulgrew answered, "We met through a mutual friend. At the time, John was newly married to his wife, Marnie, and I was also newly married. Then we had our babies at the same time. I would say he's my closest male friend. He's certainly the only man I listen to on the phone for longer than three and a half hours!"

Q finally appeared on *Star Trek: Voyager* in "Death Wish," after Michael Piller's twenty-three-year-old son Shawn solved that seemingly insurmountable problem. The proud father told *TV Guide*, "The most experienced *Star Trek* minds had been stumped by the challenge of bringing Q to *Voyager*, but my son walked in with the answer. I would have been a fool to turn it down. The record is very clear that I will buy a good idea from anybody. One Q story [on *TNG*] was from a high-school junior in North Carolina. I've bought scripts from waiters in New York and from a postman in Arizona."

Paramount aired the episode during sweeps month to boost series ratings. Q is one of the most popular characters in Star Trek. He appeared seven times on *Star Trek:*

The Next Generation, including the first and last episodes, and also on *Star Trek: Deep Space Nine*. Q's enduring popularity is ironic given that Gene Roddenberry added him as an afterthought when Paramount insisted that he expand his proposed one-hour pilot for *The Next Generation* to a two-hour debut, forcing him to pad out the plot.

De Lancie loved the script for "Death Wish." He told *TV Guide*, "There is something demoralizing about being trained to play Chopin piano concertos but being asked to play jingles. Most television shows—and a lot of movies and plays—are jingles. Now this [script] is a concerto. After reading it, I immediately called Michael Piller and said, 'If this is the kind of story you've been doing on *Voyager*, this show must really be top-notch.'"

In typical Trek fashion, the episode includes many in-jokes. De Lancie told *TV Guide*, "One was so 'in' it got cut. In the first draft, Q was supposed to say to Tuvok, 'Without Q, you would have been the engineer on the *Enterprise*.' It's known among [Trekkers] that Tim Russ, who plays Tuvok, was the runner-up for the role of the engineer Geordi [on *TNG*]."

That *Enterprise* chief engineer, Geordi La Forge, played on *TNG* by LeVar Burton, appeared in the original script for "Death Wish." Originally Q wasn't sup-

> **Emmy Award Nomination, 1994–95**
>
> Outstanding Individual Achievement in Hairstyling for a Series ("Caretaker"): *Hairstylists: Josse Normand, Patty Miller, Shawn McKay, Karen Asano Myers, Dino Ganziano, Rebecca DeMorrio, Barbara Kaye Minster, Janice Brandow, Gloria Albarran Ponce, Carol Codon, Katherine Rees, Virginia Kearns, Patricia Vecchio, Audrey Levy*

posed to materialize Will Riker, but Geordi La Forge. Since appearing in the film *Star Trek VII: Generations*, LeVar had had his head shaved and no longer looked like Geordi, so Jonathan Frakes was called instead. He told *TV Guide*, "These Trek series crossovers are handled with great trepidation. They can't be stunt casting done simply to raise ratings. They've got to make sense to the Star Trek viewers or otherwise they'll bust you. But I had no reservations about this story. I was very happy to return."

He continued, "Being on-camera is still a blast, but directing is my future." Frakes has directed three episodes of *Voyager*, as well as four installments of *Deep Space Nine* and nine of *The Next Generation*. Paramount has just signed him to direct and act in *Star Trek VIII*.

Two additional classic *Star Trek* characters will also appear on *Voyager*. George Takei will reprise his Hikaru Sulu and Grace Lee Whitney will play Janice Rand for a third-season episode. George Takei revealed to the Albert Hall Generations II convention in the UK that he had just finished filming "Flashback," in which Janeway and Tuvok meet Sulu's starship *Excelsior*. The episode, in a story by Juliann Medina, with teleplay by Brannon Braga, also features Janice Rand as well as the first officer and helmsman from the film *Star Trek VI*. KTLA in Los Angeles has reported that Tuvok will go back in time to a period when he was an ensign under Captain Sulu. Nichelle Nichols turned down an offered cameo because her role was too small. This episode is scheduled to coincide with the thirtieth anniversary of *Star Trek*.

Storywriter George A. Brozak, teleplay writers Joe Menosky and Kenneth Biller, and director Cliff Bole will bring back the Ferengi from *The Next Generation* and *Deep Space Nine* in "False Profits," a sequel to *TNG*'s "The Price." Ethan Phillips confirmed at the Generations II convention that they have shot the episode, in which *Voyager* encounters the two Ferengi lost in the Delta Quadrant. Ethan also announced that he is playing one of the Ferengi.

The cast of *Star Trek: Voyager* is very happy with the reception they've received from viewers. Tim Russ told *Sci-Fi Entertainment*, "Now that I'm being recognized, I accept that as part of the job as well. People are watching the show on a regular basis. Being recognized is just part of the deal."

What the Critics Say . . .

One significant criticism made of *Star Trek: Voyager* so far is that many episodes offer little more than a reworking of stories from earlier Trek series, the same complaint Piller, Berman, and Taylor feared would be leveled at the return of Q. They admit there is some truth to this. Taylor explained one problem, saying that most of the creative staff are not familiar with the original *Star Trek* stories.

This, combined with the 350 hours of Star Trek that have already been produced, means that it is very difficult to come up with a wholly original storyline. *Voyager* may be in the Delta Quadrant, an entirely unknown frontier, but familiar characters and "stuck on a spaceship" stories are everywhere. The challenge for the new series is taking the old and familiar and making it new and interesting again.

While most fans think *Voyager* has been at least partially successful in this, some see the show as a complete failure. Soliciting responses in a typical Star Trek Internet newsgroup drew a number of mixed replies, none of them glowing with undiluted compliments. It is worth recalling here that although *Star Trek: Voyager* received nine Emmy nominations, none were for writing, directing, or acting. Also, remember that the original *Star Trek* series only narrowly escaped cancellation after its second year and *The Next Generation* didn't hit its stride until later in its run.

David Thiel of Champaign, Illinois, wrote, "The characters are generally well-conceived, though I've never warmed to Neelix's forced, would-be comic relief nor to Janeway's command presence, which seesaws wildly between tough-as-nails and soft-as-mush. Tuvok earns my praise for taking the well-worn Vulcan philosophy out for a new spin. The performers do the best they can with the technobabble-heavy dialogue, and Robert Picardo as the Doctor frequently steals the show with his barbed delivery.

"When the series focuses on its premise—a starship cut off from the Federation with enemies all about—it can

27

really shine. The collision between Starfleet ideals and Maquis survival techniques leads to intriguing conflicts. However, all too often it settles for twice-baked *Next Generation* retreads, and somehow makes them either less interesting or entirely laughable. Worst of all, a series premise that depends on the characters being unable to get home cannot afford to allow them to discover a viable way to do just that."

Physicist and artist Jeremy Thorpe wrote, "If I may be blunt, it is tripe. I don't know whose fault it is, but I, for one, feel insulted by the fact that Paramount thinks that science fiction fans are so inane that they will swallow any and all recycled, regurgitated, pasted-together mossblossoms that happen to have 'Star Trek' in the title. I don't know where to begin . . . selective ignorance of any and all scientific principles to serve the plot, plots which seem to exist only as vehicles for long strings of technobabble resolutions and indigestible twists, a complete unwillingness to address anything which might be interesting about this situation the crew finds itself in, characters who behave completely inconsistently and who refuse to evolve (unless it is into salamanders), 'science fiction' concepts which even Piers Anthony wouldn't touch with a five-mile space station, bad guys straight out of *Days of Our Lives*. . . .

> **Emmy Award Nomination, 1994–95**
>
> Outstanding Individual Achievement in Makeup for a Series ("Faces"): *Michael Westmore, Supervising Makeup Artist; Makeup Artists: Greg Nelson, Scott Wheeler, Tina Kalliongis-Hoffman, Mark Shostrom, Gil Mosko, Michael Key, Barry R. Koper, Natalie Wood, Bill Myer*

"Then again, maybe you shouldn't have asked right after 'Threshold' aired. That left a sour taste in everybody's mouth. They've done some good things, the sets look nice, and it may improve, but right now, I can't think about *Voyager* without shaking my head in utter disbelief at the pap they think SF fans will swallow."

Michael Keane, of the University of Washington, wrote, "When *Voyager* is good, it's pretty good, but not as good as *Deep Space Nine*. When *Voyager* is bad, it's very, very, very bad. It had so much promise to start with, too. 'Caretaker' was great and the first season was strong for the most part. Then the second season hit. *Voyager* is best viewed with lots of friends to make jokes with because it really is laughable."

Pat Spacek wrote the bitterest response, "Basically, *Voyager* is an interesting concept repeatedly mired down by some of the worst writing on TV. If it didn't have the Star Trek name, it would've died a merciful death a long time ago."

Since these replies came from a newsgroup for people interested in Star Trek, so much negative commentary may not bode well for the new series. On the other hand, if a similar inquiry had been possible during *Star Trek: The Next Generation*'s second season, an even more critical barrage may have arrived. That series then found its identity, lasted another five seasons, spawned a series of movies, and left the air as the top-rated show in syndication. It may just be a matter of time before *Voyager* finds its legs and fans warm to the newest Trek—attempting to go where no show has gone before. That has always been the way of Star Trek.

29

CHAPTER THREE

Casting the Crew

First the creators develop the concepts. Then they invent the characters that will bring the story to life. Often these are synergistic, the characters bringing changes and new possibilities. Finally they hire the actors to become the characters. Characters, and those who personify them, have always been the most important element of *Star Trek*. *Voyager* is no exception. What follows are the closely interrelated stories of the characters and the actors who play them.

"Captain Kathryn Janeway is the quintessential woman of the future . . . both commanding and discerning in her warmth; she's authoritative while remaining accessible. Beneath her extraordinary control runs a very deep vein of vulnerability and sensitivity that I look forward to exploring in seasons to come."

—Kate Mulgrew

Kathryn Janeway

Forty-year-old Kathryn Janeway, the daughter of human parents—a theoretical mathematician mother and an astrophysicist father—has become one of Starfleet's finest captains. Her empathy, intelligence, sensitivity, curiosity, and amiability often provide unexpected solutions that save her ship and crew. Now, stranded in the Delta Quadrant, she faces challenges unprecedented in Starfleet history.

Janeway's parents, particularly her role-model mother, encouraged her to develop her mind, treat others with respect, and pursue the sciences. As she grew, Janeway continued her close relationship with both parents. She consciously modeled herself after her mother and enjoyed their frequent discussions, which ranged from intimate talks to debates over esoteric mathematical theorems. Janeway feels the loss of this regular contact with her mother very deeply. She fears that both her parents believe her dead after her ship, the *Voyager*, became lost in space.

Janeway also misses her fiancé, Mark, who remains behind in the Alpha Quadrant, watching her Irish Setter. Her last, hurried talk with him took place on a monitor. She intended to talk with him at greater length a couple days later, but that opportunity never came. Conscious of her leadership responsibilities as captain, Janeway keeps up a strong front, but she secretly fears that even if the *Voyager* one day returns home, it will be too late to resume her previous relationship. She fears that her fiancé, believing her dead, will find solace in a new love.

Janeway knows that her crew will begin new relationships aboard their new home. She once said, "We're a long way from home. Everyone is lonely, and all we have is each other. I think eventually people will begin to pair off." For herself, however, she doesn't want to forget her fiancé and begin anew, once noting, "I intend for us to be home before Mark gives me up for dead."

Chakotay holds a different view. He once reported a romantic indiscretion between crew members to Captain Janeway, who shrugged it off, saying that Starfleet policies are permissive and it's only natural given their circumstances. But Chakotay didn't feel it was wise to be so unconcerned, since they faced a potential seventy-year voyage with limited resources, and no teachers or day care. They finally decided to urge discretion but not forbid shipboard relationships.

Janeway enjoys "holonovels" as a release from the pressures of command. These computer-generated simulations make the user a participant in a continuing, role-playing adventure. She frequently assumes the role of Lucie Davenport, the new governess for Henry Burleigh, Viscount Timmins, and little Beatrice at the gloomy and mysterious estate of widower Lord Burleigh in a holonovel set in "ancient England." Janeway also finds Tom Paris's Chez Sandrine saloon, modeled after the real one in Marseilles, France, a worthwhile diversion. Janeway is also an expert pool player.

After graduating from Starfleet Academy, but before she became captain of *Voyager*, Janeway served in many hands-on science posts. Her family background and specialization in the sciences at the Academy give her a grasp of technology and science greater than those of Kirk or Picard. This frequently proves critical to *Voyager*'s survival, since they are far beyond the communications and supply lines of Starfleet.

Despite, or perhaps because of, her science background, Janeway knows how little is yet known about many things, and this informs her understanding of religion. She once said, "What we don't know about death is far, far greater than what we do know." She feels the other-dimensional Vhnori may go on to an energy afterlife just as they believe, and Amerindian spiritualism attracts Janeway because it may hold answers to the mysteries that surround them. Chakotay educates her in the traditions of his people, and he once even helped her discover her animal totem, a lizard. Janeway's vision quest in search of her animal guide took her to an ocean shore on Earth.

Janeway's diplomatic and tactical skills are widely respected throughout Starfleet, and these skills will be vital as she manages her crew in such a stressful situation and as they encounter many unknown alien races, including dangerous Vidiians, Botha, and Kazon. Confined for such a long period on

---

Kathryn M. Janeway

Race: Human

Gender: Female

Rank: Captain

Department: Command

Position: Commanding Officer

Janeway's mother was a mathematician, her father an astrophysicist. She started as a science officer, advancing through the ranks until she became a captain. She also serves as the science officer as well as captain on board the *Voyager*.

the ship, crew members will inevitably come into conflict, and the captain must mediate these incidents while maintaining respect. Janeway shows real compassion, gentility, and humor. Humor may be her greatest asset. She once chided Harry Kim for standing so attentive that he might "sprain something."

Unfortunately for Janeway, she cannot bare her own fears and doubts to others. She must stoically maintain an untroubled confidence that they will soon return home, serving as a pillar of strength despite her own losses and pain. Each crew member has left loved ones behind they may never see again. If Janeway falters, her crew may fall apart.

Captain Janeway has already been forced to make many difficult decisions. A transporter accident merged Neelix with Tuvok, and they became Tuvix. The Doctor finally found a way to restore them, but Tuvix didn't want to die, and Janeway was forced to make a life or death decision. When two nearly omnipotent immortals from the Q Continuum invaded *Voyager*, Janeway became judge and jury, deciding whether a Q should be allowed the right to die. Circumstances have forced Janeway to surrender her ship

> **Janeway once contacted the endangered planet Rakosa to warn them of imminent danger from an oncoming missile.**

to the Kazon, while her duplicate has surrendered to Vidiians.

Janeway, like her hero, early aviator Amelia Earhart, has the courage to confront these conflicts. When an alien made the fears of *Voyager* crew members tangible, Janeway said, "Maybe he did us a favor. Maybe it's better to look these things in the eye than to keep them buried."

But like anyone, she does sometimes make mistakes. Her Federation way of thinking and naive optimism has gotten *Voyager* into trouble. She proposed an alliance with the seemingly friendly Trabe, and their leader Mabus, but was betrayed by their treachery. More often, though, her strong convictions lead to better rewards. Janeway once contacted the endangered planet Rakosa to warn them of imminent danger from an oncoming missile. Rakosan Minister Kellen coldly replied, "Your reputation precedes you, Captain," insisting that *Voyager* was known for threatening Delta Quadrant civilizations. When Janeway later helped stop the missile, Kellen said, "I see your reputation is undeserved. For what it's worth, you've gained a friend today." Janeway, through her commitment to the codes of Starfleet, had redeemed the reputation of the Federation.

Since her ship has become lost in space, cut off from Federation contact, she has grown unsure whether to maintain distance from her crew or to allow herself to grow closer to them. She has said, "Maybe more than ever now, they need me to be larger than life. I only wish I felt larger than life." The crew feels a similar conflict.

Nonetheless, of necessity, Janeway has formed some important relationships with those who now serve with her aboard *Voyager*. Crew members respect and love their captain. She enjoys a very close bond with Tuvok. He served as her first officer for many years before Chakotay came aboard the *Voyager*. Recently, after Tuvok acted against her orders behind her back, she reprimanded him, saying, "I need you, but I also need to know that I can count on you. You are my counsel, the one I turn to when I need my moral compass checked. We have forged this relationship for years, and I depend on it."

Chakotay, a former Maquis starship captain, replaced Tuvok as Janeway's first officer. He quickly learned to respect the strong captain, and they have developed a bond of mutual respect. However, Chakotay feels that Janeway has a continuing prejudice against the former Maquis rebel crew members. When a search for a turncoat in the crew narrowed to Lieutenant Carey and Ensign Seska, she said of Carey, "He's had a distinguished Starfleet career. Seska's spent most of the last two years as an enemy of the Federation." Chakotay replied that he, too, had been an "enemy of the Federation." Chakotay has questioned the wisdom of Janeway's rigid adherence to Starfleet regulations so far from home and her unquestioning belief in them. But Janeway feels that such disagreement between them may prove useful.

Janeway and Chakotay's relationship changed dramatically when a seemingly incurable, and deadly, virus afflicted them. Janeway turned permanent command over to Tuvok and stranded herself and Chakotay alone on a strange planet. Chakotay and Janeway's relationship then took a brief romantic turn.

B'Elanna Torres, another former rebel, has reacted less favorably to the captain. She keeps her distance. Janeway once almost threw her in the brig after she deliberately violated orders, but instead she put Torres on notice, saying that one more minor infraction would bust her. After that Torres strived to prove herself.

Janeway previously served aboard a starship commanded by Tom Paris's father. She later found Tom Paris in jail and gave him a new chance aboard *Voyager*. Paris would sooner die than betray the trust of his captain. However, in one strange incident, Janeway and Paris found themselves transformed into different forms, who then created offspring together. Though they returned to normal, the experience left them both chagrined and surprised.

Janeway enjoys good relations with the rest of the crew. She is a mentor to young Ensign Kim. She once told him that he routinely exceeds her expectations and has been one of the bright spots of her tour of duty. Neelix and the captain enjoy a relationship of levity and trust. She does hate his version of coffee, though. Kes acts much like Janeway's surrogate daughter, the daughter that she now may never have. Though Janeway once considered reprogramming the Doctor, she later decided the living hologram was a sentient being deserving of respect and told the Doctor that he was a full member of the crew. Janeway once even transferred all command codes to the Doctor when an alien intruder entered the ship with the power to possess all minds but the Doctor's.

Janeway's compassion causes her to question the Prime Directive, the Federation General Order that forbids interference with more primitive cultures. Once, when the laws of an alien people prevented them from giving her access to technology that could return the *Voyager* to Alpha Quadrant, she noted, "It's the first time we've been on the other side of the fence. How many times have we been in a position of refusing to interfere when some kind of disaster threatened an alien culture? It's all very well to say we do it on the basis of an enlightened principle, but how does that feel to the aliens? I'm sure many of them think the Prime Directive is a lousy idea." Compassion once drove Janeway to violate the Prime Directive by revealing her identity and foreknowledge of a future disaster threatening a non-space faring society. She also acted to prevent the disaster. But Janeway has also followed the Prime Directive, saying, "Who are we to swoop in, play God, and then just leave without any concern for the long-term consequences of our actions?"

Janeway can be quite innovative, discarding the conventional to solve a problem. She once said, "In command school, they taught us to always remember that maneuvering a starship is a very delicate process, but over the years I've learned that sometimes . . . you just have to punch your way through."

Captain Janeway possesses diplomatic skills, strong leadership abilities, a background in the sciences, and the love and respect of her crew. Each will prove critical to the survival of the *Voyager* in the Delta Quadrant.

Kate Mulgrew

Kate Mulgrew may have been destined for the role of captain of the starship *Voyager,* but at first it was far from a sure thing. According to her, her first audition in New York City went very badly. She explained to *TV Guide*, "You can't run around screaming for taxis in the pouring rain and then be an auspicious space captain."

Paramount took a risk picking a woman to lead their new Star Trek series, and Kate told *Entertainment Weekly*, "I have a great urge to tip my hat to a large group of people who understood the financial and commercial importance of making the absolute right choice of captain. And they then transcended that. They said, 'This is what we really believe.'"

At first they believed it was Genevieve Bujold, but the actress quit after two days of shooting, walking off the set in front of the entire cast. Morale sank as everyone feared for their new jobs, and the studio sent out casting calls again. They knew that a second mistake would doom their new series. They also knew they were signing a series star to a five-year contract, a hoped-for seven-year series run, and possibly major movies after that.

After her second audition, Kate believed that the job would come to her. Though Kate was always a front-runner, a number of other experienced actresses were considered for the role, including Lindsay Wagner,

Kate Jackson, Joanna Cassidy, Tracy Scoggins, Lindsay Crouse, Chelsea Field, Patsy Kensit, Patty Duke, and Linda Hamilton. "I knew those other actresses weren't Janeway," Kate told *Working Mother*, "I was!" She was right. The producers chose the actress they had previously rejected for the job in favor of Bujold. Kate later told *Entertainment Weekly*, "They were tired, they were nervous, they were behind. They just closed the door and said, 'Who looks strong? Who can stand up to this kind of pressure for seven years?'"

Paramount announced Kate Mulgrew on September 16. The actress was suffering with the flu when summoned. "This is all about destiny and luck and timing. God knows, there are hundreds of strong actresses," she told *TV Guide*.

Things had not been going well for Kate at the time she got the new job as captain of the starship *Voyager*. She told *Working Mother*, "I needed this job. Just a couple of weeks before I got it, I was putting my house on the market. But I was in the right place at the right time. It was a magical thing. Finally all my dreams are coming to fruition. Why not give it all I've got while I have the opportunity?"

She knew her new part would require great dedication. Kate told *Orbit* at the time, "In the wake of what happened with Genevieve and the whole recasting process that ensued, which was pretty extraordinary, I feel both a great responsibility and great expectation. I've set some pretty high standards for myself because I feel what I absolutely have to do here on *Voyager* is what no woman has done before."

"Caretaker" director Winrich Kolbe told *Cinescape*, "I was shooting when Kate Mulgrew was mentioned. Then suddenly Kate Mulgrew was hired, and I had a meeting with her in the makeup trailer. When she came on the set, I was very impressed with her. She had a definite presence, and she was informed about what she had to do. She watched a lot of episodes and a lot of my episodes.

"I felt so good about her that I brought her to the set on Stage Nine and said, 'Ladies and gentlemen, the captain!' Everyone applauded. It was very nice, and I suddenly felt that we were taking off. We were just taxiing up the runway until that point."

Robert Picardo, the actor who portrays the Doctor, agreed, telling *Entertainment Weekly*, "We were blessed to get Kate. We were nervous and, literally, a ship without a captain. It truly was the eleventh hour."

Robert Beltran, *Voyager*'s Chakotay, added, "Kate has a lot of pressure on her. There's really no precedent for her situation. Except maybe Joan of Arc. And she had the anointing of God."

Kate Mulgrew was born in Dubuque, Iowa, on April 29, 1955. She is the oldest of eight children in a traditional Irish-American

> **Kate Mulgrew may have been destined for the role of captain of the starship Voyager, but at first it was far from a sure thing.**

family. Mulgrew credits her contractor father and artist mother with helping shape her into the self-confident woman she is today.

"Coming from such a large family, there was no question that I would help out around the house. Further, there was no question that if I wanted things, I went to work," Kate told *Working Mother*.

At seventeen, Kate followed the classic actor's pilgrimage to New York City to study acting. She attended New York University's Stella Adler Conservatory but left at the end of her junior year to actively pursue her craft. She finally received an Honorary Doctorate of Letters for Artistic Contribution from Seton Hall University much later in life. Kate's first major role was as Mary Ryan on the ABC daytime drama *Ryan's Hope*. She stayed with the series for two years, simultaneously acting in the role of Emily in the play "Our Town" at the American Shakespeare Festival in Stratford, Connecticut.

Kate's first major recognition arrived with her casting as Mrs. Columbo in 1979. The ill-fated series was a spin-off of Peter Falk's popular *Columbo* detective series. The then twenty-three-year-old star played the part of a thirty-nine-year-old woman and proved less than believable as the wife of a fifty-two-year-old detective. The series lasted two seasons, changing its name from *Mrs. Columbo* to *Kate Columbo* to *Kate, the Detective* to, finally, *Kate Loves a Mystery*.

Still, the series brought the actress to the attention of Hollywood studios and the American public. Kate later reappeared on television in a variety of roles. She starred in the ABC drama *Heartbeat*, from March until April 1988, then returned from January until April 1989. Kate portrayed Dr. Joanne Springstein, the head of a medical clinic. Her work won her a People's Choice Award.

She later appeared in the short-lived NBC comedy series *Man of the People* (September to October 1991) with James Garner, the ABC miniseries *The Manions of America* with Pierce Brosnan, opposite Avery Brooks in the miniseries *Roots: The Gift*, and she won a Tracey Humanitarian Award for her portrayal of an alcoholic anchorwoman on *Murphy Brown*. She also appeared as a Boston councilwoman, Sam Malone's love interest, on *Cheers*.

Her TV movies include *Jennifer: A Woman's Story*, *Love Spell*, *Fatal Friendship*, *For Love and Glory*, *Roses Are for the Rich*, Daniel Steele's *Daddy*, *A Time for Miracles*, *Round Numbers*, and *The Word*.

Although she is best known for her television work, Kate has also appeared in films. Her movies include *Love Spell: Isolt of Ireland* with Richard Burton, *A Stranger Is Watching* with Rip Torn, *Camp Nowhere*, *Remo Williams: The Adventure Begins*, and *Throw Momma from the Train* with Danny DeVito and Billy Crystal.

Kate is also a veteran stage thespian. She debuted on Broadway in *Black Comedy*, written by Peter Schaeffer and also starring Nancy Marchand and Peter McNicol. Other starring roles included parts in *Titus Andronicus* at the Shakespeare Theater in New York City's Central Park and in *Hedda Gabler* and *Measure for Measure* at Los Angeles's Mark Taper Forum.

Kate appreciates the unique nature of her new role on *Voyager* as Star Trek's first distaff starship captain to helm a series. She told the *Houston Chronicle*, "There's pressure, but I think it's alleviated by the extraordinary sense of opportunity. One waits a long time for a chance like this. And I'm at a point in my life where I can really appreciate it." She also told *TV Guide*, "This is the kind of work I do well. I'm pretty good under the gun. It suits me."

At first, Kate was unsure of the nature of her new series. She admitted to *Entertainment Weekly*, "It wasn't clear in my brain what I was doing. Is this a series, is it a spin-off, is it a movie?" Then she began to study her role and to form clear opinions about Captain Janeway and about what the Star Trek legend meant to her. The more she learned, the more she understood just how hard a job she had undertaken.

> "It's one thing to stand on the bridge and drop off the language, but to fully understand what I'm saying endows it with a deeper meaning."

"We are a different ship, a different beast. Until now, I think they [the producers] were just being circumspect and probably judicious," she later told the *Houston Chronicle*. "Let me be very frank: It's a man's job. It requires terrific physical stamina, which the sheer musculature and DNA of a male predisposes him to handle a little bit better. But I was blessed with a great constitution. So they can run me ragged, and I'll still be standing."

She understood that to portray a believable captain within such a well-defined fantasy required doing her homework. Too many fans know every niche of the Star Trek legend for her to go forth unprepared. Kate told *Sci-Fi Entertainment*, "I felt research was crucial because who is going to buy the captain if the captain doesn't know more than anyone else? It's one thing to stand on the bridge and drop off the language, but to fully understand what I'm saying endows it with a deeper meaning.

"Besides, I am a student of human nature, so it's a terrific challenge to learn all the idiosyncrasies of what something would mean. Janeway's science background has to be absolutely without question. So I decided to tackle the language."

She told *Working Mother*, "I can't work a computer and I don't have a clue what to do with a fax machine, but I have the kind of brain that has no trouble speaking fluent science fiction . . . phrases like 'evasive pattern Delta four' and 'ready the tri-cobalt devices.'"

Kate also studied the two previous Star Trek captains of the renowned starship *Enterprise*. She told *Sci-Fi Entertainment*, "William Shatner really appealed to me as a captain. I liked his style. He was easy-going but kind of rugged American. *Next Generation* had an elegance to it which I thought was lovely. You could see the evolution of the writing on *Next Generation* and all the elements coming together. The first *Star Trek* was a bit primitive technically, but now we have more graphics and opticals. You just can't believe what they have for these shows."

Kate sees clear differences between Janeway and Kirk and Picard, and she told

Entertainment Weekly, "A female captain has a lot of leeway that a male captain wouldn't have. Women have an emotional accessibility that our culture not only accepts but embraces. We have a tactility, a compassion, a maternity—and all these things can be revealed within the character of a very authoritative person. It took balls for these guys to hire me in this capacity. It's a bold choice, and an appropriate one for four hundred years in the future."

Kate has grown to like Captain Janeway more as time goes on, and she's decided that Janeway's dedication to the sciences is a key to her personality. As she told Al Roker on CNN, "Janeway is a passionate scientist; this is the foundation of her being. Her father was an eminent scientist in his own right. Her attraction to the military, I think, was born out of her love of science, and her sort of unmitigated curiosity about space and investigation. I often think of her as an exalted private eye. She wants to uncover every nook and cranny."

As the actress began to understand her character, the series writers began to mold their stories toward her. It grew into a symbiotic relationship. The writers creatively fed on the work of the actress while the actress, in turn, absorbed the nuances the writers added in their scripts. Kate told *Sci-Fi Entertainment*, "This is a marriage. I'm interpreting Janeway, so they have to write her to suit my style. I think Janeway should be very smart and strong-willed, but being a woman we should also explore her emotional depth, without ever jeopardizing her command style or authority. I don't feel she's been too emotional. I think the writers are very vigilant about that and they have a right to be. We don't want an overly emotional captain. That just won't fly. She has to be in utter command. We shouldn't sacrifice command style for humanity. We can have everything if it's done the right way.

"I'm not into that love stuff. I think we have to be very careful where Janeway goes with her amorous inclinations. I have a lover on Earth and I feel that allegiance should be respected. If and when the time comes that she has to reveal herself more as a woman, then it should be done very carefully." (Although Janeway and Paris had children in "Threshold" and she has had a couple of near-miss relationships with other characters, Janeway appears to remain devoted to her Alpha Quadrant–tied fiancé, Mark.)

Kate told *Starlog* that she finds Janeway's pioneering spirit important. She said, "It's a terrific, smart choice for Janeway. She has chosen the past, and a basic past, without letting go of her love of discovery. She's still pioneering. There's a robustness to her. She wants to get on a horse and ride. That will be a wonderful way for the audience to see her sadness, her joy, her endless possibilities that simply cannot be expressed on the ship."

After the first season, Kate felt proud of her portrayal of Kathryn Janeway. She believed she had firmly made the character her own, imprinting her stamp upon the Star Trek universe. During the second season, she was happy that the series spent more time establishing the other main characters. Kate wants her costars to share the spotlight, especially since they've become so friendly with one another. "Usually, in a group of nine people, somebody's going to be a little dubious. We're cohesive. We're professional, and we genuinely like each other," Kate told *The Official* Star Trek: Voyager *Magazine*.

Chemistry within a cast not only makes for an enjoyable work environment but it shows on screen. The dynamics between the characters often reflect the trust the cast members feel toward one another.

> **The dynamics between the characters often reflect the trust the cast members feel toward one another.**

Kate continued, "It's pure luck to begin with, and then probably a state of grace next. We have a group of disciplined, enthusiastic, and very earthy people. Nobody here is on a star trip. We all feel very blessed to have these jobs. Everyone feels very intensely about the person they are playing. All of our standards are very high. It's a marvelous thing to be able to walk into a room where you're going to be greeted by people you not only genuinely like but with whom you're going to create something that you hope will be special. I don't think that will ever change."

A romantic relationship developed between the actress and Winrich Kolbe, one of the series directors, during the first season. Working with Rick, as he's known, provides an additional pleasure during the long, tiring shoots.

Kate told the *Houston Chronicle* that she enjoys working in television. She said, "It's a great job—a great gig. I'd done this sort of thing before. I'm not a movie star. I don't have the luxury of subjective acting that takes time. I'm a shot-out-of-the-cannon person. I love it when it's a little tough. I love it under the gun."

The actress enjoys going to conventions and meeting her fans, but it can be intimidating she's found. "I try to keep a low profile, but the conventions are interesting and challenging," she told *Sci-Fi Entertainment*. "They're a total experience. They aren't something you can dance into and dance out of. I like them, but I don't think I could do a lot for them. I get asked a lot of wild questions, and when I'm asked hugely technical questions, I just handle them very politely. They're smart fans. They have an eagle eye on everything."

Kate told the *Houston Chronicle*, "All this science fiction has started me thinking more about the real universe out there. You stand outside and look up, and you see it's all another part of this vast mystery."

Kate also performs cartoon voices, including the Red Claw on *The Adventures of Batman and Robin* and a continuing character for *Gargoyles*. She reassured *Sci-Fi Entertainment*, "I'm committed to Janeway, but the cartoon people are flexible. They fit me in when I have a few hours."

Kate is also the single mother of two boys, eleven-year-old Ian and ten-year-old Alec. The family lives in Los Angeles. Like many working mothers, her job sometimes conflicts with her responsibilities to her sons, and this troubles her. She divorced the boys' father, director Richard Egan, in 1993, after eleven years of marriage. The actress has a housekeeper who watches the kids after school and helps keep things running smoothly. Kate told *Working Mother*, "I cook as often as I can, and dinner is our time to talk about school, their friendships, their dreams. The arduous hours are manageable because I am so happy with what I'm doing. In thinking about it and talking with other working mothers, I've realized that this is what makes or breaks it. If you're genuinely happy with your work, your children enjoy a mother who's fulfilled."

She told *TV Guide*, "I think that it is almost a no-win situation. So when I distill it, I say to myself, all I can do is the best I can do in the moment. If I'm on my set and I have twelve hours there, I focus on it. If I have six hours with my boys, I focus on that, because at the very least what I can say as I stagger to an early grave is: I tried to do these things excellently.

"I am a passionate actress and this is a great role. It's a role model. In a sense it's history-making, isn't it? If I can leave them the legacy that their mother was terribly, deeply passionate about what she did, perhaps then that was better than sacrificing my work to stay at home and be a rather frustrated and mediocre mother."

And Kate has indeed become a role model to growing girls throughout the world. She even has fans in the White House.

Kate visited First Lady Hillary Rodham Clinton and her daughter, Chelsea, at the White House and learned they both regularly watch her show. "The First Lady told me *Star Trek* was the one program Chelsea won't miss and that she watched it with her," Kate revealed to *Working Mother*. "She asked if I knew how important I was as a role model. She said, 'It's wonderful to see someone at the helm who I would like my daughter to become.'"

Kate told the *Houston Chronicle*, "I am nervous. This is the hardest work I've ever done, and I want it to be good. I try to set a standard on that set, and I guess on that ship, too."

Kate is dedicated to her job, feeling that she can make a real difference in the way that women are perceived. Director Winrich Kolbe agrees. He told *Cinescape*, "I think she's going to do a hell of a lot for women on TV. She is very feminine, but she can handle any situation. I would follow her. She really is wonderful."

"He also has a sense of fun and adventure, which most of the other characters don't really have because they're sad and disheartened to be lost in space. Paris is excited by that. He likes having the adventure and the fun and the fresh start."
—Robert Duncan McNeill

Tom Paris

Sometimes life offers a second chance. It happened to Tom Paris. Being trapped in the Delta Quadrant may be the best thing that ever happened to him. Before going aboard the Federation starship *Voyager* for that fateful trip, Tom's life had taken some very bad turns. As Harry Kim learned while trapped in an alternate timeline, Tom may have ended up a down-and-out fugitive in Marseilles, France, if not for the *Voyager*.

Tom came from an illustrious family. His great-grandfather, grandmother, and aunt were all admirals. That's a high expectation to live up to, and it crushed Tom. The young man grew up bright, capable, and charming, but the family legend proved too demanding. He earned average grades at Starfleet Academy, played on the Parises Squares team, and participated in extracurricular activities. That would have been enough for most cadets, but not for a Paris. The family expected more of him, and he felt guilty because he had spent most of his second semester at Starfleet Academy in a French bistro, Chez Sandrine. The bistro stocked pool hustlers, musicians, gigolos, and gorgeous women.

Tom proved a skilled pilot, and he often said he'd rather pilot a starship than captain one. After graduation, he joined a unit of Starfleet's Small Attack Vessel division. They put his piloting skills to good use. He still hadn't escaped the pressures of his famed family, though. An incident occurred during a war games demonstration that would have earned him a minor reprimand, but he panicked, fearing his family's displeasure, and lied to his officers. Predictably, his worst fears came to life, as Starfleet discovered his deception and discharged him. To his shame, Tom had blackened the name Paris.

Tom sunk into a severe depression, aimlessly drifting from job to job. He took on any commission that would allow him to keep flying, even piloting freighters and tankers. Then, one day in a port far from home, he played a fateful game of Dabo with members of the Maquis rebel underground. The Maquis desperately needed a skilled, trained pilot. Tom wanted a way out of his dead-end life. Joining the Maquis would put him in the pilot's seat of a sleek starship, his fondest dream. It would replace boring voyages aboard freighters with new missions that challenged his skills. With few other prospects, he joined up at the end of a very long night. The union was born not of conviction but of necessity, and he hoped to escape his memories of failing his family and Starfleet.

Then disaster struck a second time. Starfleet captured Tom one month after he took the helm of a Maquis starship. This time the consequences proved graver than before. The Federation didn't regard the captured rebel as a prisoner of war but as an outlaw, and instead of a discharge, he received a jail sentence. Starfleet put him in a prison in New Zealand, and Tom believed his life was at an end. Then Captain Kathryn Janeway arrived, and she offered him a new chance at life if he would serve aboard her starship, *Voyager,* and help hunt his former Maquis ship. Janeway knew the Paris family, having once served under Tom's father, Admiral Paris. Tom gratefully accepted the commission, even though it meant hunting his former comrades.

Tom helped his captain catch the rebel Maquis vessel. Then both ships were hurled into the Delta Quadrant, seventy light-years from home. The captain of the Maquis vessel, Chakotay, and Janeway combined crews aboard the *Voyager.* Of all those trapped far from home, Tom has the least reason to return. He left behind a record of dishonorable discharge and prison, and he has no great desire to face his illustrious family.

Before meeting Janeway, Tom only looked out for himself. He wasn't loyal to

> ### Thomas Eugene Paris
>
> **Race:** Human
> **Gender:** Male
> **Rank:** Lieutenant Junior Grade
> **Department:** Command
> **Position:** CONN Officer
>
> Tom Paris comes from a family of distinguished Starfleet Officers. Several family members, including his great-grandfather, grandmother, father, and aunt served as admirals. Paris was never able to live up to the high standards and expectations of his family. Paris was court-martialed, then joined the Maquis as a pilot aboard Chakotay's ship. He was caught by Starfleet during his first mission and sent to a penal colony in New Zealand on Earth. Then Captain Janeway offered him a second chance in exchange for help locating his former Maquis ship.

Starfleet and he wasn't loyal to the Maquis. Now Tom credits his new captain for his new chance at life. He would gladly stop a phaser blast for her, and he would die before betraying her trust in him. Despite the mishaps that befell him in Starfleet, his upbringing instilled a belief that rank has its privileges. When Kim once wanted to invite Janeway to join him and Paris at breakfast, Paris stopped him, saying, "Ensigns don't invite Captains to sit down. Captains don't want courtesy. They want respect. That's why they don't get chummy with the lower ranks."

Tom has all the makings of a hero. He once deliberately intercepted a bullet to save a young boy's life. As a pilot, he's proved a worthy addition to the crew. Tom also shows leadership ability. When Janeway left Tom and Neelix in charge of the ship, they successfully stared down a Kazon mothership.

Janeway once put Tom in for a commendation. She put his name along with those of Orville Wright, Neil Armstrong, and Zefram Cochrane among the Pioneers of Flight in the history of humanity. "I like the way that sounds," Tom said, smiling. "I thought you would," the captain responded.

He had been the first to fly faster than warp 10, but it had great consequences and nearly cost him his life.

As Tom's shuttle had passed transwarp speed, it had disappeared. When the shuttle returned, they learned Tom had been everywhere at once. Soon, he couldn't eat, drink, or even breathe normal air. Tom died, was reborn with an extra heart, and continued to mutate. He knocked the captain unconscious, and they left together in a shuttle. A week later, Chakotay and Tuvok found two large, sluglike beings with catfish whiskers and humanlike arms—and next to them were their offspring—in the equatorial jungle of the fourth planet of a nearby star. The beings carried the captain and Tom's DNA. After both returned to human form, Janeway told Paris, "I've thought about having children, but I never thought I'd have them with you." Flustered, Paris stumbled an apology, and swore he didn't remember. "What makes you think it was your idea?" Janeway asked, "but apology accepted nonetheless."

Tom has proven to be a good friend. When the young Harry Kim pined for home and family, Tom created a distraction on the holodeck, the Chez Sandrine, and told Kim, "It's my little piece of Earth out here in the Delta Quadrant." The bar provided a worthy distraction for Kim and is enjoyed by the rest of the crew as well. He also befriended Tuvok after the Vulcan proved him innocent of murdering the Banean scientist, Tolen Ren. The Vulcan's self-control is attractive to Tom, who still has his wild side. He remains reckless and a gambler as well as a ladies man. For a long time, Neelix feared that his Ocampan lover

Kes would betray him and begin a relationship with Tom, particularly after Tom bought her a locket necklace for her birthday. At first it appeared to be another of Neelix's jealous delusions, but Tom soon discovered that he did love Kes. However, Tom didn't pursue the romance out of respect for Neelix, going out of his way to reassure Neelix of Kes's love for him. After this incident, Tom and Neelix became close friends.

At one point, Tom appeared to have slipped back into his old, unreliable ways, increasingly prone to tardiness, brooding, gambling on the holodeck, and needling Chakotay. He was becoming a disruptive influence with the crew. After he again arrived late for his shift, Chakotay asked Janeway if she wanted to get involved in her "personal reclamation project." Janeway expressed full confidence in Chakotay, who tried to approach Paris and solve the problem. But Tom replied, "You're my problem. You won't let me do my job." Paris claimed he wasn't given the trust a pilot needs and went for Chakotay's jugular in public.

The next day when Tom arrived for duty, late again, he found someone else already at his station. Chakotay said Tom wouldn't be needed, and when Tom asked when he should return to duty, Chakotay replied, "when you grow up." Chakotay escorted Tom to the turbolift, and Tom pushed him. Janeway then ordered Tuvok to escort Tom to the brig as a confused Chakotay looked on.

Tom then asked Janeway to find him other work. He bid farewell to his three closest friends on board, Neelix, Kes, and Harry Kim, and went first to a Talaxan trading ship, then to the same Kazon vessel on which Seska serves.

But the incidents involving Tom were a ruse to flush out a traitor aboard *Voyager*. Tuvok had found evidence of illicit transmissions several weeks before and had been unable to locate the sender. He and Janeway developed the scheme to have Tom leave the ship in disgrace as an alibi for infiltrating the Kazon. Paris successfully revealed the saboteur and returned to *Voyager* in triumph.

Tom still fears his admiral father and recently realized that he's been chasing after redemption in the minds of his crewmates, but that such a goal is elusive. He's finally decided that the opinion that matters most is his own. "You've already changed a lot of minds, Tom," Janeway once assured him. "I'm sure you'll succeed."

Perhaps one day, *Voyager* will return to the Alpha Quadrant, and Captain Kathryn Janeway can bring back a glowing report about the heroic pilot to Starfleet. Then Tom can triumphantly return to his family, as well as to his collection of antique cars. He would have truly gone where no one had gone before, not even a Paris.

> **Tom still fears his admiral father and recently realized that he's been chasing after redemption in the minds of his crewmates.**

Robert Duncan McNeill

The man who brings *Star Trek: Voyager*'s Tom Paris to the screen, Robert Duncan McNeill, lives in Los Angeles with his wife, Carol, four-year-old daughter, Taylor, and six-month-old son, Kyle. Family and community rank as top priorities for this actor. He considers "family values" more than just a cliché.

Robert founded Real Play Productions with his wife when they lived in New York City, providing inner-city schoolchildren with creative ways to deal with crisis issues. It offered a diversion from bleak home lives and kept them off the dangerous streets and out of trouble. Robert and Carol's work for Real Productions made a difference in many young lives.

Robert didn't ignore his career, though. He built a very impressive résumé in theater before coming to *Star Trek: Voyager*. Robert began acting in school plays and community theater in Atlanta, the city he still calls home. His family moved to Georgia when he was twelve, after living in Washington, D.C., and Raleigh, North Carolina, where he was born. He first appeared on stage in a sixth-grade Bicentennial pageant, then followed that up as a Munchkin for a children's theater production of *The Wizard of Oz*.

Robert then studied acting for two years at Julliard in New York City. His studies prepared him for an impressive string of successes on the stage, including a stint with the national touring production of Stephen Sondheim's hit Broadway musical *Into the Woods*, an off Broadway production of *Lucy's Lapses*, a Coast Playhouse production of *Child's Play* with Gregory Harrison, *Romeo and Juliet* at the Ford Theatre—for which he received a Drama-Logue Award as best actor for his role as Romeo—and John Guare's original Broadway production of *Six Degrees of Separation* with Stockard Channing.

He left *Six Degrees of Separation* after a year because then-film producer Stanley Jaffe cast him in *School Ties*. The move from the Big Apple to Los Angeles proved to be a mistake. The film role was recast starring Brendan Frasier.

Robert also appeared in the film, *Masters of the Universe*, with Dolph Lundgren, Courtney Cox, and Frank Langella, and he made his TV debut in the "A Message from Charity" episode of *The New Twilight Zone*, about two people who fall in love across hundreds of years of time. Other TV work included the CBS sitcom *Second Chances* with Connie Selleca and playing a recurring character on ABC's *Homefront*. He also appeared in the starring role of Colin on ABC's *Going to Extremes*, a two-year stint on *All My Children* (1984–86) for which he won a Daytime Emmy nomination for his portrayal of Charlie Brent, and as a character in the ABC After-School Special *Flower Babies,* directed by actress Linda Lavin.

Then came a fateful day in Robert's life, his first encounter with Star Trek. He took what he thought would be a one-time guest-starring role, that of Nick Locarno, on the episode "The First Duty" of *Star Trek: The Next Generation*. It changed his life. Locarno leads a five-man Starfleet Academy flying team into disaster, resulting in one cadet's death, then he orchestrates a cover-up, fram-ing the dead cadet. Although Locarno is found out and expelled from Starfleet Academy, rather than from Starfleet as Tom Paris was, the similarities are impossible to ignore.

Voyager creators Jeri Taylor, Michael Piller, and Rick Berman discussed having Robert reprise the character for the new Star Trek series, then they decided against it because, as Robert told *Starlog*, "They wanted a character with a little more colorful background, and they wanted to have it be a little more open, rather than have him be locked into that accident. They wanted him to come from a family of high-ranking Starfleet officers and have him screw up left and right. So there's that pressure of living up to his family's history.

"They also felt that the way that Locarno came off in that episode didn't really open the door for the character on *Voyager*. He came off as a bad guy, not a nice guy, and they didn't want this character to be a bad guy. They wanted him to be a basically decent guy who got into a lot of trouble."

In August of 1995, Robert told a Prodigy forum, "(My audition) was very easy. They called me because I had done *TNG*. They called me in New York where I was doing a play. I did a tape and then they flew me out to Los Angeles to meet with all the Paramount executives. I got the job after two auditions."

Pilot director Winrich Kolbe told *Cinescape* that Paris "was probably the easiest character to cast. He was basically white, middle class. All we needed was someone who had a sense of being a little bit overbearing, a little bit snotty at times. A character with something in the closet, somebody who's willing to take unusual steps in order to progress themselves. What was important to me was that his father had such high expectations of him, that he thought he would be the thirty-sixth military man in the family but Paris then decided, 'The hell with that, I'm not going to play that game. I want to do something else.'"

Robert loves working on Star Trek. He appreciates his fans and enjoys the myth. He respects the acting and creative talent behind *Star Trek: Voyager*. "The thing that's so great about Star Trek," he told *Starlog*, "is there's a theatricality to it. It stays very rooted and tries to be realistic in its science, even though they're guessing at the future."

His working relationship with the rest of the cast is good, but still growing and changing. Robert told *Prodigy*, "From the first day we were all one big family. Kate is wonderful, she has a great sense of humor. I am kind of the class clown on the set. Tim is very funny, but tends to be the straight man. The joking is nonstop. It's hard to think of just one. I loved it when Tuvok broke into his James Brown impersonation during a mind meld . . . that was great."

Robert sees both good and bad in his character, Tom Paris, scion of a long line of admirals. He told *Starlog*, "The series bible says that Paris is a rebel who has gotten into a great deal of trouble before, and now has a chance, in this extreme situation, to redeem himself. When he has been in trouble, it was because he wasn't loyal. He's always sort of been out for himself. He has a sense of fun and adventure, which most of the other characters don't really have."

Robert Duncan McNeill also still has a goal: he wants to direct an episode of *Voyager*. He is scheduled to direct "Sacred Ground," an episode that will reveal more about Chakotay's heritage.

"Chakotay is a man deeply committed to his people, the Maquis. While he is passionate about the Maquis cause, he understands the discipline necessary to run the Starship *Voyager*. As a result, he is often in conflict between two worlds."

—Robert Beltran

Chakotay

Chakotay combines the traditions of the Amerindian with the experience of a trained Starfleet officer. He serves as Captain Janeway's strong right arm aboard the starship *Voyager*.

As Earth progressed, it also grew more homogeneous. Individual cultural practices slowly disappeared in a flood of fast food, television, electronic highways, easy travel, international business, pop bands, and movies. If people ate sushi and pad thai in Kansas City, others ate hamburgers and pizza in Tokyo and Bangkok. Signs in Mexico City proclaimed the availability of "American-style burritos." Deep down, people kept their differences, but surface culture changed. If Thai girls still didn't like to kiss and Japanese still bowed, everyone ate at Kentucky Fried Chicken and McDonald's (except perhaps in India), listened to the Beatles, wore Levi's, and shopped in Isetan Department Stores.

Many feared their cultures would disappear through assimilation. Diverse ethnic groups discussed solutions. Everyone shared the same problem, and, ultimately, found the same solution. Each group wanted its own world where they could remain faithful to their traditions and shut out outside influences. Many Earth cultures found their own planet and built a world in their own image.

Amerindians erected one such colony on Dorvan Five in the twenty-second century. They created a traditional home on a remote world in what later became the Demilitarized Zone between Cardassian and Federation space. They practiced traditional Amerindian religious rites and communal social organization and discouraged outside contact. They developed a new technology to allow them to experience vision quests; they mapped the unconscious and found their spirit guides. Their world flourished.

Chakotay was born and raised in that colony. Although a proud member of the Amerindian nation, he resisted communal thinking although, possibly in an ultimately impossible contradiction, he accepted communal ownership of property. His kinsmen branded him a "contrary." He loved his people and their beliefs and traditions but couldn't close his heart to the universe around him. A galaxy full of advanced technology and diverse life forms ultimately drew him to enroll in Starfleet Academy. He felt no contradiction in keeping traditional Amerindian beliefs while exploring the wonders of the universe beyond. Chakotay became the first Amerindian to graduate from Starfleet Academy with honors.

Discrimination and ethnic stereotyping had largely died out by the twenty-fourth century, but some still suffered. Few understood the history of Chakotay's people prior to the ravages brought by the coming of the Europeans. Fewer still remembered that the written constitution of the tribes of "The Long House" influenced the writing of the United States Constitution, or recalled the brilliant speeches of Chief Joseph or the military genius of Little Turtle or the mathematical advances of the Maya. Even the rescue of starving, agriculturally ignorant European colonists had been forgotten, although that event had long been celebrated as Thanksgiving by Earth's most powerful nation.

Chakotay retained his love for his people and their traditions while serving Starfleet and the United Federation of Planets. That involved no conflict of interests. His world was a Federation world, his people citizens of the Federation. In Starfleet Chakotay devoted himself to the religion of his people, spreading their traditions and rituals. He educated Vulcans, Klingons, Bajorans, hu-

mans, and many other races in the ways of his ancestors. He taught his crewmates how to go on spirit quests to find their animal guides. He explained medicine wheels and other rituals, and he continued to honor his deceased father by performing annual "Pakra" rituals.

Chakotay holds traditional nomadic Amerindian ideas about property ownership. His people taught him a person cannot own land but only courage and loyalty, the source of true power. He enjoys telling crewmates tales of his people's culture and history. They love the stories of heroic adventure and morals that sound so similar to their own belief in duty and honor. He tells of the wonders and intelligence of his people and of the problems brought by the arrival of the Europeans.

Chakotay tells many stories of the Amerindian nations, but they always end with the coming of the Europeans that destroyed their civilizations and took their land. Amerindians had warred on and killed one another, sometimes in ritual slaughter, but never with the grim totality of these Euro-

---

Chakotay

Race: Human
Gender: Male
Rank: Commander
Department: Command
Position: First Officer

Chakotay is from the Native American tribe that settled on a planet near the Cardassian border in the demilitarized zone. He follows many of their traditions, including carrying a medicine bundle; he has a spirit guide who often advises him. He completed Starfleet Academy and advanced to the rank of lieutenant commander on the *U.S.S. Merrimac*. When his people were attacked by the Cardassians, Chakotay left Starfleet and joined the Maquis soon after it was formed. He commanded the Maquis ship that was taken to the Delta Quadrant by the Caretaker. Once on board *Voyager*, he was made first officer of the joint crews and promoted to the rank of commander. He is the only crew member from the Maquis ship who has experience as a Starfleet officer.

---

peans. Europeans not only warred with the Indian nations, they attempted cultural genocide. These injustices enraged Chakotay, but he never believed the destroyer would come again.

That belief changed with the signing of the Federation treaty with Cardassia. Captain Picard and his starship *Enterprise* arrived on the Amerindian homeworld to remove the colonists in accordance with Federation rulings. Gul Evek arrived with a Cardassian scouting party. After speaking with both, Anthwara, Tribal Council leader of the Amerindians, refused to evacuate his people. Finally, Picard and Gul Evek agreed to allow the Amerindians to remain in their homes if all Dorvan Five residents abandoned their rights as Federation citizens. Gul Evek said, "I cannot speak for every Cardassian you may encounter, but if you leave us alone, I suspect we will do the same."

Not all Cardassians honored the agreement. They raided the colonies after the Federation withdrew all protection. The colonists of Dorvan Five joined a group of mercenaries and other rebels to protect their planet. The Federation outlawed the underground, which grew into the Maquis, but some Starfleet officers defected to the rebels, particularly those from worlds within the Demilitarized Zone.

Commander Calvin Hudson of Dorvan Five was one of the first. Straight-arrow Lieutenant Thomas Riker, a young half-Klingon, half-human Starfleet dropout named B'Elanna Torres, and Tom Paris, a former Starfleet lieutenant, also joined. A Vulcan named Tuvok appeared to join the movement, but he was secretly sent by the Federation starship *Voyager* to infiltrate the Maquis. Lieutenant Commander Chakotay abandoned his post aboard the starship *Merrimac* after his father died fighting the Cardassians threatening his world. Now Chakotay could not hope to one day heal the heated conflict between himself and his father and the traditions of his people. He later sought his father in "vision quests" but failed to hear his voice. Chakotay left Starfleet to defend his home, joining the rebel Maquis.

Chakotay strikes a commanding presence, overbearing, powerful, and very sexual. He quickly rose to captain his own Maquis starship and built a new life in the underground. Chakotay even entered a romantic relationship with an apparently Bajoran Maquis named Seska. The love affair didn't last. Chakotay's life among the Maquis ended when the Federation starship *Voyager* hunted his ship. Both vessels were suddenly propelled into the unexplored Delta Quadrant, stranded far from home. Necessity forced the Maquis and Federation crews to unite aboard the *Voyager*, but some Maquis proved reluctant to don Starfleet uniforms and obey Captain Janeway. Chakotay forcefully informed them that he would brook no mutiny.

He also told Tuvok only he had authority over the former Maquis. He even told Maquis member B'Elanna Torres she would be chief engineer of the *Voyager* before consulting Captain Janeway. Starfleet first officer Tuvok stepped down in favor of Chakotay.

After many new Maquis crew members proved unfamiliar with military procedures, Captain Janeway instructed Tuvok to educate them. Many objected to his rigid command and refused to attend class. Chakotay took an active role to insure Tuvok's success. He confronted Tuvok's "students" in the mess hall. When Dalby told him that they wouldn't be treated as teenage Starfleet cadets, Chakotay asked, "And you want to do things the Maquis way?" When Dalby agreed, Chakotay hauled him up and decked him with one punch. Chakotay then said, "That's the Maquis way, too, isn't it? And if you want to keep doing it the Maquis way, that's fine with me. We can do that tomorrow, the next day, every day until you want to report to Lieutenant Tuvok." This proved persuasive.

While on a mission for *Voyager*, Chakotay was once rescued by his ex-lover, Ensign Seska. She then wanted to resume the relationship they had shared aboard the Maquis starship. When he resisted, she warned him that there weren't many choices aboard the *Voyager*, and she had her eye on Kim. During another incident, Chakotay learned that Seska was secretly a Cardassian spy, altered to look like a Bajoran. Chakotay then suspected that Seska's love for him had always been false. When he confronted her, she replied, "Do you think I gave you my heart to get your Maquis secrets? Let me tell you something. Your secrets weren't good enough. I had only one agenda with you, Chakotay, and I never kept it secret."

After being discovered and fleeing with the Kazon, Seska told Chakotay she had impregnated herself with his DNA, and that he would soon be a father. She later claimed she was carrying the child of Culluh, the captain of the Kazon ship on which she serves, lying either to Culluh or Chakotay. Chakotay then received a message from Seska claiming that his newborn son had been banished by Culluh to a servant colony. Teirna, a former aide to Seska, later delivered the news that Culluh had killed Seska. It all turned out to be a trick to successfully lure *Voyager* into a trap.

Chakotay continues to practice his religious beliefs aboard the *Voyager*. It helps him feel closer to his people. He has decorated his quarters with an Amerindian altar and traditional fetishes. One wall displays traditional mural art. He celebrates the ceremonial cycle with a "habak" program in the holodeck. Chakotay reveres all living things and gives thanks to the earth spirit for food before he eats. He's a vegetarian who never takes drugs or alcohol, in order to keep his body pure.

On a *Voyager* mission, Chakotay encountered aliens who spoke the language of his ancestors. The aliens used their translator device to talk to Chakotay, then noticed that they wore the same tattoos. "I wear it to honor my father; he wore it to honor his ancestors," he told them. They asked, "Are there others on your world with this mark?" "Not many," he replied. The aliens had been told that there weren't any left. Chakotay was

> **At first Chakotay accepted the authority of Captain Janeway out of necessity.**

clearly connected to these people but he lacked the genetic memory of them the aliens expected. He learned that the aliens had visited Earth forty thousand years ago and given an enlightened tribe a nudge in the right direction. The last time the aliens had visited, they couldn't find the tribe. Chakotay told them, "We called you the Sky Spirits."

After meeting the aliens, Chakotay finally seemed at peace with himself, his father, and his tribe. The alien drew the symbol on the ground and placed his hand on it. Chakotay added his own hand. After Chakotay rejoined his Away Team, he heard a hawk screeching overhead, and the voice of his father. "Do you hear what he says to you?" his father asked. "Yes, Father, I hear him. I finally hear him," responded a happy Chakotay.

Chakotay maintains great respect for the dead and their ritual graves. He recalled the tragedy wrought when Europeans and Americans disturbed the graves of his own Amerindian people, and he objected when a *Voyager* crew member wanted to disturb the ritual graves of dead aliens. He even protested interference with the natural process of life and death when a seemingly dead woman was revived. Chakotay teaches his traditions to Captain Janeway and other crew members. He explained a "vision quest" in which he found his personal animal guide, a timber wolf. This image of a wolf appears in his dreams and helps him find inner strength.

Chakotay has observed and respects the warrior traditions of the Kazon. He and a young Kazon, Kahr, saved each others' lives and talked about what Kazon names and

Federation uniforms represent. Kahr finally told Chakotay, "You are not welcome here, you're still the enemy, and if our paths cross again, I will do my best to kill you." Chakotay said, "I understand."

At first Chakotay accepted the authority of Captain Janeway out of necessity. She then earned his respect and a strong bond grew between them, though he still resents her continuing prejudice against former rebel Maquis crew members. Chakotay also would like to change certain Federation rules, and he once told her, "I don't think we can afford to keep on doing business as usual." Janeway and Chakotay discovered an attraction between them after being afflicted with a seemingly incurable, deadly virus and then confined together on a small planet.

Chakotay and Tuvok share an ambivalent relationship. They used to bicker often, but they have since come to terms with each other. Chakotay acknowledged that it must have been difficult for Tuvok to be passed over in the chain of command when he was made first officer, and Tuvok admitted that he felt resentment and made their relationship difficult.

Legends and tales of heroism guide Chakotay. He learns and teaches important morals with these tales of heroic champions and terrible demons. Tuvok views these stories differently. Tuvok has said, "Such fables are necessary only in cultures which unduly emphasize emotional behavior. I would point out there are no demons in Vulcan literature."

For the most part, Chakotay gets along with other crew members, though he and Paris have had serious conflicts. Chakotay inspires Kim to explore his own Asian cultural heritage, and he once proclaimed his love for Torres. At another time, he attempted to contact his spirit guide with Torres holding his hand. Chakotay also explained love, jealousy, and relationships to an anxious Neelix.

The renegade former Starfleet officer Chakotay now commands all *Voyager* crew members as their senior officer. At first Starfleet members of the *Voyager* crew accepted his leadership because it was the will of their captain. They then learned to trust his judgment, fairness, and courage.

Robert Beltran

Producer-creators Jeri Taylor, Michael Piller, and Rick Berman wanted an Amerindian as second-in-command of the starship *Voyager* for their new Star Trek series. It proved to be a difficult role to cast. Pilot director Winrich Kolbe told *Cinescape* that few Amerindian actors are well known enough to be considered, but one was Robert Beltran.

However, Robert didn't like science fiction. He found TV and big screen sci-fi dry and spiritless. He wasn't a Star Trek fan. In fact, the only genre film he liked was Stanley Kubrick's *2001: A Space Odyssey* from 1968. Then he started doing his homework while he was being considered for the newest Star Trek series. "I started researching a little bit, watching *Next Generation, Deep Space Nine,* and even the old *Star Trek,*" he said. "Writing is always the crux of any program, and I found the writing on those shows to be of

top quality. I knew a lot of the same people were involved in *Voyager*. So, I got more excited about it, and by the time I got the part, I knew I'd made the right decision. And now I'm completely sure of that. When you look back at the original *Star Trek,* you can see how the relationships developed. I wouldn't say I'm a fanatic, but I now can see what is behind all of the fandom. I was impressed with the writing, the issues they were talking about, and I'm starting to like it."

Robert seemed destined for *Star Trek,* a show known for confronting moral issues. The Mexican-American actor was born and raised in Bakersfield, California, and he believes in contributing to his community. He served as a founding member and co-artistic director of the East Los Angeles Classic Theater Group. The group provides cultural enrichment to the East Los Angeles community, offering performances such as *A Touch of the Poet* and *The Price* at California State University at Los Angeles.

> *"I'm not an expert on Indians, but I'm a human being, and I know Indians are human beings."*

Robert graduated from Fresno State University with a degree in theater arts. His acting debut occurred as a spear carrier in *Romeo and Juliet.* He went on to act in *A Midsummer Night's Dream, Hamlet,* and *King Henry IV* for the California Shakespeare Festival. He also appeared in *I Don't Have to Show You No Stinkin' Badges,*

Corridos, Rose of the Rancho, and *La Pastorela* with El Teatro Campesino, the theater company of famed writer/director Luis Valdez at the La Jolla Playhouse, as well as in *A Burning Beach* and *Stars in the Morning Sky* at the Los Angeles Theatre Center.

Robert's first film role was in *Eating Raoul* in 1982. His other films include *Lone Wolf McQuade, Night of the Comet, Forbidden Sun, Scenes from the Class Struggle in Beverly Hills, Gaby: A True Story, Crackdown, Bugsy, Shadow Hunter, Kiss Me a Killer,* and Oliver Stone's *Nixon,* with Anthony Hopkins. He has appeared in a number of TV movies, including *Rio Shannon, Mystic Warrior, The Chase, El Diablo, Slowbleed,* and *Calendar Girl Murders* (a.k.a. *Victimized*).

Robert has also enjoyed an active television career, including the lead role for HBO's *Midnight Caller* and in the ABC miniseries *The Mystic Warrior.* He appeared as a guest star on *Lois and Clark: The New Adventures of Superman, Murder, She Wrote, Streethawk, Miami Vice,* and *Veronica Clare.* Robert also played Lieutenant Soto in the first ten episodes of *Models, Inc.* and appeared in the British miniseries *Shannongate,* later shown on PBS in America.

When Beltran was being cast for *Voyager,* Kolbe told *Cinescape,* "he was extremely soft-spoken in the beginning, and I think that was in part due to the script, where he was described as a calm, stoic Indian. I don't know where we got that from. It's some kind of myth that's still hanging around today, that you can throw a spear through an Indian and he won't even flinch. I'm not an expert on Indians, but I'm a human being, and I know Indians are human beings. Living on a Maquis ship and fighting a life-and-death battle with the Cardassians, he isn't going to sit around there and calmly say, 'Well, okay, now, give me full forward power and let's get moving.' There's got to be that tension there. Robert, I think, recognized this and developed during the [casting] process."

Robert told *Superstar Facts & Pix,* "I just hope they keep him actively involved in whatever adventure the crew goes on. As far as his Indian background, I don't know if they are ever going to settle on a specific tribe or culture. There are many Indian tribes and cultures to choose from and they haven't specified what Chakotay is yet. I hope they will do it a little differently and maybe go Mayan or Aztec, because they are very advanced in astronomy."

Kate Mulgrew appreciates Robert and his role as Chakotay. She told *The Official* Star Trek: Voyager *Magazine,* "I would like to see the Chakotay-Janeway relationship go further. The guy is a Maquis warrior and we haven't seen nearly enough of that side of him."

Robert enjoys his new role. He admitted, "Usually, when I work in television, it gets old very quickly, but this hasn't. The material seems to sustain and I look forward to coming to work, dealing with the plots, and learning more about Chakotay. It's been challenging and fun."

"I came into this thing, before we even started, knowing a lot about this character."

—Tim Russ, in *The Official* Star Trek: Voyager *Magazine*

Tuvok

Vulcan Tactical/Security Officer Tuvok served as Captain Kathryn Janeway's first officer and confidante for many years before the *Voyager* chased a Maquis rebel ship and found itself lost in the Delta Quadrant. He then stepped aside to allow the Maquis captain, Chakotay, to assume the role of ship's first officer after the two crews combined. Tuvok continues to serve as his captain's chief confidante and advisor. To understand him, it is first necessary to understand Vulcans. Beyond the arched eyebrows and pointed ears, he shares many mental and emotional traits with his people.

Enigmatic Vulcans puzzle other races. They will sacrifice their lives for a friend but rarely let anyone grow emotionally close. While they can appear virtually emotionless, an empathetic observer quickly realizes that they have very strong emotions indeed, under very tight mental control, lurking just beneath the surface. Ritual suicide is still in practice among aged and infirm Vulcans.

Vulcans and Terrans founded the United Federation of Planets. While Vulcans maintain their distance and few non-Vulcans have visited their inhospitable home planet, they remain staunch allies, loyal to the Federation. Vulcans appear to worship logic, but they can be compelled by religious fervor or enter a state of intense, uncontrollable sexual passion, known as pon farr,

every seven years. Tuvok is no exception. He maintains careful mental discipline and has mastered the Vulcan nerve pinch and mind meld, which, in itself, is considered a violent act by unwilling recipients, but often presents perplexing contradictions.

Tuvok married young, to T'Pel in 2304, and deeply loves his mate of sixty-seven years. They have three sons and one daughter together. The logical Vulcan once told Neelix, "being a father can have infinite rewards, far more than would seem possible." Thoughts of them clearly test his emotional control. A childlike alien, Elani, once asked him about his children, "If Vulcans don't feel anything, does that mean you don't love them?" He responded, "My attachment to my children cannot be described as an emotion. They are part of my identity—and I am . . . incomplete . . . without them." The alien could only add, "I bet they miss you, too." Tuvok then sang a "lullaby," perhaps to his own distant children as well as to the aliens.

Tuvok looks down on both humans and their love of mythology, of heroes and demons. He once told Chakotay, "Like all humans, you depend on feelings and instincts to guide you, and they invariably let you down." But Janeway has had reason to call Tuvok's vaunted logic into question. He once took very odd steps when the *Voyager* came across a world with a technology that could return them home. The Sikarian Canon of Laws, their version of the Prime

Directive, prevented the aliens from giving their spatial trajector to the *Voyager* crew. Janeway reluctantly honored the wishes of the Sikarians, but Tuvok violated his captain's prohibition to gain the spatial trajector. Though he didn't intend to use it until after winning Janeway's approval, Torres attempted to work it on her own, and Tuvok took full blame for her actions. He insisted he logically acted to spare Janeway the ethical dilemma of choosing between not violating Sikarian law and getting her crew home. He also said he expected to lose his commission and be court-martialed upon their return home.

Janeway said, "You can use logic to justify almost anything. That's its power and its flaw." Tuvok replied, "My logic was not in error, but I was." Tuvok has also admitted, "The demands on a Vulcan's character are extraordinarily difficult. Do not mistake composure for ease."

Chakotay has had similar problems with the Vulcan. He once asked Tuvok, "May I ask you to be honest with me, Lieutenant?" When Tuvok boastfully replied, "As a Vulcan, I am at all times honest, Commander," Chakotay said, "That's not exactly

true. You lied to me when you passed yourself off as a Maquis to get on my crew." Tuvok responded, "I was honest with my own convictions within the defined parameters of my mission." A baffled Chakotay could only lament, "You damned Vulcans and your defined parameters. That's easy for you."

Tuvok and Chakotay are on respectful terms now, but they have often been at odds. Before they became lost in space, Tuvok acted as a hostile spy aboard Chakotay's Maquis ship, and when *Voyager* and the Maquis ship merged their crew, Chakotay replaced Tuvok as second-in-command of *Voyager*. Tuvok eventually told Chakotay that Janeway's decision proved to be a wise one. Mutual respect has grown between them, and Chakotay's humanity and Tuvok's Vulcan logic have come to complement each other.

Before Tuvok boarded *Voyager*, he taught at Starfleet Academy for sixteen years and served aboard Captain Hikaru Sulu's Federation starship *Excelsior*. Tuvok often acts too rigidly to effectively relate to others. He isolates himself further by always eating alone because he doesn't like "short" talk, as he calls it.

Tuvok

Race: Vulcan
Gender: Male
Rank: Lieutenant Commander
Department: Security
Position: Chief of Security/Chief Tactical Officer

Tuvok is a full Vulcan. He was married to T'Pel in 2304, and his family still lives on Vulcan, in the Alpha Quadrant. He has four children who also live there, three sons and one daughter. Serving for some time in Starfleet, Tuvok returned to the Academy to teach for sixteen years. He serves with Kathryn Janeway as her security officer. Infiltrating the Maquis in 2371, Tuvok was aboard the Maquis ship taken to the Delta Quadrant by the Caretaker.

After many new Maquis crew members proved unfamiliar with military procedures, Captain Janeway instructed Tuvok to educate them. However, the Maquis rebels were reluctant and difficult pupils, unlike the eager cadets Tuvok had taught before at Starfleet Academy. The Maquis rebelled under his instruction and refused to attend his new Starfleet officer class. Neelix suggested that Tuvok was too rigid and inflexible, that if he didn't learn to bend, he would break. Taking Neelix's advice to heart, Tuvok took the hostile Dalby to Paris's bar, Chez Sandrine. There "Vulcan Slim" proceeded to trounce the young ex-Maquis at pool and to share confidences.

In the end, Tuvok learned as much from his experience as did his students. After he had violated his own order to his cadets and risked his life to rescue Gerron, Dalby asked, "I thought Starfleet rules said that it was an unacceptable risk, going back to save him." Tuvok replied, "It was. However, I recently realized that there are times when it is desirable to bend the rules."

Half-Klingon, half-human B'Elanna Torres admires Tuvok's emotional control. She hopes to learn how to restrain her own Klingon nature. Tuvok tutors Kes with her rapidly maturing mental abilities.

Tuvok has faced many dangers serving in Starfleet. He once helped a group of slaves evade capture by the Klingon-Cardassian Alliance in a mirror universe, and he had his body parts stolen by Vidiians in a duplicate existence. Another time he applied Vulcan logic to play detective and solve a crime. He has received a concussion and burns, merged with Neelix into a new being, Tuvix, been possessed by a Konar, and been forced to eat Neelix's over-spiced version of Vulcan plomeek soup! Once he even served as defense counsel for a suicidal member of the Q Continuum, although he personally abhors taking one's own life. His worst crisis will come if pon farr strikes him. Pon farr "madness" affects Vulcans every seven years. It forces them to mate in a state of blood passion. Unable to return to his wife or the planet Vulcan, it could prove fatal unless he can find a suitable substitute. Perhaps, having already fathered four children, he won't be subject to its ravages. The crew of the *Voyager* can only hope so. A superhumanly strong, mad Vulcan is a terrible sight indeed.

Tim Russ

"I've always been a fan," Tim Russ admitted to *The Official* Star Trek: Voyager *Magazine*. His first personal encounter came as a student at St. Edwards University in the '70s when he shared a college stage with visiting performer Leonard Nimoy in a production of *Caligula*. Nimoy, of course, played *Star Trek*'s most famous Vulcan, Spock, for the original television series and a string of six movies. By the time Tim met Nimoy a second time, he had won the role of Tuvok, the Vulcan aboard the starship *Voyager* for the newest series. Tim told *Sci-Fi Entertainment*, "We didn't really talk. I just shook his hand. He knew who I was, what I was playing, and he said, 'I should know your face really well.' I reminded him that we worked together in the play *Caligula*. It's quite ironic, ending up in this position."

The Trek fan seemed destined to serve aboard a Star Trek starship. He had been the runner-up for the role of Geordi La Forge, the blind engineer on *Star Trek: The Next Generation* in 1987. He later missed a shot at a regular part on *Deep Space Nine*. "I had read for Rick Berman when they were auditioning for *The Next Generation* cast," he told *The Official* Star Trek: Voyager *Magazine*, "I was second to LeVar Burton. At the time, Gene Roddenberry wanted LeVar over me and that was it. Rick has been a fan of mine since that time. He said something to my manager about it years back. Since then, my manager would keep reminding me about that. I read for a role as a regular on *Deep Space Nine*, but the role was changed."

> **A super-humanly strong, mad Vulcan is a terrible sight indeed.**

Until *Star Trek: Voyager* arrived, he had to content himself with bit parts in his favorite sci-fi universe. These included guest-starring roles as the humanoid terrorist Devor in the sixth season *Next Generation* episode "Starship Mine," the Klingon mercenary T'Kar for the first season *Deep Space Nine* episode "Invasive Procedures," and an alternate universe Tuvok that was a pro-Terran revolutionary in the third season *Deep Space Nine* episode "Through the Looking Glass." Tim even played a nameless human tactical officer for the transition film *Star Trek: Generations*.

Success finally came when he won the role of Tuvok for *Voyager*, but he almost missed that one, too. Pilot director Winrich Kolbe told *Cinescape*, "Originally Tuvok was supposed to be 160 years old. We had a problem. When we were looking for an established, older actor to play the part of Tuvok, we had some damn good actors come in and read for us, but we couldn't quite agree. So we started scaling down the age. We went from the sixties to the fifties to the forties to the thirties. A little longer, I'm sure we would have needed a tutor on the set.

"You have to understand another thing: these stoic parts like Chakotay and Tuvok are very difficult to act. What you're telling those guys is, 'I want you to withdraw. I want you to be distant, but I want you to have character. I want you to be a Vulcan, logical, but I don't want you to be boring.'" Tim was up for the challenge.

Born in Washington, D.C., to an Air Force officer, Tim enjoyed a successful career before coming to *Star Trek: Voyager*. Growing up as a military brat prepared him for the life of changes and constant relocation required of a successful actor. His family moved frequently, spending time in Asia and the Middle East before settling in Sacramento.

His first stage performance was in a musical stage show in high school and he continued to perform at St. Edwards University in Austin, Texas. Later, professional stage work included performances in *As You Like It, Dream Girls, Cave Dwellers*, and *Romeo and Juliet* at CBS/MTM, as well as roles in *As You Like It, Twelfth Night,* and *Macbeth* at L.A.'s Schubert Theatre. Tim received an NAACP Image Award as the title character in the L.A. Theater Center production *Barrabas.*

He made his television debut in "Charlie Smith and the Fritter Tree" for *PBS Masterpiece Theater.* Other television work includes guest appearances on *Seaquest DSV, Hangin' with Mr. Cooper, Living Single, Melrose Place, The People Next Door,* where he played the Answering Machine Guy alongside Jeffrey Jones, and the low budget *Freddy's Nightmares,* where he appeared as a straight-laced scientist.

He enjoyed a larger role in the short-lived series *The Highwayman,* as the sidekick to lead star Sam Jones, and he played a military type in the pilot for the never-produced series *Journey to the Center of the Earth.* Tim also had a recurring part in the syndicated drama *Arresting Behavior,* based on the reality program *Cops.*

His film debut was in *Fire with Fire,* with Virginia Madsen. Other film roles include parts in *Mr. Saturday Night* and as a rookie detective in the low budget *Dead Connection* with Virginia Madsen's cousin Michael Madsen. Tim's made-for-TV movies include *Double Cross and Bitter Harvest,* also with Virginia Madsen, for the USA Network.

Tim's big day arrived when the producers chose him to play the new Vulcan, Tuvok, for *Star Trek: Voyager.* The Trek fan was already very familiar with the legend. Tim believes in maintaining continuity in the Star Trek universe created by Gene Roddenberry. Not only was he familiar with

the three prior television series and the seven Star Trek movies, but he read all of the books that featured Vulcans to get a complete picture of their history.

Tim told Melbourne, Australia's, *The Age,* "It's a literal connection, it's a direct connection to what has already been established with Spock. I've had to fight the writers and producers on more than one occasion to make sure that they remain true to the lore, that they are true to the consistency of the culture and the philosophy of this alien race, that they understand how this character works."

He identifies closely with his Tuvok character. He said, "I tend to be very straightforward and very business-like. I do tend to be pretty logical about a lot of things. Things that don't make sense to me drive me crazy. Also, things that are inefficient drive me crazy. I don't have Tuvok's infinite patience, I wish I did. I also believe in the philosophy that we are driven by our emotions and that those things can be a problem sometimes if you allow them to get out of control."

Tim didn't want to play a stock, emotionless Vulcan. He told *Sci-Fi Entertainment,* "What I did was discover that this character, for example, had a family. He had a wife and children back in the Alpha Quadrant. We also learn about how he has to adjust to the people he works around. I think he's just going to have much more understanding about the ways of human beings and how they live and communicate, and he'll try to become more tolerant to some degree."

Tim is pleased to work within the Star Trek universe created by Gene Roddenberry. He appreciates the IDIC—Infinite Diversity in Infinite Combination—symbol central to the Vulcan culture of his character. Tim told *The Age*, "In my recent past as an actor I've had to play and read for certain parts that were contemporary stereotypes of blacks from the inner city and the ghettos. Some of those projects I refused to read for because they were just caricatures. With this particular part in *Voyager*, I am very proud and very lucky to have the opportunity to play a role that is nontraditional for blacks. It is absolutely at the other side of the spectrum, far away from the contemporary image of blacks in this country and what had been perpetrated on television."

Tim told *Sci-Fi Entertainment* that he believes *Star Trek: Voyager* has been well received. "So far the remarks and comments have been that I've fulfilled this Vulcan character pretty much to the highest degree. The believability is there that he is a Vulcan, so they're happy about that. However, the fans are much more critical about the details and consistency of the show and what's been done in the past. There are rules you have to follow that have been established by the previous series, so it's quite interesting how you have to make the whole process work."

Many cars in Los Angeles display a bumper sticker with the classic Hollywood cliché: "I'd rather direct." Tim, like most actors, would like to get behind the camera, just as *Star Trek* actors Leonard Nimoy, William Shatner, LeVar Burton, and Jonathan Frakes have already done. Tim told *Sci-Fi Entertainment*, "I don't know if that's going to happen, but it is in the back of my mind, and I may want to use the opportunity on *Voyager* to expand my skills behind the camera. It's a different kind of work. Directing is more about being in charge of making images come together with some degree of imagination, and because of the show, it would have to be a certain way, no matter what you want to do. So I'd have to gear myself up for that challenge if I want to take it. It's a big step away from what I'm doing. You have to be objective in directing. It's an entirely different approach."

Tim is also aware that there is a price for being on a high-profile series. Tim told *The Age*, "I will be identified with this role very closely and it will be very difficult to try to break that pattern, so this summer my partner and I are producing a low-budget feature film that we're going to be shooting here in Los Angeles. That is going to start a line of feature projects that we're going to be producing on our own and this is how I intend to bridge that gap from my role in *Voyager*."

"He's the rookie on the ship. He's a pro, but he doesn't have any
real starship experience under his belt, and he is a little insecure."
—Garrett Wang, in *The Official* Star Trek: Voyager *Magazine*

Harry Kim

In every crew there is a golden boy (or girl), and Harry Kim—the young, twenty-one-year-old Ops/Communications Officer on *Voyager*—is that person. He has enjoyed such status all his life. His parents had tried to conceive a child for years before Harry was born, and since he arrived as they approached their golden years, his proud parents called their only child "golden boy" ever after. They showered him with love, warmth, and support. It was a sheltered childhood, protected from the normal cares and concerns of life. Harry rarely experienced adversity and so failed to develop coping tools.

His parents just knew he would excel in whatever field he chose. Faithful to their Asian traditions, they stressed the importance of education. Dedicated to fulfilling their expectations, he graduated from Starfleet Academy with honors after a shining academic career. Ensign Danny Bird was his best friend at the Academy.

Harry had distinguished himself as editor of a Starfleet Academy journal. Like everything else, he took the job seriously, monitoring subspace communications, and he even broke the story of the Maquis rebellion. In a rare burst of enthusiasm, Harry once told Neelix, "Opinions were polarized, debate was sparked, people got passionate, we learned and we communicated." Apparently history was not a strong subject, though. Harry knows little about the early twentieth century, including aviation pioneer Amelia Earhart.

After graduating from Academy, Harry lived in San Francisco with his fiancée, Libby. He plunged himself into a standard San Francisco lifestyle, frequenting a coffee shop and playing a musical instrument, the clarinet. Then Starfleet awarded him a rare honor. They assigned him as Ops/Communications Officer aboard one of the newest, most modern, ships in Starfleet, *Voyager*. His proud parents saw him off on his first voyage.

Their support meant a lot to him. The young Asian remained close to his parents, frequently communicating with them. Then, in the midst of a voyage he thought

---

Harry Kim

Race: Human

Gender: Male

Rank: Ensign

Department: Operations

Position: Chief of Operations/Communications Officer

Harry Kim is fresh out of the Academy. The *U.S.S. Voyager* is his first assignment. Kim is very close to his family. He wrote them every week before the Caretaker incident. He plays the clarinet.

---

would last a month, his ship was propelled to the Delta Quadrant, seventy light-years from home. Feeling truly lost, he believes his parents and fiancée will think him dead. He also knows that his mother and father will be dead of old age long before he returns. This realization leaves him scared and lonely.

Often he feels trapped in a bad dream from which he hopes to awaken—to find his mother singing in the garden and his father hammering copper plate for sculpture. Only dedication to normal routine saves him from madness. Young Harry suffers more than anyone else in the *Voyager* crew, though he is well-liked by everyone. He misses his clarinet, which his mother had tried to send to him but Captain Janeway had not allowed it. Other crew members protect the young, inexperienced man, and they are more charmed than annoyed by his eager-beaver attitude. Tom Paris created Chez Sandrine, a bar and billiards hall, primarily to entertain Harry. Chakotay keeps Harry's nose to the grindstone to keep him distracted. Captain Janeway often acts as a substitute mother.

Harry has already experienced many adventures aboard the *Voyager*. He died in a Vhnori cenotaph pod but was restored to life aboard the *Enterprise*. It was quite an experience for someone who doesn't know if there is an afterlife. Another adventure pulled him into a subspace vacuole dimensional distortion. He created a "Beowulf" holonovel on the holodeck that came to life, and he, Tuvok, and Chakotay were all dematerialized by "Grendel," an energy being.

An adventure trapped him in an alternate time stream. There he continued his life in San Francisco, working as an engineer for Starfleet, and living with his fiancée, Libby. In that world, Paris ended up down and out, living in Marseilles, France. Harry sacrificed the opportunity to return home from the Delta Quadrant to restore his friend to a better life aboard the *Voyager*. Sacrificing his fiancée and parents a second time was a difficult decision for Harry.

Now the real Harry can never return. He died when a hull breach sucked him into the vacuum of space. The Harry Kim now aboard *Voyager* is a stranger in a strange land, an exact duplicate. "We're Starfleet officers," Janeway told him with a smile. "Weird is part of the job."

Garrett Wang

Garrett Wang (pronounced *Wong*) breathes life into Harry Kim for *Star Trek: Voyager*. The young actor, a son of immigrant Chinese-American parents, considers his role an important one, particularly for Asian-American viewers. He told *A Magazine*, "If my presence makes it better for some Asian kid who's susceptible to the kind of pain I felt, that's the most important thing."

His character, Harry Kim, has become almost as popular as series star Kate Mulgrew's Captain Janeway, but Garrett still doesn't feel secure in his acting career. He noted the paucity of roles for Asian Americans, telling *Star Trek Communicator*, "There's plenty of roles for Asian males in

63

Vietnam movies, or as bad guys, or Chinatown guys, but when it comes down to ensemble casts, they'll throw into the loop an Asian female because it's less threatening."

Star Trek: *Voyager*'s Harry Kim is Garrett's first major role. He made his movie debut in *Angry Cafe*, a short film made by fellow student Eric Koyanagi while they were both attending UCLA. He won critical acclaim for his first performance outside college as lead role John Lee in Chay Yew's *Porcelain* at the Burbage Theatre. Other theater work includes *Modle Minority* for the Los Angeles Theatre Center, *Woman Warrior* for the Mark Taper Forum, and *A Language of Their Own* for the Intiman Theatre.

Garrett also had a role in the low-budget film *Flesh Suitcase*, and he turned down a part in the film *Cruz* to do *Star Trek: Voyager*. His only television series appearance occurred as the conservative boyfriend of Korean-American series star Margaret Cho in the premiere episode of her ABC comedy series, *All American Girl*. He has also appeared in various television commercials.

Garrett turned to acting at least partly because of his experiences growing up in Memphis, Tennessee. He was born in Riverside, California, but his botanist father soon moved the family to Indiana, then Bermuda, then they ended up in Memphis, where Garrett spent his teen years.

Garrett recalled in *A Magazine*, "It's a nice town with Southern hospitality, but there was also a heavy dose of conservatism. I became painfully aware of my ethnicity in Memphis. I aspired to be as Caucasian as possible, but it was never enough in the eyes of some individuals. No matter what I did, I was always a chink to them."

Garrett remembers after one particularly bad experience, "I told my mother that I wished I had been born to white parents. She said the Chinese had thousands of years of tradition and that Americans only had five hundred. I told her I still thought the Chinese were a subrace. She turned away for a second and I could see she was crying. I didn't care because I was so bent out of shape. I was happy I hurt her."

Garrett moved to Los Angeles to attend UCLA. He graduated in Asian studies after first switching majors from pre-med to economics to political science. He also began rediscovering his Asian cultural roots, going on a cultural tour of Taiwan with other Chinese Americans. He began to think about changing the perception of Asian Americans, and that led to an interest in acting. Garrett told *A Magazine*, "I started thinking that these Caucasian kids who had picked on me weren't born that way. They learned their behavior from their parents or from TV and film. I really feel that TV and film are powerful mediums; that's where I thought I could make a difference."

He credits Jenny Rountree, a UCLA theater professor, with heavily influencing his career decision. He said, "Jenny was responsible for my first breakthrough. She inspired me to go beyond the status quo."

Garrett began appearing in plays on and off campus. He also began to take part in Asian-American activities, once meeting George Takei at a gathering of Asian-American actors in Los Angeles. He sees Takei as a "ground-breaker" for an Asian-

American actor in a non-ethnic specific role. Takei played the popular Sulu for the original 1960s *Star Trek* series and in the movies that followed.

Ethnic rediscovery, acting, and an encounter with Takei all led to Garrett's own Star Trek role. He began with clear ideas about Harry Kim. Garrett told *The Official* Star Trek: Voyager *Magazine*, "He's the rookie on the ship. He just graduated from Starfleet Academy. Unfortunately, for him, there's no easing into it. He thought he would just be running some maneuvers in space, doing routine stuff. He's a pro, but he doesn't have any real starship experience under his belt, and he is a little insecure."

> "He's a pro, but he doesn't have any real starship experience under his belt, and he is a little insecure."

Pilot director Winrich Kolbe told *Cinescape*, "Harry Kim is probably the most inexperienced, naive character of them all, and probably the character who will have to fight hardest to stay in the forefront. When we were casting, we said we wanted a young, Asian male, and there are not that many Japanese or Asian actors here. It was a very hard role to cast. Garrett is a young, up-and-coming actor, but he needs to learn, and that's going to take some time. He's one of the actors who has to really work hard on his craft in order to keep up with the others."

Garrett told *A Magazine*, "The first day of shooting was supposed to take place on the bridge of the ship. I had only one line in that scene—'Thrusters ready.' But we had some problems finding a captain, so the schedule was rearranged and the first day ended up becoming 'Harry Kim Day.' I remember walking onto the set that first day of shooting and thinking to myself, 'Why are they doing this to me? I need more time.'"

Though he has no prior musical training, Garrett is currently studying clarinet to play his role more authentically.

Voyager has quickly thrust the young actor into the limelight—to much public acclaim. He once substituted for Kate Mulgrew at a Star Trek convention and received a standing ovation from over four thousand fans before he even began to speak. Garrett told *A Magazine*, "Usually with actors there's a slow and steady progression they make in their careers, but I went from sea level to three thousand feet right away. When you take such an abrupt climb up, the altitude changes. It's harder to breathe up here. People don't understand that."

The actor still has a couple of non-Star Trek items on his agenda. He wants to tackle the lead in Korean-American director Clifford Son's film *Helium* if time permits. And Garrett Wang and Taylor Bernard, an actress, became engaged in May of 1995. They haven't set a date yet for the marriage, but, according to Taylor, "Since it will have to be on his hiatus, it will either be next year or the year after."

"B'Elanna is strong-willed, independent, and confused, caught between worlds. She attempts to deny and suppress her powerful Klingon side."

—Roxann Biggs-Dawson

B'Elanna Torres

Every person has conflicting sides, but B'Elanna Torres is a woman at war with herself. The twenty-five-year-old daughter of a Klingon mother and human father, she has never reconciled her two heritages, but she favors her humanity and rejects her Klingon nature. B'Elanna's father and mother divorced when she was five, and she never saw her father again. Her Klingon mother raised her in the primarily human colony on Kessik Four during a time when Federation relations with the Klingon homeworld remained strained. She wore scarves, hats, anything to hide her distinctive Klingon head.

Like many children of broken homes, she felt responsible for the divorce of her parents. B'Elanna once said, "I finally decided that he left because I looked like a Klingon, and so I tried to look human." Her peers taunted her, and she learned to hate everything Klingon, idolizing all that was human and turning her father into a perfect fantasy figure.

Still, her Klingon side often compelled her to act in a Klingon way, much to her dismay. She possessed a hot temper. She disliked herself and turned a belligerent attitude toward others. She walked around "with a chip on her shoulder" that often kept her from reaching her goals.

B'Elanna affirmed her human over her Klingon side by entering Starfleet Academy. Few Klingons enrolled in the Federation Academy. She excelled in the sciences, but she rebelled against authority and was generally antagonistic toward others. She found it impossible to follow orders and struggled with the structure and discipline demanded by the Academy. This constantly put her in trouble with her teachers and administrators, and B'Elanna washed out of Starfleet Academy in her second year.

After leaving the Academy, she joined the Starfleet Engineering Corps, but her inability to take orders again led to problems and she quit Starfleet. B'Elanna next joined the Maquis rebel underground. Fighting the Cardassians allowed her to become a warrior. Her captain, Chakotay, understood this need. His style, perhaps due to his own Amerindian background, proved compatible with the talented engineer. Still, B'Elanna refused to credit her Klingon side for her prowess as a courageous soldier.

B'Elanna flourished fighting against the Cardassians. War appealed to her Klingon side. The crew of the Maquis vessel grew to depend upon her, as did her captain. She had finally found a place where she felt she belonged, but it would not last. When *Voyager* gave chase to her rebel Maquis ship, both vessels were propelled into the Delta Quadrant, unable to return home. The

Maquis and Starfleet crews then joined forces aboard the *Voyager*.

On *Voyager*, B'Elanna's past seemed to catch up with her. She no longer had an enemy to fight, the Cardassians, and she was once again serving in Starfleet, under the command of a Starfleet captain. Her previous failure in the Academy began to haunt her, and she cursed her hot Klingon blood for being the cause of it all.

The sullen, pouting half-Klingon was ready for a fight. Inevitably, B'Elanna wound up in a clash of wills with Lieutenant Carey, who served as chief engineer of the *Voyager*, the same position B'Elanna held on the Maquis ship. Before she could stop herself, B'Elanna beat up Carey.

Though First Officer Tuvok wanted her thrown into the brig, Chakotay said he'd take responsibility for her, since he'd asked for sole authority over all ex-Maquis serving aboard the *Voyager*. When he found B'Elanna, he reprimanded her, saying, "You're going to need support from people like Carey." B'Elanna insisted, "I don't need support from anybody!"

B'Elanna Torres

Race: Half-Klingon, half-human
Gender: Female
Rank: Lieutenant
Department: Engineering
Position: Chief Engineer

Torres's father is human and her mother is Klingon. Her father left when she was young, and her mother raised her on a colony far from Qo'noS, the Klingon homeworld. Her conflicting human and Klingon ancestry often frustrates her. Torres has not kept in touch with her estranged mother, even before the Caretaker incident. She has had no contact with her father since he divorced her mother. Torres attended Starfleet Academy but dropped out during her second year. She joined the Maquis and became the chief engineer on Chakotay's ship. She is now chief engineer of the *Voyager*.

Then Chakotay took a gamble. Without checking with Captain Janeway, he told B'Elanna he was making her chief engineer of the *Voyager*, Lieutenant Carey's superior. Janeway resisted the idea at first, then relented. But the gambit has paid off, and B'Elanna has risen to her new responsibilities.

Later, B'Elanna confessed to Captain Janeway her failure at Starfleet Academy and her belief they wanted nothing to do with her. To B'Elanna's astonishment, Janeway revealed that she knew some of her history and that B'Elanna's instructors had been sorry to see her go. B'Elanna had nurtured a misconception for years.

Another incident from B'Elanna's past also returned to torment her, though it provided her with an opportunity to partially redeem herself in the eyes of Captain Janeway. While B'Elanna was a Maquis in the Alpha Quadrant, the Cardassians constructed a guided missile to destroy a Maquis installation. B'Elanna reprogrammed it to go after a Cardassian target, but the missile became lost and later appeared in the Delta Quadrant. Torres had redesigned it to resist all known Federation and Cardassian weapons. B'Elanna had anticipated thirty-seven possible security breaches and programmed them all into the computer. The system did the rest, adapting to new situations.

Voyager then discovered that the missile threatened an inhabited world in the Delta Quadrant, and B'Elanna beamed over to the dreadnought to try and convince it to stop. Though this worked for a time, the missile's computer became convinced that B'Elanna had been coerced by the Cardassians to stop it, and it resumed its mission. B'Elanna returned to the missile and engaged the guidance computer in a battle of wits, trying to use logic to convince it that it's mission was an error. Despite her best efforts, the computer finally perceived B'Elanna as an enemy spy and a threat, and it cut off life-support in the missile.

Facing certain death, B'Elanna worked feverishly to access the Cardassian file and her original programming. She activated the Cardassian control program which immediately tried to gain control of the missile but failed. B'Elanna then phasered a core breach and established a transporter lock. The computer tried to convince her to stop, but she continued relentlessly, saying, "Who'd have thought, back when we spent all that time together, that we'd be out here trying to kill each other?" Then the warp core went critical, Janeway beamed B'Elanna out, and the missile blew up. Since then, B'Elanna has acted often to save the ship, and this has won her Captain Janeway's respect, though not her full trust.

B'Elanna has become a masterful engineer, one of the best in Starfleet, but unlike the others on the *Voyager*, B'Elanna misses no one in the Alpha Quadrant. She hasn't seen her father since she was five, and she is estranged from her Klingon mother. B'Elanna also left no serious romantic relationship behind. She has begun to win friends aboard the *Voyager*.

B'Elanna admires the Vulcan Tuvok for his emotional control, although she can sometimes be quite hostile toward him. From him she hopes to learn how to restrain her own Klingon nature. Paris likes B'Elanna, but she hasn't yet responded. Torres has confided personal matters in Harry Kim. Janeway still intimidates her, but she'll go to the wall for her captain.

B'Elanna has studied traditional Amerindian rituals with her ex-captain, Chakotay, with whom she has had a brief romantic liaison. Chakotay said she is the only person he's ever known who's tried to kill her animal guide during a vision quest, but she once helped Chakotay save the *Voyager* using Amerindian implements.

Phage, the disease killing off the Vidiian race, once infected B'Elanna. A greater danger faced her in the Avery system when the chief surgeon of the Vidiian Sodality divided her into two people, one fully Klingon, the other fully human. The incident helped her to understand herself. The Klingon form enjoyed killing, while the fully human form lacked her instinctual genetic predisposition for battle.

At one point, her Klingon side asked her human side, "If I hadn't come along, were you just going to waste away in that prison camp until they killed you for your body parts? Were you too frightened to act?" Her human side replied, "That's the way you respond to every situation, isn't it? If it doesn't work, hit it. If it's in your way, knock it down. No wonder I got kicked out of the Academy." To which the Klingon replied, "For which you should be eternally grateful." The human then insisted, "Well, I'm not. Your temper has gotten me in trouble more times than I . . ."

Ultimately, the Klingon side died saving the human side, and the dying Klingon B'Elanna said, "You showed true courage. It makes my death an honorable one."

Later, aboard the *Voyager*, the Doctor insisted on reuniting B'Elanna with her Klingon side against her wishes, saying she needed her Klingon genes to survive. B'Elanna finally accepted being reunited, admitting, "I came to admire a lot of things about her. Her strength. Her bravery. I guess I just have to accept the fact that I'll spend the rest of my life fighting with her."

Roxann Biggs-Dawson

Actress Roxann Biggs-Dawson was an immediate fit for the part of the half-Klingon, half-human B'Elanna Torres, and she is well respected by the other cast members. Kate Mulgrew said of her in *The Official* Star Trek: Voyager *Magazine*, "I love Roxann Biggs-Dawson's intensity and her talent."

Pilot director Winrich Kolbe told *Cinescape*, "Roxann came in on day one and we just cast her. Not that we didn't keep looking, but she was pretty well set from the first day. I think she and Kim are going to be the two characters who are going to have to fight for airtime. One thing she has going for her is a volatile temper, which could go off at any time. She's the only one who challenges Captain Janeway's final decision in the pilot. B'Elanna Torres is a land mine—a hand grenade with the pin pulled out."

> "B'Elanna was trying to fit into a human world, and being different automatically made that difficult for her to do."

The actress has a very clear image of her character in mind. Roxann told *Starlog*, "I've created all these different reasons in my head about why she hates her Klingon half so much. I think it has a lot to do with her relationship with her mother, who I don't think she got along with too well. Also, B'Elanna was trying to fit into a human world, and being different automatically made that difficult for her to do. She wound up with the Maquis because they were probably the only group that would accept her for who she was. Her aggressive side had a very good outlet there. They listened to her. They respected her differences and her ideas, which were maybe a little off-center; they didn't quite fit into the Starfleet mode. She always thought in different ways, and the Maquis respected that.

"B'Elanna is a character that you can look forward to watching as she grows and progresses. The more conflict, the better, as far as I'm concerned. She's basically at war with the two sides of herself. She wants to be identified more with her human side and very much resents her primitive Klingon side, but she doesn't acknowledge that this is what gives her an edge over a lot of other people."

Roxann possesses a strong thirst to learn about philosophy and religion. This desire for self-understanding provides a strong link between the actress and the Starfleet officer she portrays.

At one point, Roxann told *Wired* she was in the middle of reading both *A Concise History of the Catholic Church* by Thomas Bokenkotter and *The Great Divorce* by C.S. Lewis. The actress said, "I'm interested in the study of religions and their effect on society. There's a lot of ritual in any formal religion, and understanding where those rituals come from, how they often developed in response to political and social events throughout history, can help you understand how and where they can fit into your life."

She characterized Lewis's book as "a philosophical and religious book that describes a soul on a bus ride between heaven and hell. It's about what is good and bad, how we might be judged in the afterlife, and who makes those judgments. Lewis brings up questions without answers, and some of the images are so intense and otherworldly that it takes a few readings to understand them." These questions are clearly important to Roxann.

Roxann's training as a theater arts major at the University of California, Berkeley, helped her learn how to bring life to *Star Trek: Voyager*'s most volatile character. She told *Starlog*, "I think that people love creating an alternative reality. People do it all the time, but this is an accepted way of doing it. This is a very popular way of doing it. It's fun. It's interesting. It's a universe within itself. It has integrity. It is respected. You step on board knowing that your role is not only to create but to continue the legacy, and that's an amazing feeling."

The actress has spent almost her entire life in Los Angeles. She was born and raised in L.A., and she still lives there with her husband, casting director Eric Dawson. After graduating from the University of California, Berkeley, Roxann hit it big. Her first professional role was as Diana Morales in the Broadway production of *A Chorus Line*. The successful play brought professional recognition to the young actress.

She continued to work in theater, appearing in such plays as *The Early Girl* and *V & V Only* for the Circle Repertory Company, *The Tempest* for the Classic Stage Company off-Broadway, *Accelerando* at the American Contemporary Theatre, and in plays at many regional theaters.

The actress has also worked in television, as Adrienne Morrow on NBC's *Another World*, as a regular on the NBC series *Round Table* and *Nightingales*, and in leading roles for USA Network's movies-of-the-week, *Mortal Sins* and *Dirty Work*. Roxann has appeared as a guest star in *The Untouchables*, *Matlock*, and *Jack's Place*. Her film work includes roles for *Guilty by Suspicion* with Robert De Niro, *Bound by Honor*, and *Darkman II* (which went directly to video).

"Doc Zimmerman is programmed with all the medical knowledge to make him a good doctor; however, with one flip of a switch, he can disappear. He is extremely competent and efficient, but he doesn't see the purpose in humor or irony. As the show develops, so will his bedside manner."

—Robert Picardo

The Doctor

When the Starfleet vessel *Voyager* and the Maquis rebel ship it was chasing were propelled into the unknown Delta Quadrant seventy light-years from home, the two ships had to merge crews onto one vessel. Though for the most part this meant that there were two officers for every one position, it was soon discovered that both ships had lost their medical officers. *Voyager* was suddenly without a doctor.

The *Voyager*'s Emergency Medical Program temporarily assumed the role of ship's physician, creating a sentient living hologram called only "the Doctor." However, it was soon clear that "the Doctor" would have to remain at his new job for a long time. This is the first time in Starfleet history that an EMP has had to serve as a ship's doctor.

The Doctor has a brusque, sarcastic attitude and lack of bedside manner. He quickly resented being treated as a piece of medical equipment rather than a doctor. Perhaps his arrogance showed most when someone asked how he had solved a particular medical problem. The Doctor replied, "I would be happy to take you through the process, but it would take at least ten hours to explain it all to you. Needless to say, it was a remarkable procedure."

At first, his only friend was Kes. She sees him as a living, self-aware entity, the same as any sentient being. After Kes demonstrated an aptitude for medicine, he made her his assistant. When the crew complained about the Doctor to Captain Janeway, who was considering reprogramming him to make him more congenial, Kes pleaded his case. She pointed out that he deserved the same rights as any sentient being, and Janeway reconsidered.

Janeway later made the Doctor a full member of the crew with sole control over turning himself on and off. She told him that he should no longer think of himself as an emergency medical program but as a crew member. The *Voyager* captain has learned to trust the Doctor. She gave him all the command codes when an alien intruder entered the ship with the power to possess all minds but his. When she tried to impress upon him the importance of the codes, he replied, "I make life and death decisions every day."

Janeway sent him on his first "Away Mission" to the holodeck because he was the only one who could rescue Kim, Tuvok, and Chakotay from a "Beowulf" holonovel. Already composed of energy, he couldn't be dematerialized but could be solid or intangible at will. Kes suggested it was his chance

71

to be treated as a full crew member, and that he should choose himself a name before beginning his first mission. He chose the name "Schweitzer" after the famous Terran healer.

The Doctor enjoyed being acclaimed as a hero by the characters in the holonovel. Freya, a beautiful maiden, offered herself to him, but she died intercepting a dagger meant for him before he had a chance to accept. After that, he decided not to keep his new name, since "the last time I heard that name spoken was a painful one."

Another holonovel brought an odder adventure to the Doctor. A kinoplasmic radiation surge in the imaging system created a feedback loop between the holodeck computer and his program. It almost convinced him that he was a human Dr. Zimmerman and the *Voyager* and its crew were all holograms.

The Doctor was once challenged by Kes to show more compassion toward his patients. He programmed himself with a simulated flu virus to experience the discomforts living beings feel. The Doctor also helped Kes in her time of elogium, acting in her father's place. Later the doctor advised her on having a child.

The Doctor often surprises B'Elanna Torres, who is not accustomed to being surprised. When Torres misplaced a stone in a medicine wheel she had hung over Chakotay's bed in sickbay, the Doctor corrected it, saying, "You've placed the Coyote Stone at the crossroads of the Fifth and Sixth Realms, which would divert Commander Chakotay's soul, that is, his consciousness, into the Mountains of the Antelope Women, according to his legend, an extremely attractive locale he might not

want to leave." The Doctor told a surprised Torres that he knew about medical treatments "including those based on psycho-spiritual beliefs."

The Doctor has endured a number of ordeals aboard *Voyager*, but he is especially vulnerable since he is completely dependent on *Voyager*'s computer system. When Kim and Torres tried to project the Doctor into engineering, the first attempt shrunk the doctor. When the antimatter supply drained from the ship, and a proton burst shorted out systems, he started to fade. Perhaps his most pain-filled incident was when he fell in love with a lady hologram, Denara, a Vidiian doctor transformed into a holographic lifeform. They once went to Paris's holodeck Marseilles tavern. Denara gave him a new name, Schmullis, named after her favorite uncle. "I think I like the sound of that," he said.

She was puzzled because the Doctor wouldn't dance. He replied, "It's not in my programming." However, the Doctor considered Denara his patient, not his date, and he refused to admit his attraction to her. Kes later found him in sickbay running a self-

> *The Doctor has endured a number of ordeals aboard Voyager, but he is especially vulnerable since he is completely dependent on Voyager's computer system.*

diagnostic. He thought there was something wrong with him because he couldn't concentrate on his job. Kes said, "You're attracted to Denara!" Though the Doctor insisted such a thing wasn't in his programming, Kes reminded him that his programming was adaptive.

The Doctor bluntly told the lady hologram, "I'm romantically attracted to you and wondered if you felt the same way." Denara blurted out, "I think we should keep our association professional." Lieutenant Paris counseled the heartbroken Doctor on the pitfalls of romance, but later he was able to meet the real, flesh and blood, Denara. He caressed her face and activated a dance program, as they shared a tender moment.

The Doctor now has greater mobility aboard the *Voyager*. New holographic emitters on critical decks allow him access to most of the ship through holoprojection. The gruff, sarcastic Doctor has grown very fond of his crewmates. If they find a home and leave him alone on *Voyager*, he plans to turn himself off as he doesn't want to go on without them.

Robert Picardo

Born and raised in Philadelphia, actor Robert Picardo now resides in Los Angeles with his wife and two children. If Robert wasn't destined to be a doctor, he was at least destined to play one on TV. He switched to theater arts after entering Yale University as a pre-med student, and he has already appeared as Dr. Dick Richards on the ABC

series *China Beach* and as Dr. McCaskill in the theater production *The Waiting Room* at the Mark Taper Forum. Now he brings Doc Zimmerman to life for *Star Trek: Voyager*.

Picardo never wanted to be *Star Trek*'s holographic doctor. He wasn't a Star Trek fan, even if his wife was. He found the description of the doctor on the front of the script for the pilot episode "colorless, humorless." He admitted, "I read the lines and thought, 'This isn't funny!' The role didn't sound terribly interesting." Robert said, "I was not really knowledgeable about the other Star Trek shows, so I didn't get the analogy to other well-loved Star Trek characters, like Spock, Data, Odo—the nonhuman characters who reflect on humanity. I didn't understand that at all. I just thought this was going to be basically a machine-type guy with no personality, and I thought that joke would get tired fairly quickly."

Instead his friend, fellow actor Megan Gallagher, who guest-starred in the *Deep Space Nine* episode "Invasive Procedures," convinced him to audition for the role of Neelix, but he lost out to another friend, Ethan Phillips. Meanwhile the studio couldn't find an actor to portray the Doctor. They asked Picardo to read again. "We had a lot of different actors come in once we decided we were going to go with a comedian. Nobody else seemed to get it," Director Winrich Kolbe told *Cinescape*. "They all played it too holographic and computerlike. Robert Picardo has that almost insane-at-times look that we desperately wanted. There is a certain sardonic twist to that man. That's going to be an interesting character to follow."

Jeri Taylor later told Robert that when they heard his voice, they thought, "The Doctor!" Picardo nearly turned down the role at first. After Robert took the part, he began to explore the Star Trek myth, and his interest in his new role grew. With his wife at his side to interpret the finer points of the Star Trek characters, Robert began to see the possibilities for Doc Zimmerman. The contradictions of the character left many possibilities for an interesting screen portrayal.

He told *Comics Interview*, "Data was very lovable, and they certainly did all the questions of what constitutes artificial intelligence and real intelligence with him. But this guy, they sort of programmed some emotion into him that doesn't quite work, and I think that's going to be a source of a lot of amusement. Doc aspires to be human, but he would not admit it to himself. Data would admit it to himself."

Robert has began a mutual admiration society with series star Kate Mulgrew. He told *Entertainment Weekly*, "We were blessed to get Katherine." Meanwhile, Mulgrew told *The Official* Star Trek: Voyager *Magazine*, "Robert Picardo is a genius, and a great energy exists between the two of us."

The Doctor most often appears on screen with Jennifer Lien's alien Ocampan Kes. Kes became Zimmerman's medical assistant and he her teacher. He has promised her knowledge equivalent to a degree in medicine. Robert told *TV Guide*, "If I'm the most armored personality in the cast, Kes is the most available. It's interesting that the writers chose to pair us."

Robert has enjoyed a significant acting career prior to *Star Trek: Voyager*, beginning at Yale in Leonard Bernstein's *Mass*, a musical theater piece originally commissioned for the 1972 opening of the Kennedy Center in Washington, D.C. He brought it across the Atlantic Ocean, playing the leading role in the play's European premiere at age nineteen. Robert then enrolled at the Circle in the Square Professional Theatre Workshop, whose alumni include Kevin Bacon and Ken Olin. Other theater work followed, including roles in David Mamet's *Sexual Perversity in Chicago*, with Diane Keaton, and in *The Primary English Class*. He costarred with Jack Lemmon in Bernard Slade's *Tribute*, appeared in *Beyond Therapy* and *Geniuses* at the Los Angeles Public Theatre, and in *The Normal Heart* at the Berkeley Repertory Theatre, for which he won the Drama-Logue Award. His Broadway debut came in the leading role for the comedy hit *Gemini* with Danny Aiello.

Robert has won several awards for his work in television, including an Emmy Award nomination for the part of Mr. Cutlip on the ABC series *The Wonder Years* and two Viewers For Quality Television Founder's Awards, one for *The Wonder Years* and the other for his portrayal of Dr. Dick Richards on *China Beach*. He's been a guest star on *VR-5* on Fox and *Tales from the Crypt*, had a starring role opposite Helena Bonham-Carter in NBC's movie-of-the-week *Deadly Deception: The Marina Oswald Story*, and been in the HBO movie *White Mile* and the NBC miniseries *Deadly Matrimony*. He's had recurring roles on *Home Improvement* and *L.A. Law*. His film work includes appearances in *The Burbs, Back to School, Star 80, Loverboy, Total Recall* (voice only), *The Howling, Explorers, Legend, Tribute, Gremlins 2, Wagons East*, and *Innerspace*.

All of this, of course, led to the role Robert expects to change his life, the part of the Doctor on *Star Trek: Voyager*. Robert is very optimistic about the series. He told *Entertainment Weekly*, "Does the prognosis look good to me? Yes, it does. I am definitely looking forward to the possibility that these characters could go beyond tele-vision. As an actor, I've never had a job like this, where you think in terms of something lasting that long."

Robert appreciates the devoted following of Star Trek's many fans, even if he sometimes tells a joke at their expense. He once sardonically told *TV Guide*, "I'm sure it's only a matter of time before I'm asked to contemplate the cosmic connection between Picard and Picardo."

"Everything is new to Kes. It's all wondrous and different for her, and I love playing that."
—Jennifer Lien, in The Official Star Trek: Voyager Magazine

Kes

First the *Voyager* found the Talaxan Neelix. Then he led them to his Ocampan lover Kes. They both have made worthy additions to the starship's crew, even if they had never before heard of Starfleet or the United Federation of Planets. Neelix, among other things, has become the resident cook aboard the starship *Voyager*. Kes proposed, then created and tended, a garden to grow fruit and vegetables for the crew. This would save wear and tear on the replicator during their long trip, but the promise hasn't been kept up, and replicated vegetables have been necessary. Kes has also assumed the role of assistant to the Doctor.

Kes is a short-lived Ocampan. Her people normally live nine years. Although Kes looks to be twenty years old, she is less than two. Kes's father is Benaron. The Caretaker's race almost ended Ocampan society, destroying the atmosphere of Ocampa, turning a garden world into a desert. The repentant aliens then built an underground cavern to shelter the natives. The Caretaker provided them with energy, and the society grew dependent, later facing extinction when the energy began to run out.

Captain Janeway saved them. She warned them of the imminent disaster and told the Caretaker that they should be allowed to fend for themselves. Kes had already fled from her people's underground city to the surface. She wanted to learn what waited outside their protected society. Curiosity burns very bright in Kes and drives many of her actions.

On the surface she met and fell in love with Neelix, but she was captured by a savage tribe. Neelix led the *Voyager* to Ocampa to rescue her. Kes and Neelix share a deep love. She once donated a lung to save his life. Although he used to fly into fits of jealous rage, especially at Tom Paris's attentions to her, she never betrays their trust. Kes once told Neelix, "Before I met you eight or nine years seemed like an eternity. It never occurred to me that anyone could live longer. Now that we're together no matter how many years we have left, it doesn't seem like enough. But the important thing is to cherish whatever time we have together, whether it's a day or a decade." Kes did have to struggle with the loss of her Talaxan lover when a transporter accident merged him and Tuvok into a new entity, Tuvix, but Neelix was later restored.

Kes and Neelix once almost had a child together. *Voyager*'s contact with strange energy beings caused her elogium to begin. Female Ocampans experience a time of change know as elogium when their body prepares for fertilization. Body temperature elevates and increased electrophoretic activity occurs in their nervous system. Their eyes turn yellow green and a sticky yellow ooze called ipasaphor comes from their hands that makes mating possible. They also develop a mitral birth sac on their back. They often also exhibit odd behavior. Kes ate dirt, spawn beetles, and flowers.

She was surprised to be undergoing the change because it normally occurs between the ages of four and five, and she was not yet two. The elogium occurs only once. She believed that if she didn't have children then, she could never give birth. Kes asked Neelix to be her mate. He acted reluctant at first, but finally agreed. She cautioned that she only had fifty hours in which to begin and that they must remain joined for six days to insure conception.

The rolisisin ritual requires a father to rub the woman's feet until her tongue swells. Kes described the ritual as being the time when a father and daughter enter a new phase of their relationship, saying that it's the father's opportunity to dispense wisdom before another becomes the most important man in her life. The Doctor filled in for her absent father, and he now often serves as a father figure for her, much as Janeway acts as a surrogate mother.

Eventually, Kes decided not to become a mother, and the Doctor said her condition may have been a false elogium brought on by the proximity to the ship of energy crea-

> ### Kes
>
> **Race:** Ocampa
> **Gender:** Female
> **Rank:** Civilian
> **Department:** NA
> **Position:** Hydroponics Bay, Medical Assistant.
> Kes is an Ocampa. Like Neelix, she was picked up by *Voyager* in the Delta Quadrant and is a civilian on the starship. Although she appears about twenty years old in human years, she is actually only two years old, with a life span of nine years. She has limited telepathic powers that have emerged because of her transition to living in space.

tures. He felt Kes and Neelix may still retain the opportunity to have a child at a later date.

At one point Neelix's relationship with Kes was tested when it was revealed that Neelix had fled his homeworld to avoid being part of what he felt was an unjust war. Neelix had refused to join the defense forces, then Neelix's entire family, and 300,000 Talaxans, were killed in an attack on his home moon—and others were being slowly poisoned to death by radiation. Neelix had to go into hiding to avoid a death sentence, and he now felt he had been a coward. For fifteen years he had hated himself for living while his colony died. He had been living in self-exile as a hermit on an asteroid when the *Voyager* found him.

Kes told him, "You think that makes you a coward? What an awful burden you've carried all these years. You have to stop hating yourself." They later learned Neelix was dying from a fatal degenerative blood disease caused by the attack.

Ocampan bury their dead, believing that the soul, or Komra, is released into the afterlife. Perhaps the doomed lovers, short-lived Kes and dying Neelix, will be reunited in another place. Their love is certainly strong enough.

Kes's other close relationship aboard the *Voyager* is with the Doctor. She serves as his assistant while he teaches her medicine. At the beginning, the Doctor doubted her ability. When she wanted to borrow advanced texts on anatomy and physiology, the pleased Doctor warned her that they were difficult. She promised to do her best, then memorized the books in less than a day. The Doctor told her that she might have the equivalent of a medical degree by the time they returned to the Alpha Quadrant.

Despite him being a holograph, Kes sees the Doctor as a living, self-aware entity. She came to his rescue once when Captain Janeway threatened to reprogram him to eliminate his rude behavior, but Kes has also been less than patient with him herself. When the Doctor acted efficiently but compassionless toward the pregnant Ensign Wildman, whose husband was in the Alpha Quadrant, Kes suggested that he should get sick for once in his life, so he could know what it was like. Later a frantic and whiny Doctor urgently demanded immediate attention when the twenty-four-hour flu he had given himself lingered. He begged Kes to stay in sickbay with him. But Kes had reprogrammed the flu to last an extra couple of hours, and she told Harry Kim, "It's not a fair test if you know when it's going to end, now, is it?" The Doctor settled into the diagnostic bed and groaned to a smirking Kim, lamenting, "She's far more devious than I ever expected."

Kes has had many strange adventures since leaving Ocampa and boarding the *Voyager*. She disappeared into a "spatial rift," defeated an alien invader of the starship, and even met a duplicate incarnation of herself. Paris is teaching her to fly a shuttlecraft.

Kes has begun exhibiting strange mental powers. She receives images and feelings, and she once detected both a seemingly vanished Janeway and an ethereal alien entity that no one else could perceive. Tuvok, her tutor in honing her rapidly maturing mental abilities, has concluded that her burgeoning powers have been extremely underestimated. As these powers, and her control over them, grow, Kes may become an even more important addition to the crew of the *Voyager*.

Jennifer Lien

Jennifer Lien was only twenty years old, barely an adult herself, when the studio chose her for the role of Kes, the two-year-old Ocampan, a race that lives for only nine years. She enjoys her work and shares many personal traits with her character. Jennifer told the *Charlotte Observer*, "Most of what Kes sees and encounters in each episode is entirely new and fresh for her. She is just so open and alive and interested in everything that happens around her. I love that. It's so freeing for me as an actress to come in here every day and play her, because there's always something new for me to react to, to feel, to experience."

Kes and Neelix share a very dedicated love relationship. Kes is very loyal to him despite his sometimes overwhelming jealousy. Jennifer explained to *The Official Star Trek: Voyager Magazine*, "I think it helps that they're both not from Starfleet. They're two people who said, 'Hey, we want to join you.' They have a different perspective on things."

Jennifer and Ethan enjoy a good working relationship. Jennifer told the *Charlotte Observer*, "Ethan is a total professional, so giving, and he's a very funny man too. I love sharing so many of my scenes with him. Kes and Neelix have a relationship that is very much one of the give-and-take kind." Phillips agreed, telling *Starlog*, "I love playing those between-the-lines moments with Jennifer. She's unbearably sexy as Kes."

Jennifer's character Kes also enjoys a good relationship with the holographic doctor. Jennifer told *The Official* Star Trek: Voyager *Magazine*, "Kes is sharing her understanding of humans, of humanness, of all the good things she has learned about them, with the Doctor, and he is sharing his knowledge of medicine with her. There's also a strong friendship there."

Kate Mulgrew told *The Official* Star Trek: Voyager *Magazine*, "Kes is a lovely character and I enjoy a nice chemistry with Jennifer Lien. Kes could be Janeway's surrogate daughter, the daughter that perhaps Janeway will never have. Jennifer is a constant and wonderful surprise."

Pilot director Winrich Kolbe admitted that Kes proved very difficult to cast. They interviewed many actresses before settling on Jennifer Lien. He told *Cinescape*, "Kes was the usual problem you have when you try to cast twenty-something actresses or younger. There are a lot of beautiful women around, especially in Hollywood, but not a lot of them can act. We went through quite

a procession of beautiful girls, not bad as actresses but not good enough. We wanted somebody who could be fragile but with a steely will underneath. Jennifer Lien gives us that."

Star Trek: Voyager presents both a major opportunity and challenge to Jennifer. The twenty-year-old Illinois native began her career at age thirteen, appearing in such Shakespearean plays as *The Tempest* and *Othello*. She credits two of her teachers with encouraging her interest.

> **"Kes could be Janeway's surrogate daughter, the daughter that perhaps Janeway will never have. "**

Jennifer's television debut came on Oprah Winfrey's *Brewster Place*. At age sixteen, in 1990, she moved to New York to appear in the NBC daytime drama *Another World* as Hannah, a misfit orphan. She stayed with the series for a year and a half. She later appeared in the recurring role Roanne on the short-lived ABC series *Phenom* and in a short, independent film trailer, *The Hairy Bird*.

Jennifer's voice has appeared in more places than her face has. She can be heard on *Saturday Night Live* regular Adam Sandler's comedy album and as a guest voice on television's animated series *The Critic*. She even dubbed lines for the English version of the French film *Baby Blood*.

All of this has prepared her for her role as the youngest regular character to appear in the history of any Star Trek series. Jennifer enjoys her work on *Star Trek: Voyager*. She told *The Official* Star Trek: Voyager *Magazine*, "I've gotten a chance to know everybody in the cast on a personal level, and we have a great team here. I'm really lucky to be involved with this group of people. Everybody has been telling me how rare this is. The actors do their jobs and then so many other people have to do their jobs to make it all work. It's a huge group effort, and I like being a part of this group. The fans seem to be very pleased with the show, and I think they like Kes, so that makes me very happy."

She told the *Charlotte Observer*, "Acting is just such an incredible art form. It has let me do and be so many different things. Really, I don't know where else I'd be able to play an alien like Kes. So I'm one of those rare people who loves what they do and can actually make a living doing it."

"Neelix is a loner and a lover. He's manipulative and brave, sexy and silly. You might say he's an alien of many colors . . . an eccentric odd-ball who never ceases to amaze me."
—Ethan Phillips, *The Official* Star Trek: Voyager *Magazine*

Neelix

The Talaxan Neelix serves as morale officer, cook, scavenger, con man, trader, and sage aboard the Federation starship *Voyager*. He's an expert on the aliens, animals, and plants on all worlds of the Delta Quadrant, and he helps guide the Alpha Quadrant *Voyager* through this strange land.

Captain Kathryn Janeway found the trustworthy and versatile alien living alone on an asteroid. The starship technology, different from any in the Delta Quadrant, impressed him. He immediately guided the starship to rescue his Ocampan lover, Kes, from her abductors. Neelix and Kes both proved to be valuable additions to the *Voyager* crew. At first Neelix complained that Janeway didn't make full use of him, then he promptly turned her private dining room into a crew galley and appointed himself chef on the *Voyager*. Janeway appreciated his efforts because she did not wish to overtax the food replicator on their long voyage.

His foods range from the strange to the inedible. His attempts to create familiar dishes often fail. Tuvok doesn't like Neelix's over-spiced version of Vulcan plomeek soup. Janeway, who only wants coffee, not breakfast, in the morning, hates Neelix's gloppy seed extract substitute. He used schplict in an effort to make macaroni and cheese to please Ensign Ashmore, until Tuvok noted that he must cultivate bacteria to make cheese. His cooking once even endangered the ship because his foods carried viruses that sickened the bio-neural circuitry.

Neelix truly loves the Ocampan Kes. Although she always acts faithfully, for a long time he flew into fits of jealous rage, especially at Tom Paris's attentions to her. Tom and Neelix have now become friends, but only after Paris reassured the Talaxan that Kes loves no one else.

After Neelix learned he was dying of Metremia, a form of radiation poisoning, he told Kes, "When I first met you, I didn't know that your species only lived eight or nine years. I fell in love with you without knowing how lonely it would be to live without you after you're gone. Now that I'm going to die first, I don't have to worry about it."

Haakonians had conquered his homeworld Talax more than fifteen years before, when he lived on the moon Rinax with his family. The enemy employed the Metreon Cascade, a weapon of mass destruction conceived and built by Dr. Jetrel. It enveloped the moon in a horrible cloud, blocking out sunlight forever. The weapon instantly killed 300,000 Talaxans, including Neelix's family. Many more Talaxans later slowly died from radiation poisoning. Talax surrendered to the Haakonians.

At first Neelix told the *Voyager* crew he had been on the homeworld with the defense forces, who were preparing for the invasion when the attack came. He finally revealed to Kes that he had actually been in hiding from the defense forces under threat of a death sentence because he had never reported for duty. He had believed the war unjust and avoided service. He now saw himself as a coward.

Dr. Jetrel paid a visit on a reluctant Neelix and informed him that he had developed the fatal degenerative blood disease called Metremia, a result of exposure to the Metreon isotopes, which Neelix had contracted while doing rescue work on his home moon. Dr. Jetrel was also dying from the effects of his invention.

Neelix hated Jetrel, though after the war the doctor had devoted his life to helping radiation victims. Dr. Jetrel felt that, in the end, use of the Metreon Cascade had killed fewer people than an invasion would have. As Dr. Jetrel lay dying, Neelix forgave him, and he also made peace with his own actions.

Neelix, ever the optimist, acts as the ship's morale officer, constantly cheering up others despite his own tragic past. A transporter accident once merged Neelix with Tuvok into one entity, Tuvix, creating a humor-filled, logic-defying fusion until the two beings could be separated again. Neelix acts as the ship's counselor, and everyone likes his

Neelix

Race: Talaxan
Gender: Male
Rank: Civilian
Department: NA
Position: Cook, Guide, Morale Officer
Neelix is a Talaxan from the planet Talax in the Delta Quadrant, where he was picked up by *Voyager*. He is a civilian passenger, with no connection to Starfleet.

upbeat, humorous nature. Neelix now films his own talk show, "Live from the Delta Quadrant, it's A Briefing With Neelix!" for the *Voyager* crew. The Doctor contributes a recurring health segment.

Neelix's homespun anecdotes are funny and sometimes surprisingly pertinent. One time Torres, Kim, and Paris were discussing their attempt to exceed warp 10, a theoretical impossibility. Neelix offered to help. Simply to humor him, they listened while he told a seemingly unrelated story about something that happened to him in a nebula. However, his story helped solve the problem. Another time he gave similar sage advice to Torres. He even helped Tuvok when the Vulcan was failing in his efforts to run a Starfleet officer course aboard ship.

Another time Janeway left Tom Paris and Neelix in charge of *Voyager*, and they successfully stared down a Kazon mothership. Neelix showed an eagerness and an aptitude for sly strategy and courage that served the ship well.

Neelix believes that Captain Janeway relies on him. He once said, "She'd be lost without me. She's come to depend on me a great deal."

After the Haakonian War, Neelix went into exile until the *Voyager* found him. The starship has brought happiness back into his life. He now has a lover, satisfying work, and many new friends. The likable Talaxan will never let his captain or his crewmates down.

Ethan Phillips

Pilot director Winrich Kolbe told *Cinescape*, "Neelix was rather easy to cast," but it didn't feel that way to actor Ethan Phillips. In fact, Phillips was a bundle of nerves and worry till he finally got the fateful call.

Kolbe said, "We narrowed it down to three actors, and Ethan Phillips was the one we pulled out. He was an inspired choice, and he's the life of the party on the set."

Meanwhile, Ethan sat by the phone, hoping and waiting for his agent's call to come. Waiting and hoping are a normal part of the job, he's found, as he told the Vulkon Convention audience in Towson, Maryland, "You audition for a lot of series when you're in New York and then they tape it and fly the tape out to L.A. Then you never hear from them again!" He said he suspects that the tapes must fall out of the airplane somewhere between the two coasts.

After he auditioned for Neelix, he didn't hear anything for three days. Then he got another call asking him to come back and audition for the role of Doctor Zimmerman, and he figured his shot at the Neelix role was completely dead. He went back and read for the Zimmerman part, doing his best to sound like a hologram. Two weeks later they called him back again, this time for Neelix, and he learned there were only two other actors in the running for the part. One of them was

his friend Robert Picardo, who, of course, went on to play Doc Zimmerman.

An anxious Ethan learned that he had won the part in early August. He called his agent at three on a Monday afternoon only to hear there was no news yet. Then he called his agent again at six that evening and his agent put him on hold because he had another call. When his agent came back on the phone, he told Ethan the part was his.

When Ethan told his friend Rene Auberjonois, who has a role on *Star Trek: Deep Space Nine,* Rene said happily, "Welcome to the franchise!" Rene had long told Ethan how great it was to be part of the only show in the world where you meet the fans. Ethan had originally worked with Rene on the *Benson* television series, and he still regularly sees his friend. There is a place called Star Trek Alley, which is the part of the Paramount lot where they shoot *Deep Space Nine,* and across the alley is where they shoot *Voyager.* Ethan said he is always bumping into Star Trek people.

When he was in graduate school, Ethan used to watch the original series every night for about two years. He thought it was the best show in the world. Then he didn't watch it again until he played the part of Dr. Farek for *The Next Generation* episode "Ménage à Trois." He wanted to see what he looked like and started watching the series. When Rene was on *Deep Space Nine,* he started watching that show, too, and soon became a big fan.

Regarding his character, Ethan told *The Official* Star Trek: Voyager *Magazine,* "Neelix is a loner and a lover. He's manipulative and brave, sexy and silly. You might say he's an alien of many colors, an eccentric oddball who never ceases to amaze me. He can be pretty brave and I think he's incredibly optimistic. He's somebody who loves life and loves things that are alive. He's fairly emotional, too. Neelix gets away with an awful lot with the captain, and he's just the cook. That makes it funny. That makes him Neelix. He's impulsive. He's centered around the food. When we get around food, we tend to be gregarious and relax a little bit. We get to see some colors of people that we might not otherwise see.

"Those kinds of scenes are going to be lighthearted. Is he comic relief? I don't think so. He's not an alien Seinfeld. He's not hysterical. He might have a few moments that make you chuckle, but for the most part he brings a lightheartedness to the scenes he's in."

Perhaps the biggest drawback in playing the role is the incredible amount of makeup. Ethan says it's not as complicated as what Armin Shimerman wears in his role as Quark on *Deep Space Nine*, but Phillips still has to be at the studio at 3:30 A.M. It takes about two and a half hours to put on the makeup and about an hour and fifteen minutes to remove it. Mike Westmore created it and Scott Wheeler applies it. Mike Westmore told Ethan that it's the first Star Trek makeup that's motile in the forehead. Its very thin rubber allows him to wrinkle his forehead. However, Ethan has developed a love-hate relationship with all the goop. He loves the illusion and was stunned the first time he looked at it in the mirror. However, his head can't breathe because it's glued to rubber, and after about eight hours it gets really warm.

Ethan enjoys working with his costars. He especially enjoys working with Jennifer Lien, who plays his on-screen love interest, the Ocampan Kes.

Star Trek's built-in popularity surprised Ethan. The news media and millions of fans all had their eyes on the starship *Voyager* and its crew from the start. Before the premiere hit TV, the stunned actor told *Entertainment Weekly*, "We haven't even aired yet. We're getting interviewed, our pictures are being taken. It just doesn't make any sense to me. I'm not really prepared for this." He told *TV Guide*, "I'm getting fan mail, and we haven't even finished shooting the first episode. If it all goes right and they keep me, it's a security you don't often get as an actor. But just in case, I'm keeping my 1980 Honda with the 150,000 miles."

> **Neelix gets away with an awful lot with the captain, and he's just the cook.**

Ethan revealed that he and his wife sit down and read every single letter. He believes Star Trek appeals to people because we want to feel that we have some hope as a species. He thinks that *Star Trek: Voyager* offers that.

Ethan decided to devote his life to acting when, as a little boy, he used to watch a horror show on television called *Panic* back in 1956. The CBS show only lasted one season. He was watching a particularly scary part when he turned to his mother and told her he was scared. She explained to him that they were actors and they were being photographed. They would do the scene and when the scene was over they would go have a coffee break. Then they'd come back and do the scene again. Ethan was fascinated that these adults were getting paid to pretend!

Ethan said that the best way to get started in acting is to do stage work, because on the stage you learn to do your own close-ups, your own editing, and you get to build a character in the span of two hours. When Ethan first started his acting career, he had to support himself by working in a mental institution as a psychiatric aid, driving a cab, cleaning toilets in bars, and waiting tables. He loves theater and has been doing that his whole life. He's played leading roles in many regional theater productions. He's also appeared in *My Favorite Year* at the Lincoln Center, *Measure for Measure* at the Delacorte, *Lips Together, Teeth Apart* at the Lucille Lortel, *Modigliani* at the Astor Place, and new productions for Horizons Ensemble Studio Theatre and Hudson Guild Theatre. He really likes Shakespeare. Ethan has also published and produced plays, including *Penguin Blues,* published by the Samuel French Company. His plays have been produced more than 150 times throughout the United States and Canada.

Ethan's love of the stage is strong, and he sees theater as a celebration of simply being together and telling stories, which is something we've been doing for thousands of years. He wishes people would write more plays instead of just television and movies, and he would love to see Meryl Streep do a play. He thinks she is "the best actor alive today."

Ethan has also acted for films and television. He played a sexaholic in a 12-step group meeting in *Jeffrey,* a film that also featured *Star Trek: The Next Generation* star Patrick Stewart. He also appeared in *Wagons East, Bloodhounds of Broadway, Lean on Me, Glory, Green Card, Man Without a Face*, and *The Shadow.*

For television, Ethan has appeared in five seasons of the sitcom *Benson,* playing Pete Downey, the Governor's press aide, alongside Rene Auberjonois. He's also had a recurring role on the nighttime drama series *Werewolf* and appeared on *Law and Order, L.A. Law, Murphy Brown, The Mommies,* and *NYPD Blue.*

Ethan was born and raised in Garden City on Long Island, along with five sisters. He is a distant relative of Joe Phillips, a well-known stand-up comic in the 1920s. Ethan received a Jesuit education in New York before earning a degree in English literature from Boston University and a master of fine arts degree from Cornell University. He currently lives in Los Angeles with his wife, fashion magazine stylist Patricia Creswell, and their West Highland terrier, Frank. Ethan is an avid backpacker and rock climber and an amateur ornithologist and botanist. He says his unfulfilled dream is to hike the Appalachian trail from end to end.

CHAPTER FOUR

Placing Voyager in the Star Trek Universe

In January 1995, *Star Trek: Voyager* became the fourth series set in Gene Roddenberry's universe, appearing almost three decades after the first classic series hit the airwaves. Everyone wanted to see how the newest entry would compare with its three siblings, *Star Trek*, *The Next Generation*, and *Deep Space Nine*.

Fans and critics analyzed every detail: stories, settings, characters, special effects, costumes, the ship. Even the actors and creators, from Mulgrew and Russ to Berman, Piller, and Taylor, publicly compared their series with its predecessors. This chapter looks at each of the Star Trek series, their underlying philosophies, and the heroes who gave them life.

Star Trek

The starship *Enterprise* embarked on its first *Star Trek* mission in September 1966. It never attracted many viewers, and in the days before sophisticated demographics, the networks remained unaware they had successfully captured a select audience highly desired by advertisers. They wanted to cancel the series after the second year. A fan campaign forestalled the inevitable for one year. But the original *Star Trek* was canceled after only three seasons.

Then, just as *Star Trek* entered syndication, man landed on the moon. Science fiction suddenly became reality. Neil Armstrong's small footsteps changed everything. The impossible suddenly appeared possible; the stars seemed ours for the taking. Viewers looked for a television series offering a positive view of our future in space, one that showed that next step. *Star Trek* filled the bill.

In syndication, the series won not only viewers but faithful followers, perhaps true believers in Gene Roddenberry's optimistic philosophy. They put on conventions, launched magazines, started clubs, and wrote thousands of stories about their favorite heroes. Some even fell in love with their on-screen heroes and chronicled tales of romantic, and even sexual, encounters.

> The characters and underlying philosophy drew millions to the adventures, and misadventures, of the starship Enterprise.

The characters and underlying philosophy drew millions to the adventures, and misadventures, of the starship *Enterprise*. Stories ranged from the humorous "The Trouble with Tribbles" to the grim "The City on the Edge of Forever." Fans developed a fine-tuned sense for the Star Trek world and philosophy. When a story violated a character's reality, such as the third season's abysmal "Spock's Brain," the wrath of the fans knew no bounds.

Fans began to clamor for more *Star Trek*, and producers obliged. *Star Trek* led to an animated series featuring new stories, with both scripts and voices supplied by the original series veterans. An attempt to launch a new live-action series followed, but it failed. One script spawned a movie, which was so successful it led to a series of six films: *Star Trek: The Motion Picture, The Wrath of Khan, The Search for Spock, The Voyage Home, The Final Frontier*, and *The Unexplored Country*. Later, a seventh film was made, *Generations*, which served as a transition from the old, original *Star Trek* characters to the characters of the new series *The Next Generation*.

The Star Trek movies, faithful to the Star Trek philosophy, continued the original portrayals of the classic TV characters as they aged and grew. With fans religiously filling theater seats every two years and faithfully tuning in to watch repeats of the original series, which continued its strong run in syndication, the time seemed ripe to attempt a new TV series. Everyone— fans, station owners, and advertisers— wanted more. However, rather than reprise the original, Paramount decided to move forward into the Star Trek universe. They named the new series *Star Trek: The Next Generation* because that's what it was, in terms of story, cast, and crew.

The Philosophy

If Gene Roddenberry's founding philosophy attracts viewers, just what defines that philosophy? Two words: cautious optimism.

Wesley Eugene Roddenberry, the former World War II combat pilot and Los Angeles policeman, was hopeful for our world. Despite the bitter war in Vietnam, the riot wracked world cities, and the continued threat of nuclear bombs ending the Cold War with a bang, Roddenberry set his starship in the twenty-third century. And the future looked pretty good.

In his story, humanity survives for another three hundred years, overcoming its immediate crises. Even better, humanity makes it in high style. Far from slipping back into the Stone Age or a subsistence-level agrarian society, civilization progresses. Unlike the advanced Minoan civilization after the Thera volcano blew its top, the future proves more glorious than the past. People make peace with both the Earth and with one another. Tribal nation states unite into a world federation. Individual worlds further unite into a United Federation of Planets, which is founded in 2161.

Other social ills—crime, disease, and poverty—almost disappear. No one starves to death in a civilized world. Racial and gender equality is the norm. Religious prejudice also largely disappears. The crew of the starship *Enterprise* becomes a utopian vision of the melting pot, mixing people of all races, blacks with whites, Vulcans with Terrans. A woman serves aboard the bridge in a command position. (Roddenberry had originally wanted the *Enterprise*'s first officer to be a woman, but studio executives, reflecting the imperfect social standards of twentieth-century America, vetoed that choice. That shortsightedness wouldn't be rectified until the fourth series.)

War still exists in Roddenberry's universe, but it is not promulgated by the United Federation of Planets. It might occur on or between unenlightened worlds outside of the

UFP, or alien aggressors might attack or instigate a battle with the UFP, but the UFP clearly wear the white hats. While the paramilitary Starfleet might appear warlike, Roddenberry makes clear this is not the case. Starfleet runs defensive and exploratory missions only. The mission of the Starfleet ship *Enterprise* is to look for new worlds and new civilizations, not to engage in combat. The Prime Directive of the Federation prohibits interference in alien worlds. Of course, many, including certain Klingons, dispute this.

Gene Roddenberry's philosophy predicts a better universe through technology and understanding. The benevolent UFP sends out advanced starships peopled with harmonic, multiracial crews to ply the spaceways and advance the frontiers of knowledge. Considering the social unrest and racial tensions of the '60s and '70s in America, it is small wonder that such a philosophy attracted many in search of hope. *Star Trek* offered a better tomorrow with stories that supported humanistic values through the courageous actions of its well-meaning heroes.

The Heroes

James T. Kirk captained the starship *Enterprise*. He led his crew "where no man has gone before" expanding the frontiers and often saving the Federation and Earth. He and his crew became legends.

As time progressed in the Star Trek universe, Kirk and McCoy became Admirals. Sulu, Scotty, and Spock got their own starships. Spock joined the diplomatic corps, then went underground to work for peace with the Romulans. Nurse Chapel assumed a career as a doctor of medicine. Uhura and Chekov attained the rank of full commander.

For fans of Star Trek, these characters became heroes. Viewers came to identify with and relate to them; they grew to know their heroes as full human beings. Their heroes won and lost. They laughed and cried. They acted heroically and made mistakes. They formed warm friendships, bickered, fell in love, and even hated.

These same heroes acted as icons, as symbols used by the governing philosophy of Roddenberry's universe, which was steeped in the contradictions and history of Western, American culture.

Kirk was the key "hero": the classic, womanizing, man of action. Sulu and Uhura showed that all races would serve together without discrimination. Uhura also symbolized a woman on the bridge in a command position—even if *Star Trek* wasn't ready to hand her full command. Chekov foresaw an end to the Cold War—a Russian serving alongside Americans and others.

McCoy, as the backwoods, Southern doctor, offered old fashioned wisdom and humanism. But, while steeped in modern medical technology and learning, he still could rely on a hunch. Spock, at least at first, represented the polar opposite. He was the being of pure logic—always in complete control (or supression) of his emotions. Although Spock grew beyond this as the series of movies progressed, he and McCoy offered the yin and the yang of the Western Renascence, the so-called age of reason. This conflict played with resonance for American and European audiences.

However, non-western audiences failed to understand the nuances of the Star Trek heroes. Their culture did not suffer the dichotomy of character presented in classic *Star Trek*. Just as those cultures never abandoned reason to a Dark Ages, they also never abandoned spirituality to worship on an altar of reason. There are other paths a civilization can take. But Roddenberry and crew failed to see this. Even as Star Trek postulated about life between the stars, it remained rooted in Roddenberry's twentieth-century western civilization.

The Next Generation and Deep Space Nine

Star Trek: The Next Generation grew from the popularity of *Star Trek*. For a variety of reasons, Paramount chose to return to the universe and philosophy of the original series but with a new set of protagonists. They asked Roddenberry to repeat his magic. With much help, he did. *The Next Generation* grew even more popular than the original series, proving that the first series was more than a lucky fluke—the universe worked. New stories could be told about new heroes placed in the familiar setting.

The Next Generation ran for seven seasons and has continued in movies. A sister series, *Deep Space Nine*, later appeared every week alongside *The Next Generation*. *Voyager* began even as *The Next Generation* left the air.

The Next Generation and *Deep Space Nine* are set during the same time period in the Alpha Quadrant. As *Voyager* clearly shows, they all share one corner of the universe, and this has allowed characters to cross over between the series. Rumors persist that *Deep Space Nine* characters will appear in future *The Next Generation* movies. And both classic *Star Trek* and *The Next Generation* characters have appeared on *Voyager*.

The Philosophy

The Next Generation continues Gene Roddenberry's philosophy. The series even brings a Klingon aboard the new Enterprise. During the one hundred years from Kirk's first *Enterprise* mission until that of Picard, the Klingons have made peace with the UFP. Mention of the alliance first appears in *Star Trek: The Motion Picture*. Friction still exists, particularly with die-hard warhorses on both sides, such as Kirk, but Picard and his crew accept Klingons more readily.

However, the basic formula hasn't changed. Picard and his *Enterprise* crew are still the good guys, while others portray clear enemies, such as the Romulans. New dangers, such as Borg, the Dominion, and the Cardassians, also appear.

The Next Generation stories center on a mixed crew of humans, aliens, and even an android. They are all admirable people who become an extended family of friends despite any friction. Their starship expands the frontiers, discovers new worlds, and meets alien races and fascinating civilizations. Technology offers new wonders. Little has changed from the mission of Kirk's *Enterprise*, but cracks begin to appear in Gene Roddenberry's golden universe. While the series diverges from Roddenberry's philosophy in only minor ways, it presages larger changes to come. While Roddenberry provided the initial guiding hand for *The Next Generation*, he soon abandoned his active role. Rick Berman and Michael Piller took the helm, and they began to blur some of the lines between good and evil.

The UFP provided the foundation of Roddenberry's universe. *Star Trek* presented a virtually blemishless UFP, truly the white hats of the galaxy. *The Next Generation* began testing underlying assumptions. The series even questioned the Prime Directive. Kirk may break the rules, but the more dangerous Picard questions the rules themselves. If the Prime Directive prevents the righting of a clear wrong or the saving of a people, perhaps it should be changed, not just ignored. Perhaps it only provides a convenient screen for the UFP to hide behind to evade difficult decisions.

The rebel freedom fighters known as the Maquis think so. They fight the Cardassians in defiance of the Federation government. Federation officers, even starship captains, covertly assist the Maquis, and some Starship officers even abandon the UFP to openly join the rebels. A larger crack appears in the pristine UFP, with the possibility that much of the highest leadership conspires to bad ends. Suddenly the white hats have become various shades of gray. While *TNG*'s new storylines offered interesting possibilities, they also changed Gene Roddenberry's universe. Shining Avalon becomes a world much like our own. It no longer offers a golden grail at the end of our path.

Deep Space Nine takes this a step further. Gene Roddenberry played almost no role in the series, and the rifts are deeper. Storylines center on a crew plagued with various tragedies in their pasts. They man a rundown space station near a ravaged world rather than a gleaming starship plying the spacelanes. Their rundown space station no longer represents the triumph of technology, as do the *Enterprise* starships. Many stories involve internecine conflicts between the UFP and Starfleet, the Cardassians, and the Bajoran inhabitants of the ravaged world. Episodes pit good guys against each other in very ambiguous moral tales. *Deep Space Nine* diverges very far from the vision of the original *Star Trek*. Perhaps significantly, this series is the least popular in the *Star Trek* family.

The Heroes

The Next Generation characters, while fleshed out human beings, also serve as symbols, and they form a melting pot of races, cultures, and personalities that is similar to the original *Star Trek*. Picard is the thinking person's captain, a man of strong convictions who prefers reason and persuasion over force and violence. He doesn't get into fist fights or chase women across the galaxy; he is an older father figure who governs his ship wisely and acts judiciously at all times. Riker, his first officer, is similar to Kirk, a handsome, two-fisted man of action and champion poker player. A variety of nonhumans form the nucleus of the crew: Betazoid Deanna Troi is the intuitive, empathic ship's counselor, Klingon Worf is the gruff, no-nonsense head of security, android Data is the voice of reason and logic, and the mysterious, wry Guinnan is the crew's confidante, the owner of the ship's bar who is as close as the show comes to a spiritual advisor. Beverly Crusher, a human woman, is the ship's competent medical officer.

Geordi La Forge is a blind, black human in charge of engineering, and he provides a nod to the handicapped, showing that they, too, can play a part aboard starships, at least so long as they have a high-tech visor. Interestingly, no Asian was chosen as part of the core ensemble, but clearly the same goal has been achieved: women and men of many races and cultures share the responsibilities of command.

These heroes follow in the tradition of their predecessors. Picard's crew proves every bit as noble, endearing, and interesting as Kirk's crew. Both crews reflect their gleaming starships, proud, self-confident, and assured (most of the time, at least).

Deep Space Nine changed all of that. These space station–bound characters suffer grim pasts and labor in much grayer circumstances. Although many leading characters act heroically and possess admirable traits, all are haunted by dark histories. This makes the *Deep Space Nine* characters grimmer as befits their setting and stories, but it runs counter to the Roddenberry protagonist.

Benjamin Sisko, nominally the Kirk/Picard counterpart, buried himself for three years working in the Mars Utopia Plentia Shipyards after his wife died in a Borg attack. His son Jake watched his mother die and his father flee Starfleet service.

O'Brien suffers from traumatic memories, racial bigotry, and a gambling habit. Nerys grew up as an underground terrorist on Bajor, always hiding and running—hardly a nourishing childhood. The greedy, cowardly, lusting Ferengi Quark runs a casino and a brothel. He possesses all the less-than-endearing qualities of his race. Perhaps Odo, the shapeshifter, proves the most lucky, but the symbiont has suffered watching the deaths of virtually all of his friends for three hundred years. Clearly, the noble hero of Roddenberry's original vision is nowhere among the crew of *Deep Space Nine*.

> *Picard's crew prove every bit as noble, endearing, and interesting as Kirk's crew.*

Voyager

The first Star Trek series put together after the death of Gene Roddenberry has yet to attract a large audience. The creators—Rick Berman, Michael Piller, and Jeri Taylor—intended *Voyager* to return to the spirit of the original *Star Trek*, but to do so with a different set of problems. *Voyager*'s primary mission is not to discover new worlds and new civilizations but to get home from a far-flung, unknown part of the galaxy.

One of the reasons *Voyager* was created was because *Deep Space Nine* proved unpopular with the loyal Star Trek audience. Perhaps the gray characters and grim setting failed to fit into Gene Roddenberry's universe and philosophy. Perhaps it was simply less interesting for the series to be rooted on a space station instead of voyaging across the universe. For whatever reason, it failed to attract the audience that *The Next Generation* had, and the studio wanted to protect their Star Trek franchise with a new series. *Voyager* began even as *The Next Generation* ended its run.

So the creators decided to play it safe by returning to the roots of the original series but with a twist. They set *Voyager* at the same time as *The Next Generation* and *Deep Space Nine* but in a different, unexplored space quadrant. *Voyager* is a smaller starship, crewed by a personable collection of humans and other beings, and with a Kirk-like, action-oriented captain at the helm. However, this time, the captain is a woman.

The Philosophy

Voyager offers a proper extension to the Star Trek universe and restores the cautious optimism of Gene Roddenberry's original *Star Trek*. The crew of the starship *Voyager* mixes all races and beings: whites with blacks with Asians, Vulcans with Terrans with Klingons with Talaxans with Ocampans, and even a sentient hologram. A woman serves as captain, finally fulfilling Roddenberry's wish to show a woman in a primary command po-

sition, and her starship *Voyager* holds no hostile intentions. The crew simply wants to return home and explore on their way. These white hats willingly sacrifice their own interests to help others.

Voyager supports Gene Roddenberry's philosophy of building a better universe through technology and understanding. The starship *Voyager* features the most advanced technology seen in any Star Trek series. Once again, an advanced starship run by a friendly multiracial crew traverses the galaxy, discovering unknown worlds and spreading knowledge and understanding.

The philosophy attracted many in search of hope once before. The original *Star Trek* supported humanistic values through the courageous actions of its heroes. Now *Voyager* offers the same hope.

The New Heroes

Captain Kathryn Janeway, the first woman as a starship commander and Star Trek series lead, brings a spotless service record, a strong background in the sciences, and a happy, well-adjusted childhood to her job as captain of the *Voyager*. Janeway, although female, is cut from the same cloth as Kirk and Picard, the classic hero and ship's captain familiar to Star Trek and previously represented by Horatio Hornblower and James Kirk.

Voyager's crew offers the traditional mix of races, cultures, and beings, but with some twists to avoid complete stereotyping. American Indian Chakotay, black Vulcan Tuvok, and Asian Harry Kim help balance one another on the bridge. Tuvok is a too-logical, often too-rigid Vulcan, while Chakotay is a headstrong rebel Maquis leader. Now first officer of the *Voyager*, Chakotay combines the technological knowledge of a starship commander with the spiritual beliefs and traditions of his people. Kim is an eager young officer who is still a bit wet behind the ears, a recent honors graduate from Starfleet Academy who desires to prove his worth.

B'Elanna Torres is half-Klingon and half-human, bringing together in her person these two antagonistic races. The rebellious engineering genius struggles to reconcile her Klingon side with her human side, and she and Harry Kim provide the *Voyager* with traditional rite-of-passage heroes.

Tom Paris represents the blemished hero. The prodigal son of a highly respected and honored Starfleet family, Paris struggles with the burden of his legacy, determined not to fail on *Voyager* as he so often has in the past. In fact, Captain Janeway pulled him out of jail to get him aboard her starship, and he doesn't want to let her down.

Neelix and Kes represent two new alien races for Star Trek, and as devoted lovers, they bring true love to the series. The Doctor, a living hologram created by the ship's computer, is an odd mix of emotion and logic. If Tuvok echoes Spock and Janeway recalls a distaff Kirk, then the Doctor oddly reminds us of the very human, curmudgeonly McCoy.

Which Is Best?

Which Star Trek wins as best series? Before *Voyager*, the answer was clear—the original, classic *Star Trek*, although *The Next Generation* has its strengths. Gene Roddenberry poured an undiluted vision into the first series. The stories told fables of the future, faithfully based on his philosophy. The heroes represented Roddenberry's vision.

The Next Generation falls close to the mark while *Deep Space Nine* misses entirely. Perhaps, in a strange twist of fate, the first series without Roddenberry, the first created by his disciples, so to speak, rings truest to his vision. While it is too early to tell, we may be witnessing the best Star Trek of all. The producers, witnessing the failure of *Deep Space Nine*, chose to return to the roots, and to take a step forward, but just as with earlier series, it may take a couple of seasons for it to grow into its potential.

Recapturing Roddenberry's founding philosophy and concept of heroes, *Voyager* also takes advantage of what followed. They make excellent use of existing concepts, including Klingons, Vulcans, Starfleet Academy, hologram technology, Maquis, and much more. They even put a woman at the helm of the starship and the series. They also take good advantage of the latest special effects techniques and larger budgets to work on-screen magic impossible in the original series.

They successfully return to the roots of the original *Star Trek*, including the best of what has been added since and moving forward. In doing so they have answered the oft-asked question, "Can there be Star Trek after Roddenberry?" Happily, the answer is a resounding, "Yes!"

CHAPTER FIVE

Meeting the Women of Star Trek

Gene Roddenberry's belief was that by the twenty-third century gender equality in employment as well as in life would be the norm of society. And so he originally cast a woman, Majel Barrett, to play second-in-command to James T. Kirk's captain on the original *Star Trek*. It's hard to imagine now what *Star Trek* would have been like, or how the womanizing Kirk would have handled it, if studio executives hadn't forced Roddenberry to cut her role. Since then, despite the initial setbacks, Star Trek writers have populated the future universe with many interesting, capable women in various positions of responsibility and power.

By the time of Roddenberry's twenty-third century, the male domination common to virtually every human society for at least the past five thousand years has ended. It may be worth noting that the starship *Enterprise* serves in Starfleet, a paramilitary organization, and it's relatively unclear if female equality exists throughout the rest of society, in government and industry. The military has traditionally offered opportunities to minorities or the disenfranchised that are unavailable in society as a whole. Armies as separate in time and space as those of ancient Egypt and modern America have offered minorities advancement otherwise impossible outside

Fifty Reasons Why Captain Janeway Is Better than Captain Picard

1. More hair than all previous Star Trek commanding officers combined.
2. Drinks coffee, not that sissy Earl Grey tea.
3. Beams down to the planet like real captains should.
4. Mutes the Doctor when the Doctor gets out of line.
5. Hasn't let an adolescent pilot the Federation flagship—yet.
6. *Voyager* needs a female captain. Its captain must be willing to admit they're lost and pull over for directions.
7. Picard likes to talk his way through. Janeway likes to punch her way through.
8. Hasn't quoted Shakespeare—yet.
9. Looks better in sleepwear.
10. Gives guilt trips that would make a Jewish mother proud.
11. Isn't French with an English accent.
12. Will give you two days off to ponder your life-shattering experience.
13. When Janeway lands her ship, it can take off again.
14. Janeway says "I don't like you!" to her enemies instead of trying to convince them to behave better.
15. To comfort children, Janeway cares for them in a loving motherly way. Picard sings a song in French about a monk who can't wake up for morning bells.
16. The only children on *Voyager* can be turned off at will.
17. Janeway has a first officer "boldly go where no one has gone before" and took them to the extreme.

military life. Joan of Arc could lead the French military rebellion against British rule but not a France at peace. However, given Roddenberry's utopian vision, it seems clear that he would have extended equality to all parts of society.

But America in the 1960s wasn't ready. They had yet to see the incredible breakthroughs that women would make in the coming decades. Studio executives doubted that television viewers would accept a woman in such a position of authority. Ironically, space travel, alien races, transporters, tricorders, and phasers all seemed plausible to them in a twenty-third century world, but not women in leadership roles.

Today, women serve as governors, senators, and mayors. They are elected in their own right rather than only when continuing the political careers of famous husbands. Women also lead or have led nations as diverse as Israel and Pakistan, Britain, India, and Turkey. And now, finally, a woman has been allowed to take the helm of a twenty-third century starship as the lead in a fictional television series. Curiously, in 1996, no woman has yet headed a major Hollywood studio—unusual in a state that has two female United States senators. Clearly, some institutions take longer to change than others.

18. Picard could never act like a prostitute to gain a tactical advantage.

19. Janeway doesn't have any pesky Federation admirals to get in her way.

20. Three words: Compression Phaser Rifles.

21. Acknowledges freely when she breaks the Prime Directive, instead of trying to weasel her way out of it with philosophical ramblings.

22. Janeway's holoprograms create useful things like doctors and lungs. Picard's holodecks create maniacal evil geniuses who yet again take over the ship.

23. She doesn't need to straighten her uniform every time she stands.

24. Janeway has never worn green tights and frolicked about in Sherwood Forest. If she did, however, she would look fantastic!

25. She doesn't waste time learning foreign languages. All lifeforms in the Delta Quadrant speak perfect English.

26. Her engineer does not wear a banana clip over her eyes.

27. Slouches in her chair even in critical life-threatening moments.

28. Doesn't have a counselor on board (thank God!).

29. Her telepath only lives nine years.

30. Janeway heard the words

31. Forty-five thousand light-years is one thing. Every point in the universe instantaneously? That's excessive!

32. Picard tells alien cultures, "I hope our two cultures will one day come to a greater understanding." Janeway threatens them with "the deadliest of force," with a tattoo.

33. Janeway's security chief would never grow a ponytail.

Star Trek

The *Star Trek* series continued to introduce capable women as protagonists and antagonists. Uhura proves capable of serving competently on any bridge station when needed. She enjoys good character moments, including when she locks "Mr. Adventure" into a closet in *Star Trek: The Search for Spock*, goes looking for nuclear vessels in San Francisco with Chekov in *Star Trek: The Voyage Home*, and performs an exotic dance to distract men in *Star Trek: The Final Frontier*. Uhura ultimately rises to the rank of commander. Many believe she presented the best female role model on *Star Trek* before Captain Janeway.

Other female protagonists include Christine Chapel and Janice Rand. Chapel first appears in "What Are Little Girls Made Of" as McCoy's nurse, and she becomes a doctor by the time of *Star Trek: The Motion Picture*. Captain Kirk's personal yeoman, Janice Rand, receives a promotion to transporter chief before *The Motion Picture* and to commander by the time of *Star Trek: The Undiscovered Country*. Rand and Chapel occasionally receive opportunities to excel. They are always competent professionals whose gender holds no significance.

Many other intriguing female characters appear. Vulcan-trained Dr. Miranda Jones

---

Fifty Reasons Why Captain Janeway Is Better than Captain Picard
(continued from previous page)

34. Janeway doesn't have to point which way to go when they set off.
35. Maintains an elaborate hairdo that would baffle even Princess Leia.
36. Has mastered facial expression understood by all to mean, "Boy, Paris, are *you* ever stupid."
37. Hugs her Vulcan from time to time.
38. Has a more manly voice.
39. Doesn't have a starship that splits in half when it's in a tight spot.
40. Has a dog and a significant other, not some damn fish!
41. Kes. Troi. No contest.
42. At least she doesn't have to yell "Hot!" at her cook every time she wants something to drink.
43. Her ship has neat-looking folding warp nacelles.

44. Her CONN officer actually went through the Academy.
45. Her first officer has a hallucinogenic device.
46. Her security officer draws his phaser at the first hint of trouble. Picard's security officer gets beat up by half the aliens who come aboard.
47. None of the crew members' relatives have ever tried to take over the ship, invade the Federation, steal a starship, or enslave all humankind.
48. To help her relax, Janeway's first officer helps her contact her spirit guide. Picard's first officer helps him get…to Risa.
49. Riker never smiled at Picard that way.
50. Q asked Janeway to run away with him and she refused. Q asked Picard's girlfriend to run away with him and she accepted.

serves as translator for the Medusan, Kollos, in "Is There in Truth No Beauty." Dr. Ann Mulhall loans her body to the conscious mind of Thalassa, Sargon's beloved in "Return to Tomorrow." Odona risks death to save the lives of her people in "The Mark of Gideon." Doomed Lenore Karidian murders to protect her father's reputation in "The Conscience of the King." Android Rayna Kapec in "Requiem for Methuselah," Edith Keeler in "The City on the Edge of Forever," Losira in "That Which Survives," Marlena Moreau of the mirror universe in "Mirror, Mirror," and Natira in "For the World Is Hollow and I Have Touched the Sky" all show power equal to that of any man.

The final story of the original series delivers a strong message. "Turnabout Intruder" tells the tale of the mentally unbalanced but brilliant lady scientist, Dr. Janice Lester, who switches minds with Kirk. The episode shows that a woman can rise to a captaincy even as the womanizer experiences being female. While many argue that the episode strikes a blow in favor of liberated women, it should be noted that the petulant, headstrong, over-emotional Janice Lester personifies many of the worst clichés about women.

The Next Generation and Deep Space Nine

Two decades after the original *Star Trek* pilot, "The Cage," first appeared, contemporary society had changed, and women in positions of authority had become more common. *The Next Generation* and *Deep Space Nine* show women as starship captains and even as admirals. Aboard Captain Jean-Luc Picard's *Enterprise*, women serve as doctor (Doctor Beverly Crusher), ship's counselor (Counselor Deanna Troi), and security chief (Lieutenant Tasha Yar). Each represents Starfleet at its best.

Perhaps the most powerful person aboard the starship is a woman, the head of the bar, Ten Four. Guinnan, a mysterious member of an alien race, has already lived over one thousand years at the time of the series.

The *Next Generation* episode "Yesterday's Enterprise" offers a third Enterprise that preceded Picard's, the *Enterprise-C*, captained by Rachel Garrett. "The Best of Both Worlds" offers another memorable female Starfleet officer, Lieutenant Commander Shelby. The series finale, "All Good Things," predicts that chief medical officer Beverly Crusher will one day captain her own starship.

Voyager

Voyager takes the final step and puts a woman at the center of the series and at the head of a starship. Captain Kathryn Janeway possesses the same special spark that illuminated Captain James Kirk and propelled him to become a Starfleet legend. She commands one of Starfleet's most advanced vessels, the starship *Voyager*. Janeway exhibits unique strengths and weaknesses. She combines the talents of

Kirk with the more patient, strategist's mind of Picard. Janeway's crew never questions her authority on any level at any time. The captain can be both warm and completely authoritative, compassionate and commanding, funny and powerful. Like Kirk, Janeway is quick to anger.

Janeway's ship is lost in an unknown quadrant of space. They are true pioneers, unable to turn home for help. Starfleet stocked *Voyager* for a one-year mission, but they will soon run out of parts and supplies. Janeway must find solutions to save her ship. Unlike Kirk or Picard, she has an education in the sciences that gives her more than courage and drive. This distinction may become critical to the survival of *Voyager* and its crew.

With *Voyager*, the captain is finally a woman. Roddenberry's original dream, of a starship with a woman in command, has come to fruition.

CHAPTER SIX

Speaking Trek Tech

Star Trek, to state the obvious, is science fiction. And the scientific technology in Star Trek is, indeed, fictional—for the most part. In the '60s, Roddenberry would never have imagined how outdated his twenty-third century computers would become in thirty years. And one of Star Trek's signature technologies, the transporter, may be a reality very soon—for amoebas, at least. It's technobabble, surely, but a good bit of the futuristic technology envisioned by Star Trek's creators has turned out to be not so wacky after all, and some of it may become reality sooner than we think. Hand-held lasers seemed quite exotic when the original *Star Trek* aired, but who would question their reality today?

A Star Trek transporter permits disassembly of an object or living being from matter to energy and then reassembly at a distant point. The *New York Times* has recently reported that two scientific research teams

> "That's our ship, that's *U.S.S. Voyager*. Intrepid-class, sustainable cruise velocity warp-factor 9.975, fifteen decks, bio-neural circuitry. Some of the traditional circuitry has been replaced by gel packs that contain bio-neural cells. They organize information more efficiently, speed up response time."
>
> —Lieutenant Stadi, "Caretaker"

U.S.S. Voyager

An Intrepid-class vessel capable of holding two hundred crew members, the *U.S.S. Voyager* is one of the fastest and most powerful starships in Starfleet. Although at 1130 feet long it is about half the size of the *U.S.S. Enterprise* NCC-1701-D, the *Voyager* is more technologically advanced than previous *Star Trek* vessels. Superbly equipped for exploration and research, the *Voyager* has an equally impressive array of defensive and offensive weapons, making it ready for action.

Voyager is the second of only four Intrepid-class starships built by Starfleet to date, launched stardate 48038.5 (the year 2371).

have almost accomplished this. Dr. David E. Pritchard at MIT has converted a sodium molecule into wave form, enabling it to be manipulated, altered, recombined, and analyzed. This accomplishes the transporter process, the conversion of matter to energy and then back to matter. The new process can already accommodate unicellular life, and perhaps a creature as large as an amoeba could be turned into a wave and propagated and then recombined. A human being is obviously much more complex than an individual molecule, but since all living creatures are composed of molecules, expanding the process may be indeed be possible.

Another Star Trek technology that is now becoming a reality is the hypospray, which allows a starship's medical officer to administer medicine without using needles to pierce the skin. The *New York Times* has reported that a device is being created that uses ultrasound-induced cavitation effects to deliver drugs through the lipid regions of the skin without breaking the skin barrier. Clinical trials could begin within a year.

The sickbay diagnostic bed moved from fiction to reality years ago. We seem to catch up with our science fiction very quickly these days, and this chapter looks at the state-of-the-art technology in use on *Voyager* today. For Captain Janeway and her crew, this is everyday reality.

> United Star Ship *Voyager*
>
> Naval Construction Contract 74656
>
> Intrepid class, second of four as of SD 48315.6
>
> Commissioned stardate 48038.5
>
> 154 crew
>
> 15 decks
>
> 1130 feet long
>
> Maximum sustainable speed: warp 9.975
>
> Dedication plaque quote: "For I dipp'd into the future, far as human eye can see / Saw the Vision of the world, and all the wonder that would be." From Tennyson's *Ulysses*

Transporters

Transporters are matter-energy conversion devices that take an object or being and transform it into a pattern of phased energy that can be transmitted as a complex trans-barrier signal through the first-level subspace (hyperspace) domain to a set of desired coordinates and then retransformed into its original form. They employ Heisenberg compensators, pattern buffers, phase transition coils, biofilters, matter streams, confinement beams, matter-energy converters, and phased matter. An entity remains conscious during transport and can be held in stasis. While in transport, you seem whole to yourself.

The "annular confinement beam" locks onto, then disassembles, a subject into phased matter via the phase transition coils, causing it to take on an energylike state somewhat akin to plasma, called phased matter. The matter stream is then fed into the pattern buffer, piped through waveguide conduits to one of the beam emitters on the hull of the starship, and then relayed to a point on the ground where the annular confinement beam reconstructs the subject.

The annular confinement beam maintains a "lock" on the subject to identify what to beam out and what to leave behind. The beam also transports the intact subject.

The "pattern buffer," a cyclotron-like tank, holds the whirling matrix of phased matter in the annular confinement beam while the subject is beamed out and beamed in. It keeps track of the subject's particles in the beam.

"Virtual focus molecular imaging scanners" perform a trace at the quantum level. The transporter ID trace keeps a verification record of the trace after transport. This compressed sample also includes the subject's name and logs of the transport cycle.

Ionizers and phase transition coils perform the quantum matrix manipulation to transform an object into phased matter in what is known as the "dematerialization process." This is what produces the familiar gold "sparkles" of the older-style Federation transporters and the red-and-blue effects of later Federation systems, as different dematerialization and phase transition processes were developed.

The Heisenberg Principle states that you cannot know both the location of a subatomic particle and its direction of motion. This has changed by the twenty-fourth century. The Heisenberg compensators help keep track of the particles in the beam by compensating for what is not known.

The biofilter identifies elements of the pattern and erases unwanted particles. It can be used to filter out unwanted viruses or bacteria and to manipulate DNA strings.

Pattern degradation occurs because annular confinement beams aren't perfect, even when amplified by Heisenberg compensators. The matter stream shifts out of alignment. A subject can be suspended in transport for up to 420 seconds before degradation becomes too severe to reform the subject. Locking the transport controller in a diagnostic loop keeps pattern degradation to a minimum, but phased-matter "bugs" reside in the plasma environment.

Emitter array pads reside at various sites on the surface of the *Voyager* hull. "Long-

Deck 1

Main Bridge

The command post and braintrust of *Voyager*, this area serves as the location to view other starships, to negotiate with leaders of rival races, and to learn about the unfamiliar area of the galaxy into which the starship has been thrust. The command area at the center of the bridge features seating and information displays for the captain and first officer. Captain Kathryn Janeway is in command of this communications hub. Major stations on the bridge include flight controller, operations officer, security/tactical, engineering, mission operations, and science.

The captain's ready room and the briefing room are located directly adjacent to the main bridge on Deck 1, the uppermost deck of *Voyager*'s primary hull.

Captain's Ready Room

The captain's ready room is located just starboard and aft of the main bridge. Here, the captain can meet with officers and communicate privately with other people outside the *Voyager*. The ready room is also sometimes used for briefings when the briefing room is not available. The captain can relax here, also, away from the activity of the bridge, but she is nearby in case she is needed. There is also a replicator in the ready room.

The ready room is located to the starboard side of the main bridge on Deck 1, and it's accessed through the doorway just forward of the tactical/security station.

Briefing Room

Inside the briefing room, the entire senior staff can gather to make important decisions and hold negotiations with other aliens or opposing forces.

The briefing room is located to the port side of the main bridge on Deck 1, and it's accessed through the doorway just forward of the operations station.

range virtual focus molecular imaging scanners" handle remote disassembly of the subject and facilitate reassembly.

Replicators

Replicators use the same technology as transporters. They use more energy because they create new objects rather than manipulate existing objects. An object is sampled at a molecular rather than quantum level. The computer then applies a lossy compression algorithm to save computer memory. This gives the computer a pattern from which to produce copies.

Starships keep a small supply of recycled bulk material from which to create new objects. A waveguide conduit system sends bulk material to the replicator, which reforms it into the requested objects, then it transmits the new object to the terminal.

"Quantum transformational manipulation" allows the creation of new elements. Energy costs are high for all forms of replication, thus making practical alchemy, such as creating limitless ladium, impossible, but food (normally simple arrangements of water, proteins, and lipids) is more practical to replicate from bulk matter than to store.

Warp Drives

Warp speed is fast, and that's all some care to know. But the warp drive on a starship is perhaps its most important and complex part; without it, getting across galaxies would be functionally impossible. Perhaps our biggest obstacles to inhabiting other solar systems as envisioned by Star Trek are the physical limitations of space and time.

Warp travel is a non-"propulsive" technology. It moves the ship, but it doesn't propel it in any particular direction. "Impulse power" operates in the same way as twentieth-century rocket technologies and is thus propulsive with inertial effects; that is, once you turn off the rockets you keep moving forward. Warp drive does not share propulsive effects or the additive advantages of inertia. Since it operates by creating a separate

---

Deck 2

Mess Hall

The mess hall, located on Deck 2, provides a social atmosphere as well as a dining facility for the crew.

Captain's Private Dining Room

When Kes started producing vegetables in her air garden on board, Neelix commandeered Captain Janeway's private dining room adjacent to the mess hall, turning it into a kitchen. Appointing himself chief cook, Neelix prepares creative concoctions for the *Voyager* crew, which he serves here.

Deck 3

There's nothing here yet.

107

subspace field, you could instantly stop a ship under warp drive if you could kill the subspace field rapidly enough.

The "stress-energy tensor" mathematically describes each point in four dimensional space-time. It is linked to the mass and energy distribution of normal space (non-subspace). This distribution and flow of the stress-energy of matter is dependent on the surrounding stress-energy tensor, which defines the curvature of four-dimensional space-time. Matter-energy within the warp (or subspace) field is disassociated from the matter-energy outside of the field due to the violent change in the frame of reference produced by the plasma stream within the warp field coils in the nacelles.

This violent change in the local stress-energy within the subspace coils would rip the fabric

Deck 4

Transporter Room

The transporter converts matter into energy and reconverts it back to matter at another location, allowing crew members to travel quickly from the ship to a planet's surface and back again. The transporter is most often used to beam people or objects to or from this room; direct beaming to another location (sickbay, for example) consumes nearly twice the power and is only used in emergencies.

There are two personnel transporters on Deck 4 of the *Voyager*'s command section, plus two cargo transporters. In addition, four small emergency evacuation transporters are available for one-way beaming off the ship only.

Nicaletti's quarters are on Deck 4.

Deck 5

Sickbay

Sickbay is a fully equipped medical facility, complete with a surgical center, recovery units, and specialized treatment rooms. Sickbay is prepared for any challenge—including the loss of a doctor. Inside this medical chamber lives the emergency medical holographic doctor, capable of the same medical experiments and procedures as "living" doctors.

Sickbay and the adjacent doctor's office are located on Deck 5.

of space except that nature produces a subspace field around the event to gradually fix the tear. This in effect spreads the event over a general area in a subspace field that looks similar to a gravity field originating from a gravity well and protects the space-time continuum. It can be manipulated into asymmetric propulsive fields.

Matter within the field is removed from normal space and anchored to the frame of reference of subspace. The effect of this is to allow matter within the field to almost completely bypass relativity's obstacles and allow phenomena such as FTL travel. The limiting factor is the energy required to disassociate the matter from normal space. This energy must be continuously applied or the subspace field gradually dissipates and brings the matter back into normal space.

Subspace is a field that defines a particular frame of reference at all points in known space. It is composed of an infinite number of cells like a honeycomb. A ship entering warp uses subspace so as to keep its frame of reference regardless of speed. The asymmetrical peristaltic warp field propels a ship by pushing against each anchored reference frame of subspace. The first field coil anchors the ship to the occupied position in subspace, then passes the field along to the next coil along with its anchored position in subspace, and so on down the nacelle.

It is not necessary to add extra nacelles to increase warp speed. Once a warp field is established, it takes pure engine power to push toward warp 10. The nacelles create the warp field and sustain it. The number of nacelles is determined by the size and mission of the starship, although three nacelles is a very unstable design (the *U.S.S. Tritium Warp 4 Cruiser*, designed with three nacelles, was canceled in 2155 due to severe instability during warp flight). Two extra nacelles made the Constellation-class starships very agile.

Before the current environmentally friendly, movable warp coils on the Intrepid-class starships, ships that went faster than warp 5 polluted space with localized "rifts." The *Voyager* can safely reach a top speed of warp 9.975 for short periods. The new warp drive technology is top secret, but it has been publicly speculated that the drive could eliminate the risk of pollution because of the orientation of the warp fields (nacelle position), new materials, the configuration of the warp coils in the nacelles, or by computer

---

Deck 6

Holodeck

The Holographic Environment Simulator, familiarly known as the holodeck, can duplicate any environment in the computer's memory with startling reality. These simulations are remarkably useful for crew training, recreation, and exercise. Since the *Voyager* is lost in an unfamiliar part of the galaxy, many crew members seek refuge from this harsh twist of fate in the holodeck, creating memories of what was and fantasies of what's to come.

The crew has attempted to tap the holodeck's power supply to augment the *Voyager*'s dwindling main energy sources. They have learned that the power used in the holodeck is incompatible with that required for the ship's other operations; therefore, the holodeck can be used for training or recreation as needed without regard to the energy used.

Lieutenant Kyoto's quarters are on this deck.

Deck 7

Security personnel quartered on Deck 9 were moved to this deck so that Deck 9 could be shut down and its power rerouted to the warp drive.

When the ship was heated to eliminate the infection of the bio-neural gel packs, Deck 7 lost the gravitational net as a result of system failures.

Hargrove's and Lieutenant Iota's quarters are both on this deck.

---

manipulation of warp formula to synchronize and shape the warp fields. Dedicated warp coils may produce a subspace distortion field around the nacelles to facilitate moving them quickly. Gravimetric force fields may also be used to move the nacelles.

Bio-Neural Circuitry

The bio-neural computer network aboard the starship *Voyager* consists of "bio-gel packs." The network is faster than the *Enterprise-D*'s computer core. The *Enterprise*'s core is encased in a subspace field to allow the optical circuitry to operate faster than light. The gel packs composing the bio-neural computer network are located in a main core on the *Voyager*. They are not encased in a subspace field. A computer core similar to the one on the *Enterprise* would be too big to fit into *Voyager*, so they had to revolutionize the computer system to have a computer with equal capability. A "neural network" is a computer designed to function like the human brain.

> ### Deck 8
>
> Kes's quarters are on this deck.

> ### Deck 9
>
> Security personnel on Deck 9 were relocated to Deck 7 and this deck was shut down, so that the power it used could be rerouted to the warp engines.

> ### Deck 10
>
> There's nothing here yet.

"Bio-neural" circuitry is made of organic substances that function as a learning machine. The circuitry is a synthesized neuron grouping modeled on a very large computer to act as a shipwide organic "brain." Neurons are efficient transmitters, but, like any organic being, they must be continuously fed with nutrient solutions or they will die.

The neurons may be fed with electrical power or other readily available energy. A low DC voltage that reverts food into a usable form could "feed" a gel pack. The gel pack would convert the energy in food during normal operation. A circulator system could fuel the packs. Neuron activity is faster than cell metabolism for data processing, but the artificial neurons would need a cell metabolism to survive, including programmed DNA to control all activity.

Isolinear chips remain as resident backup. Nothing has to be physically replaced for the ICs to be brought on-line. Because of its bio-neural network, the computer on the starship *Voyager* may develop consciousness and experience dreams. It is subject to disease and even potential emotional disorders.

Holodecks

Holodeck walls can generate holographic images that appear to extend for an unlimited distance. Holograms can also be projected into space. They can be augmented with force beams to simulate solid, tangible objects or with replicator technology to create actual solid matter such as foodstuffs.

Holodeck matter can impersonate real matter even at the molecular level. Molecule-sized magnetic bubbles replace molecules in full-resolution holo-objects. The computer can manipulate them individually in three dimensions. The computer may use large magnetic bubbles to simulate surfaces and textures rather than create an object at the molecular level.

Computers cannot duplicate the complexity of electron shell activity and atomic motions that determine biochemical activity in living creatures. This prevents replicators from duplicating life and resurrecting the dead. Advances in computer technology may allow this, permitting a person to live forever in any chosen environment while interacting with real people and objects visiting the holodeck. On the other hand, a person can be injured on the holodeck.

All foods eaten on the holodeck are replications. No other type of simulation would survive outside of the holodeck.

The holodeck includes a force-field treadmill. Approaching a wall causes an instant shift away. The holodeck can change gravity in three dimensions, so occupants don't notice the change.

Any technology has limitations. "Reality gaps" can become apparent.

The *Voyager* crew once tried to hook the holodeck power systems to the main power systems and blew out a conduit. This explains why the crew uses the holodeck despite the limitations on power supplies aboard the lost starship.

Deck 11

Main Engineering

Main engineering, on Deck 11, is the home of the *Voyager*'s warp drive system, more advanced and efficient than that of its predecessors. The *Voyager*'s folding wing-and-nacelle warp drive system allows the starship to exceed the warp 5 "speed limit," imposed in the *Star Trek: The Next Generation* episode "Force of Nature," without polluting the space continuum. The *Voyager* can reach a speed of warp 9.975, but only for short periods.

Deck 12

Navigational Control
Deck 12, section B-7

Deck 13

There's nothing here yet.

Holodocs

The *Voyager* has the only holographic doctor. The Holodoc is an empty shell with nothing beneath the apparent surface to avoid wasting computer power simulating unnecessary internal organs.

Holodecks use "omnidirectional holographic diodes." The *Voyager*'s sickbay is fitted with a system of OHDs that project an image of the Doctor. Each projects a complete image. Visible portions change as the Doctor moves, creating an illusion of fluid motion.

Magnetic containment fields allow the Doctor to interact with physical objects. These force fields move as the Doctor moves to create the appearance of solid matter. He can shut off the containment fields, allowing objects and people to pass through him.

Similar OHDs and magnetic fields were added to other parts of the ship, allowing the Doctor to leave sickbay. The Doctor's first mission away from sickbay took place on the holodeck.

His cohesion can range from solid to intangible. He appears human in other ways. He eats, drinks, and exhibits a dry sarcasm.

The Doctor possesses a data bank of medical information. He is slowly developing his own personality. The Doctor now possesses the emotional range of an average human crew member. He can become proud, caring, lonely, happy, indignant, annoyed, and angry. He even once confessed that he was anxious before going on his first "away" mission out of sickbay. The Doctor has begun to interact with other crew members in an intimate way. He has enjoyed two, brief, romantic relationships.

He now has sole control over his own on/off command. He not only doctors patients but also keeps records, maintains equipment, and performs other duties in sickbay.

Deck 14

There's nothing here yet.

Deck 15

When the ship was heated to eliminate the infection of the bio-neural gel packs, this deck lost life support as a result of system failures.

Hydroponic Garden

The hydroponic garden is in one of the unused cargo bays. Here, Kes grows vegetables and other foods that Neelix uses to cook with.

CHAPTER SEVEN

Examining the Prime Directive

Science fiction writers, and people in general, have a habit of coining short rules explaining the mysterious ways the universe works, bringing sense to chaos, giving instructions, or simply summing up despair in pithy phrases. There's (Theodore) Sturgeon's Law, Robert Heinlein's wisdom of Lazarus Long, and Arthur C. Clarke's law of science and magic. Isaac Asimov's Three Laws of Robotics provided a foundation for both artificial intelligence researchers and other science fiction writers.

The writers of Star Trek are no exception. The Prime Directive, first met in the classic series three decades ago, has become fundamental to science fiction, and it provides an underpinning uniting all the Star Trek series.

The Prime Directive, also known as General Order Number One, forms part of the governing law of the United Federation of Planets, including Starfleet. It forbids anyone from interfering with the natural growth of less-developed alien civilizations.

The Federation Council first passed a series of executive orders. These General Orders provided specific direction to Starfleet vessels operating without immediate communication with Starfleet Command.

These General Orders include the following:

General Order Number One: This forbids anyone from interfering with the natural growth of less-developed alien civilizations.

General Order Number Six: A ship's self-destruct sequence must automatically activate twenty-four hours after the entire crew has died (shown in the animated "The Albatross").

General Order Number Seven: No vessel, under any circumstances, may approach Talos IV, and any vessel that does so, must be destroyed (*Star Trek* "The Menagerie").

General Order Number Twenty-four: A world must be destroyed if the galaxy is threatened by it (*Star Trek* "A Taste of Armageddon").

Six of these General Orders form the basis of the Prime Directive. When a ship loses contact with Starfleet, its captain acts as ambassador and military commander. He or she makes decisions on behalf of the Federation. The General Orders establish strict guidelines for relations with alien cultures.

Bjo Trimble's *The Star Trek Concordance* first defined the importance of the Prime Directive in the 1970s. She called it "a wise but often troublesome rule which prohibits Federation interference with the normal development of alien life and societies. It can be disregarded when absolutely vital to the interests of the entire Federation, but the commander who does violate it had better be ready to present a sound defense of his actions."

The Prime Directive raises as many questions as it answers. It can provide protection to less-developed cultures or be abused as a shield to hide behind to avoid making difficult moral decisions.

History

The original *Star Trek* introduced the Prime Directive, but it has grown more important in the more settled twenty-fourth-century of *The Next Generation, Deep Space Nine,* and now *Voyager.* It has become a key guide for decision-making.

If Kirk often ignored the Prime Directive, Picard and Sisko cannot. Janeway's *Voyager* offers an interesting situation, since it is lost in the Delta Quadrant and cut off from Starfleet. Janeway is potentially the first Star Trek protagonist with a freer hand than Kirk.

> **The Prime Directive grew out of errors committed by Federation citizens against newly met alien civilizations.**

The Prime Directive grew out of errors committed by Federation citizens against newly met alien civilizations. The incident described in *Star Trek*'s "A Piece of the Action" appears to have taken place before the adoption of the Prime Directive. In that episode, the *U.S.S. Horizon* has left behind the book *Chicago Mobs of the Twenties* on Iotia. The Iotians read the book and remodel their society based on twentieth-century Chicago gang life. Obviously the book severely disrupts normal development of the civilization. This incident, and others like it, lead to a directive designed to prevent cultural contamination. The directive commands that a society must be sufficiently advanced to prevent disruption before contact can be made.

It isn't that simple. The Directive also inevitably commands Starfleet personnel to watch threatened worlds, and their sometimes human inhabitants, die without them being able to interfere. Strict interpreters of the Directive insist that this complies with the natural law governing the universe. They maintain that objecting to this universal governing law is akin to protesting the laws of physics. More liberal interpreters insist that circumstances can overrule the Directive. Strict constructionists call this cultural imperialism, insisting that Starfleet has no right to judge which civilizations are worthy of survival. Loose constructionists accuse their opponents of hiding behind the Prime Directive to avoid making difficult moral choices. Most often, those who work aboard starships in direct personal contact with alien worlds become loose constructionists.

Rule Bending

The Prime Directive links all the Star Trek series, and bending or ignoring the Prime Directive links the lead Star Trek captains. Each have wrestled with it and had to find their own middle road, adhering to it or not given their circumstances. When does exploration itself become interference? When is helping worse than leaving people to their own fate? These issues are timeless and persistent, and it's no wonder the Star Trek captains are seen frequently struggling with them.

Captain Janeway had her most memorable struggle with the Prime Directive in the premiere episode of *Star Trek:*

Voyager, "Caretaker." In that episode, the garden world of Ocampa has been turned into a desert by the Caretaker's race, and feeling guilty for having nearly destroyed their world, the Caretaker has built an underground cavern to shelter the natives, providing them with energy. Over time, the Ocampans have grown dependent on the Caretaker.

When Captain Janeway arrives, it's discovered that the energy is running out, and if something isn't done to save them, the Ocampans will die. Captain Janeway decides to interfere. She warns the natives of the imminent disaster and tells the Caretaker to allow them to fend for themselves from now on.

Though Captain Janeway violates the spirit of the Prime Directive, because the Caretaker had already interfered in the normal development of Ocampan society, her actions actually free the Ocampans from dependence on another. This justification of her actions echoes earlier decisions of Kirk, while the Caretaker recalls the memories of classic guilt-ridden aliens such as the Organians in the classic *Star Trek*'s "Errand of Mercy."

> *A science fiction cliché postulates that giving a peaceful, primitive society advanced technology, such as atomic power, before it is ready can lead the society to destroy itself.*

The flip side to the Prime Directive appears in *The Next Generation*'s "Homeward." Captain Picard, adhering to the Prime Directive, abandons the last survivors of a dying race to their fate. Worf's foster-brother saves the people without violating the spirit of the Prime Directive, but everyone is angry with him for violating the letter of the law. The Captain, seemingly heartless and rigid, supports the Federation rules, feeling he is right to turn his back on helpless people in this instance.

But Picard deliberately alters the development of an alien culture in the fifth season of *The Next Generation*. Though the Borg are waging war on the Federation, rather than destroying the Borg race, Picard plays god by trying to change their nature. He calculatedly sends back a Borg named Hugh with knowledge of individuality, a concept alien to Borg culture, hoping that this virus will alter the natural development of Borg society and make them more peaceful. When Starfleet Command discovers Picard has allowed the Borg to survive, they reprimand him.

In another *Voyager* episode, "Prime Factors," the Prime Directive is used against the Federation itself. Lost, and needing a miracle of technology to get them home, the *Voyager* stumbles upon an alien people who possess the technology they need. However, the laws of the alien people prevent them from sharing their technology. Janeway notes, "It's the first time we've been on the other side of the fence. How many times have we been in a position of refusing to interfere when some kind of disaster threatened an alien culture? It's all very well to say we do it on the basis of an enlightened principle, but how does that feel to the aliens? I'm sure many of them think the Prime Directive is a lousy idea."

Starfleet Rules

Starfleet Command will judge Janeway's actions in the Delta Quadrant upon her eventual return. In *The Next Generation* 's "The Drumhead," Starfleet Command accuses marionette Jean-Luc Picard of violating the Prime Directive nine times. Picard fights the accusations.

A starship captain may assist a culture with sufficient technology to produce a vessel capable of spaceflight. Bajor requested assistance from the Federation after the Cardassian occupation ended. Previously, the Federation had ignored decades of brutal occupation by the Cardassians because the Bajorans didn't yet fit within permissible rules.

The Prime Directive protects the natural development of cultures that might misuse knowledge gained too early. A science fiction cliché postulates that giving a peaceful, primitive society advanced technology, such as atomic power, before it is ready can lead the society to destroy itself. The Prime Directive forces the Federation to study such cultures without interference. It leads to respect for all life, but it shouldn't demand turning a blind eye on holocaust. Application of the Prime Directive raises many questions.

These questions have arisen frequently on our own world, particularly since the end of the Cold War. Bosnia, Cambodia (Kampuchea), Somalia, Iraq, Haiti, and South Africa offer examples of similar problems. The debate over so-called "Asian values" provides another example. The original *Star Trek* used the Vietnam War, the Cold War, and 1960s racial conflicts as springboards for excellent stories. *Voyager* could create excellent episodes using the Prime Directive to question when and if the United Nations, NATO, or the United States should interfere in local conflicts. One of the reasons Star Trek has remained relevant for as long as it has is because it uses dramatic conflict to offer imaginative commentary and solutions to problems in our world today.

117

CHAPTER EIGHT

Understanding the Maquis

Since the rebel Maquis form half the crew on the starship *Voyager*, it's worth having a look at who they are and how they developed. *Star Trek: The Next Generation* introduced the Maquis, and their importance grew on *Deep Space Nine*. Then *Star Trek: Voyager* began a new page of their history. The story of the Maquis begins with the Cardassians, whose aggressive, territorial actions eventually gave rise to the rebel group.

The Cardassians

The warlike Cardassians love to conquer. They are a humanoid race with ridges that appear to connect their necks to their shoulders and ridged foreheads. This gives them a martial look that is quite appropriate.

Years ago, the Cardassians engaged in a long conflict with the United Federation of Planets (UFP). An uneasy truce between the two adversaries was signed in 2366. During negotiations, Ambassador Spock, and his father, Ambassador Sarek, publicly disputed the treaty.

Starfleet captain Benjamin Maxwell, commanding the *Phoenix*, promptly, and illegally, violated the treaty. Starfleet authorities believed Maxwell's suspicions of illicit Cardassian military activity to be accurate. Captain Picard fled from a Cardassian warship while in command of the *Stargazer* in 2355.

The Cardassians were once peaceful, spiritual people living on a poor world. Starvation and disease led to the rise of

military power. They then embarked on the conquest of richer worlds, and they acquired more advanced technology by force or stealth. The desperate Cardassians lost millions of lives in the war effort, but this was acceptable to them. Bajor, one such conquered world, was annexed by the Cardassians in 2328; the Cardassians then robbed it of all its resources and forcibly resettled most Bajorans on other worlds.

> The Cardassians were once peaceful, spiritual people living on a poor world. Starvation and disease led to the rise of military power.

Peace for Some

The peace treaty of 2366 established an armistice between the Federation and the Cardassian Union. Historians credit Starfleet captain Edward Jellico for the success of the negotiations. The treaty guaranteed all prisoners the right to see a representative from a neutral planet following their imprisonment.

Many believed that the Cardassians were developing a metagenic weapon in 2369. They feared Cardassia planned to use it in an invasion of the Federation. *Enterprise-D* captain Jean-Luc Picard, Chief Medical Officer Beverly Crusher, and Security Officer Worf covertly entered Cardassian space to investigate. The rumors proved to be a trap. Also in 2369, the Bajoran resistance movement forced the Cardassians from Bajor after years of terrorist activity. The retreating Cardassians abandoned orbital space station Deep Space Nine. The station offered a strategic base for scientific investigation and trade after discovery of the Bajoran wormhole.

The border provisions of the peace treaty unveiled in 2366 defined a demilitarized zone within which the Federation extended no protection. The UFP ordered all inhabitants of Federation colonies within the demilitarized zone to abandon their worlds in compliance with the treaty. Some colonists refused to abandon their homes to serve Federation political interests. Cardassians often preyed on these worlds and continued to harbor secret plans for their conquest. The Cardassian Obsidian Order even planned to build a secret fleet in violation of the treaty.

The UFP honored the treaty and withdrew aid from colonists who refused to evacuate. The *Star Trek: The Next Generation* episode "Journey's End" introduced one such world colonized by Amerindians. These colonists wanted a world to preserve their culture. They lived in peace until the treaty, when the Federation ordered them to relocate and then withdrew their protection when they would not. The Cardassians took that opportunity to invade their settlements. The Federation refused to assist the colonists, insisting that they honor the evacuation order.

Birth of the Maquis

This drove the colonists into alliance with similar rebels. They organized a resistance, taking the name "Maquis" to honor past heroes of Earth. The first Maquis were an actual WW II, French resistance group, who fought against the puppet Vichy government that the conquering Germans had imposed on France. The name "Maquis" refers to "the bushes" where they hid. The Maquis band of Federation rebels defended their homes and property against Cardassians, believing that Starfleet had failed them for reasons of politics.

> The border provisions of the peace treaty unveiled in 2366 defined a demilitarized zone within which the Federation extended no protection.

The Federation often refers to Maquis and Bajoran freedom fighters as "terrorists," but many Starfleet officers secretly support the Maquis. Ensign Ro Laren, of the starship *Enterprise*, identified with the Maquis because their plight resembled that of her own Bajoran people.

Despite Federation condemnation, the Maquis continue their fight against oppression, aided by many sympathizers, including former officers of Starfleet. Commander Calvin Hudson of Dorvan Five, Lieutenant Thomas Riker, former Starfleet officer

Chakotay, B'Elanna Torres, and Tom Paris, a former Starfleet lieutenant, are among those who defected to the Maquis. The sympathizers helped the Maquis acquire a small fleet of ships to carry bootleg arms to fight both Cardassians and Starfleet.

This situation has close parallels to the real-world incidents that led to the creation of Israel in 1948. While the withdrawing British Army turned arms over to the Arabs, many British officers secretly aided the Jewish Haganah and Irgun underground. Ships carrying bootleg arms slipped into ports. The grateful new nation of Israel later named streets after respected sympathetic British military officers, including a major road in Tel Aviv named after General Allenby.

Different Times

The politics and entanglements surrounding the Maquis in the Alpha Quadrant are partly the result of the inevitable development of society. When James T. Kirk's *Enterprise* first flew through the Alpha Quadrant, it was a frontier unknown to the UFP, and as a result, Kirk enjoyed a greater freedom to act as he saw fit. Jean-Luc Picard and Benjamin Sisko find themselves in a more settled star system, one that is now filled with established relationships and governments.

One generation has brought many changes. Trailblazers lead different lives than settlers. Kirk now finds himself out of place in the brave new world of the twenty-fourth century, which he has done so much to bring about. History has repeated this process many times. The American Declaration of Independence and the United States Constitution were drafted thirteen years apart, in 1776 and 1789 respectively. However, only three people signed both documents. The men who ran the new nation replaced the men who made the revolution, much as "space cops" such as Picard and Sisko have replaced pathfinders such as Kirk.

In dealing with the Maquis, Picard and Sisko are constrained in ways that Kirk never was. Picard, though apologetic, accepts Federation decrees. Sisko, commander of Deep Space Nine, privately opposes Federation policy while officially treating the Maquis as outlaws. He lives with the carnage the Cardassians have wrought on Bajor, but he feels restrained by his position.

On *Voyager*, the situation is different yet again, for though the crew is nearly half Maquis and half Starfleet, they are all far removed from their normal context. What do the old politics mean in this unknown part of the galaxy? Forced together for an unknown period of time, possibly for the rest of their lives, Starfleet officers and Maquis must learn to trust and rely upon one another. Cooperation offers their only chance of surviving and returning home.

CHAPTER NINE

Navigating the Delta Quadrant

When cocreators Rick Berman, Michael Piller, and Jeri Taylor sat down to plan their new extension to Gene Roddenberry's Star Trek universe, the Delta Quadrant, they knew they wanted to leave the familiar Alpha Quadrant far behind. But how far behind, and what would we find in this new area of the galaxy? What are the physical parameters of this new quadrant, and who inhabits it? This chapter looks at what the creators have come up with.

Just How Far Is Far?

First the creators had to decide where the starship *Voyager* was, how far from home in the Alpha Quadrant their trip to the Delta Quadrant had taken them. They put the *Voyager* seventy thousand light-years away from Federation space, but just what does that mean in practical terms? There are 31,536,000 seconds per year and light moves at 186,000 miles per second equaling 5.87e12 miles in one year, or 4.11e17 miles in seventy thousand years. So that means the *Voyager* has to go 4.11e17 miles to get home unless it finds a shortcut.

At warp 8, the *Voyager* travels a thousand times faster than the speed of light. That means it travels a thousand light-years per year. The ship traveled for six and a half months at an average of warp 8 in stardate 530.9 (season one), thus traveling 3.10e15 (3.1015872e15) miles, or 193 days (16,675,200 seconds) at an average of warp 8 (186,000,000 miles per second). That's making pretty good time,

but it still leaves 4.079e17, or 407,900,000,000,000,000 miles to go. Home is indeed a long ways away!

Meet the New Aliens

Berman, Piller, and Taylor wanted to populate the Delta Quadrant with new faces. If they only filled it with Vulcans, Klingons, Romulans, Cardassians, Bajoran, and Borg, they wouldn't be bringing Star Trek where it had never been before. They already had a half-Klingon and a full Vulcan aboard their ship, so they needed interesting new aliens. Piller said, "We'd gotten to know our territory—and the Romulans, Cardassians, Ferengi, and Klingons—just a little too well... The first Enterprise crew had no idea what was 'out there,' and neither will *Voyager*'s. And it's allowing us to create fresh, and frankly, intimidating story material." Taylor agreed, adding, "It is our responsibility to populate the Delta Quadrant with fascinating new aliens that will be

> "It is our responsibility to populate the Delta Quadrant with fascinating new aliens that will be just as interesting to the audience eventually as the Klingons are to them now."

just as interesting to the audience eventually as the Klingons are to them now."

Star Trek: Voyager delivers on the promises of its creators. At the time of writing, the series has offered the following possibly significant additions to the Star Trek universe.

Baneans ("Ex Post Facto")

Baneans are at war with another race, the Numiri, even though the two races once co-existed on one planet. Baneans possess the technology to extract memory engrams from the dead, providing an account of how they died. The engrams are used in murder trials; punishment for murder is an implant that causes the killer to repeatedly experience the event through the victim's eyes. Numiri framed Lieutenant Tom Paris for murdering the Banean Minister of Science, Tolen Ren.

Botha ("Persistence of Vision")

This race of paranoid isolationists decloaked and attacked the *Voyager*. They also cast a bioelectric psionic field around the ship, causing all crew members except telepathic Kes and the holographic Doctor to hallucinate. A resonance burst counteracted the effect.

Caretaker ("Caretaker," "Cold Fire")

The Array are mysterious, active pieces of space hardware. One pulled the starship *Voyager* to the edge of the galaxy. Ocampa call their technologically advanced protector a "Caretaker." He once had a mate who became bored with a stationary lifestyle and took off to explore the galaxy. Now close to death, the Caretaker looks for a new mate. Tanis, a male Ocampan colonist, led the *Voyager* crew to an entity they call Suspiria, the female mate of the Caretaker.

Drayans

This isolationist race shunned outside contact for decades. They age in reverse and fear "morrok," the messenger of death. The race appears to be opposed to technology. Tuvok crashed on a moon they consider to be sacred territory.

Energy Creatures ("Elogium")

These beings resemble and flagellate like protozoa, and they appear to absorb nutrients through their skin. They exist in varying sizes, leave magnetic wakes, change colors, and are capable of emitting powerful electrically charged plasma streams. They fly independently through space, without a starship, to find food. Some of these creatures once induced elogium in Kes and were sexually attracted to the ship, *Voyager*.

Haakonians ("Jetrel")

The Haakonians conquered the Talaxan homeworld in 2356. They employed their Metreon Cascade, a weapon of mass destruction conceived and built by Dr. Jetrel, against the Talaxan moon, Rinax. Talax surrendered unconditionally. The attack killed Neelix's family.

Katarian ("Deadlock")

This Alpha Quadrant race possesses head spikes and teething fangs that grow in a few days. One half-Katarian/half-human baby has been born in the Delta Quadrant aboard the starship *Voyager*. The difficult birth, due to the human mother's body's unfamiliarity with head spikes, caused the Doctor to perform a fetal transport beaming the baby girl out of her mother.

Kazon ("Caretaker," "State of Flux," "Initiations," "Maneuvers")

Kazon are a reddish hue and have a coxcomb that runs down the front of their forehead. Honor and name are greater than life for the Kazon, and being shown compassion is the deepest disgrace. A Kazon must perform heroic deeds or suffer glorious failures to earn a name. Their slow ships possess no cloaking device and only weak weapons. Kazons use towing emitters as their tractor beams, but these can be destabilized by feedback loops. They now possess a transporter. "Enemy's Blood" is a Kazon drink.

There are eighteen separate Kazon sects in the Kazon Collective, each only vaguely connected with the others. Known Kazon sects include Ogla, Sari, Nistrum, Relora, Hobii, Mostral, and Oglamar. The Relora and the Ogla are, or were, the leading sects. Kazon sects don't get along with one another, causing daily changes in maps and alliances, although Jal Sankur once united the sects. Kazon-Ogla have an M-class moon where young Kazon are trained to survive rigorous combat conditions. Kazon attacked the peaceful Ocampa for their water, a scarce resource. Sestra, a Cardassian with the appearance of a Bajoran, who previously served aboard Chakotay's Maquis ship and the *Voyager*, now serves aboard a Kazon vessel. Kahr, a Kazon, once saved Chakotay's life. Jal Razik, a Kazon war hero, told Chakotay, "Everything you are is a threat to us. The Kazon fought long and hard for their independence from uniforms like yours—

> There are eighteen separate Kazon sects in the Kazon Collective, each only vaguely connected with the others.

your uniforms, your laws, your technology. You are not welcome here."

Konar ("Cathexis")

Trianic-based energy beings, the Konar are noncorporeal life forms that extract the neural energy of other beings to sustain themselves. They live in a dark matter nebula. On stardate 48734, a Konar took over Tuvok's body in an attempt to lead the *Voyager* into the nebula to extract the crew's neural energy.

Numiri ("Ex Post Facto")

Although the Numiri once coexisted on the same planet with the Baneans, the two races are now at war. Numiri ships, comparable to the *Voyager* in power and possessing tractor beams, regularly intimidate visitors to the Banean homeworld. Numiri patrols engaged the *Voyager* in 2371 while that ship was visiting the Baneans. They attempted to frame Lieutenant Paris for murdering the Banean Minister of Science, Tolen Ren.

Ocampa ("Caretaker")

This alien species, formerly protected by the array, has a life span of only nine years. Ocampa possess telepathic abilities. Female Ocampa experience a time of change when their body prepares for fertilization called elogium. Body temperature elevates and in-

creased electrophoretic activity occurs in their nervous system. Their eyes turn yellow-green and a sticky yellow ooze called ipasaphor comes from their hands that makes mating possible. They also develop a mitral birth sac on their back and often exhibit odd behavior. Elogium normally occurs between the ages of four and five, and only once. They have fifty hours in which to begin and must remain joined for six days to insure conception. The rolisisin ritual requires a father to rub the woman's feet until her tongue swells.

Several hundred thousand Ocampa reside miles underground a hot, desert planet, where they have lived for over a thousand years. Their below-the-surface habitat originated when a mysterious global warming began, and their planet turned into a desert. At this time the Caretaker ordered the Ocampa to leave the surface to find refuge and water underground, with strict instructions never to return to the surface. Kes is a member of the Ocampan race.

The Q Continuum ("Death Wish")

Q and others of his kind exist in the Q Continuum, an extradimensional domain. Q are immensely powerful entities, possessing near-godlike powers. In the Q Continuum lies a paved road in the middle of a desert. The road leads everywhere else in the universe, and all roads lead back to it. By the road is a small house, where several people sit or stand, reading books, smoking pipes, playing croquet or pinball. A rocking chair, front steps, a scarecrow, a hound dog, and a beat-up pinball machine complete the picture. A book that says "the old," a magazine that says "the new," and croquet balls that look like planets add the final touches. The dog is mostly ignored. No one has spoken for millennia. This describes the Q Continuum, a place where one easily grows bored.

The first contact with a Q occurred in the Alpha Quadrant with the *Enterprise-D* in 2364. A Q was also responsible for the first encounter with the Borg when the *Enterprise-D* was transported some seven thousand light-years beyond Federation space to system J-25. The *Voyager* encountered a bored, suicidal, ex-philosopher of the Q race and a redeemed ex-prankster who chose to return to his former ways.

> *Vhnori are a race of humanoids whose belief system centers on entrance, after they die, into what they term the "Next Emanation," a higher level of consciousness.*

Sikarans ("Prime Factors")

This advanced society can travel forty thousand light-years in seconds. Their Canon of Laws, a local version of the Federation Prime Directive, prevents this benevolent race from sharing this technology, which could return the *Voyager* to Earth in minutes. Sikarans are interested in friendship, pleasure, science, and the arts. They prize stories above all else, and they wanted the *Voyager* crew to remain with them.

Sky Spirits ("Tattoo")

This Delta Quadrant race visited Earth in the Alpha Quadrant over forty thousand years ago. They assisted in the cultural progress of an Amerindian tribe. The tribe, Chakotay's ancestors, called them Sky Spirits. Chakotay, and the *Voyager* crew, encountered them.

Talaxans ("Caretaker," "Jetrel")

These fun-loving scavengers may not be courageous but they are clever, kind, and helpful. Haakonians waged war on the Talaxan star system. Talax surrendered to the Haakonians after they destroyed the Talaxan moon colony, Rinax, in 2356. Neelix is the first Talaxan ever encountered.

Vhnori ("Emanations")

Vhnori are a race of humanoids whose belief system centers on entrance, after they die, into what they term the "Next Emanation," a higher level of consciousness. Vhnori leave this life for the Next Emanation voluntarily. The individual is placed in a cenotaph, which transports the body through a subspace vacuole to a different area of space. On stardate 48623, the *Voyager* determined that the bodies release neural energy after passing through the vacuole, and that energy becomes part of an ambient electromagnetic field, supporting the Vhnori concept of the Next Emanation. Harry Kim was inadvertently transported to the Vhnori homeworld, while a Vhnori, Ptera, found herself on the *Voyager*. Contact caused both Vhnori and the *Voyager* crew to reevaluate their beliefs.

Vidiians ("Phage," "Faces")

Long ago, Vidiians were educators and explorers before a fatal disease, phage, ravaged their planet, infecting the race. It destroys genetic codes and cellular structures, causes severe pain, and leads to deterioration of the body and death. These beings, although not evil, now threaten the Delta Quadrant in their quest for survival. They possess force fields that simulate rocks and walls, and they have weapons that incorporate medical scanning and advanced surgical functions, giving them the ability to harvest and transplant organs to replace their own. Their piecemeal faces and bodies remain in a constant state of decay. They stole Neelix's lungs. Danara, a Vidiian doctor, once spent time aboard *Voyager*.

CHAPTER TEN

Nit-Picking the Episodes

Even to the most sympathetic viewer, many Star Trek episodes display distinct lapses of reason, sense, and/or attention. What follows is a critique of *Voyager*, with all of the plot misfires, equipment malfunctions, and memory lapses duly noted. Following each entry are ratings from two systems. One is the Spoiler-free Opinion Service, which is a rating system that operates on the Internet and tabulates from one hundred to three hundred votes on each episode. The other is the Nielsen ratings, in which one rating point is equivalent to 954,000 television homes.

A few statistics from the Nielsen ratings: the highest rated show was "Caretaker," which got a 13.0 rating, 19 share. The lowest rated show was a "Heroes and Demons" rerun (July 9, 1995), which got a 2.7 rating, 6 share.

Season One: January Through June 1995

Episodes 1 and 2: "Caretaker"

Production number: 721
Stardate: 48315.6
Air date: January 16, 1995
Teleplay: Michael Piller and Jeri Taylor
Story: Rick Berman, Michael Piller, and Jeri Taylor
Director: Winrich Kolbe

Guest Stars: Josh Clark: Lt. Carey; Alicia Coppola: Lieutenant Stadi; Bruce French: Ocampa Doctor; Stan Ivar: Mark; Eric David Johnson: Daggin; Basil Langton: Banjo Man; Scott MacDonald Rollins; Jeff McCarthy: Human Doctor; Gavan O'Herlihy: Jabin (Kazon); Jennifer Parsons: Ocampa Nurse; Angela Paton: Aunt Adah; Richard Poe: Gul Evek; David Selburg: Toscat (an Ocampa official); Armin Shimerman: Quark; Keely Sims: Farmer's Daughter

Spoiler-free Opinion Service Rating: 8.3
Nielsen Ratings: 13.0

The Federation starship *Voyager* tracks a Maquis vessel until both are transported to the Delta Quadrant. Captain Chakotay then sacrifices his Maquis ship to save the *Voyager,* and both crews unite aboard the Federation vessel, which is now lost seventy thousand light-years from home.

The combined crew meet Neelix, a Talaxan, on an asteroid. He guides them to a world with a Caretaker that has the power to get them home, and it just happens to be his lover's homeworld, Ocampa, where she is being held prisoner by the Kazon.

The episode introduces all the main characters, the new ship, and four new alien races, including the powerful Caretakers and the ongoing menace of the Kazon. Janeway violates the Prime Directive, then justifies it by saying her interference only undid prior interference by the Caretaker.

Key Quotation

The Caretaker: "Well, aren't you contentious for a minor bipedal species?"

Plot Misfires

This show made a point of introducing several characters on the *Voyager* only to kill them with the displacement wave. Most die in freak accidents, but not the first officer. Upon Janeway's order to brace for impact, he leaves his current position (that of holding to some handrails) so he can run across the bridge in a very unbraced fashion. Lo and behold, he's toast.

After the crew is transported aboard the array, Paris gives a report that everyone is accounted for. How can he be so sure? They just suffered a major catastrophe, and an unknown portion of the crew is dead. They didn't have enough time between the wave smacking the ship and the crew boarding the array to make an accurate assessment of who is alive and who isn't. And unless the Caretaker kidnapped the corpses as well as the live crew, there couldn't have been a suitable roll call made.

Tuvok explains that the Caretaker examined the *Voyager*'s library computer banks to create a suitable holographic environment for the crew to wait in, presenting problems. The environment is centered around Earth, yet many of those kidnapped are not human. Further, it is centered around southern white Americans. Is Dogpatch, USA, really the most comfortable setting for everyone?

When the Caretaker starts to seal the conduits, the *Voyager* reports that it is unable to beam up the Away Team through the holes in the shield. This forces the team to find their way outside of the security field, which they do. But then they break through to the surface of the planet with their phasers. Why? They're outside the shield, *Voyager* should have no trouble locking onto their signals.

When Chakotay runs his shuttle into the Kazon Warship, he stays in the ship until the last possible second. When he finally does call to be beamed out, the Kazon ship fires several times at the small craft. But in order to beam out, the shields have to be down. And if the shields are down, how could that beat-up little thing sustain direct hits without exploding?

Equipment Malfunctions

The holographic doctor picks up a bad habit. When the Caretaker beams everyone off the ship, he calls the bridge. No answer. So he taps his communicator twice and tries again. The comm badge is not real; it's a hologram like the rest of him. What good does double-tapping it do?

Harry's tricorder must be broken. When scanning the barn, he reports that he's found human life signs and a Vulcan's. What about B'Elanna? She's right next to the other Maquis folks, and she definitely isn't human.

The transporter room doorway isn't very courteous to visitors—at least not to Neelix. He walks up to the door, and faces it, but it doesn't open until Tuvok walks up next to Neelix and points to the door.

After the array stops sending energy pulses, the *Voyager* puts the array on screen at a very unusual angle. They can see *behind* the array. They are in orbit around the planet, where

133

the pulses are being sent, but in the picture, the array is firing away from *Voyager*. The pulses should be flying toward *Voyager*.

Memory Failures

Voyager clearly takes advantage of old *Next Generation* models. The shuttle that takes Tom to *Voyager* first has *Voyager*'s number on the side. Paris and Stadi talk a bit, and then the shuttle reads "1701-D." The model people just relabeled it.

After Paris rescues Chakotay and takes him to sickbay, something odd happens. Chakotay isn't wearing shoes! He had them on when Tom saved his life, and twenty-fourth-century medicine doesn't require disrobing to fix broken limbs, so what happened to them?

Episode 3: "Parallax"

Production number: 103
Stardate: 48439.7

Air date: January 23, 1995
Teleplay: Brannon Braga
Story: Jim Trombetta
Director: Kim Friedman
Guest Stars: Josh Clark: Lt. Carey; Martha Hackett: Ensign Seska; Justin Williams: Jarvin
Spoiler-free Opinion Service Rating: 7.1
Nielsen Ratings: 9.2

A quantum singularity traps *Voyager* in a story reminiscent of early *Star Trek: The Next Generation*. The crew must figure a way out of the trap.

This is a background story intended to deliver a lot of information to the viewer in a short amount of time. To avoid distraction, no new elements are introduced and the entire adventure is confined to the ship.

Lots of character bits. B'Elanna Torres becomes chief engineer, Janeway readily accepts Chakotay as her first officer, and Kes begins her friendship with the Doctor, while sharing good scenes with her lover, Neelix.

Technobabble Alert

What follows is some pure, undistilled technobabble from the first season of *Star Trek: Voyager*. By the time the second season concludes, it will certainly have expanded on this depressing collection.

magnacite, subspace transponders, reconstituted Jenum, enhanced mitosis, band-width modulation-adjustable phasers, microfissures, genetron, phase resistant nucleotide sequences, a dermal stimulator, a biomatrix, polaron burst, fluctuating neuclionic patterns, neuclionic radiation, neosaurium composite, pyrocite replacement, culitane, Orkit's disease, Vinian N-grams, neural pathway damage, neuro-implants, dorsal phase emitter, LN2 exhaust conduits, falmerite explosives, columnator, radiation stream phase variance, a covariant isolator, verteron exit vector, verteron emanations, reactant injectors, neucliogenic peptide bonds, neuclionic beams, multipolar charges, electroplasma leaks, hydroxil radicals, barrier thoron emissions, shield polarity reversal, EM hull pressure, polycyclic structures, folding space, spatial trajector, neutrino dispersion pattern, phased neutrinos, neutrino envelope, antineutrinos, photonic energy, matter conversion nodes, data stream protocols, protostar photonic activity, annular confinement beam breach,

Plot Misfires

Chakotay informs B'Elanna that she could have killed Mr. Carey because the bone fragments nearly entered his cerebellum. This is unlikely; the cerebellum is in the back of the head. I'm sure Chakotay meant to say cerebrum; that part is right up front.

Neelix suggests to the captain that she go to a nearby star system for help in freeing the distressed ship. He says that they are "less than three light-years away." We can presume that means "more than two but not quite three light-years away." After the subspace tractor beam fails, she decides to head for this system. Yet she orders Mr. Paris to proceed at full impulse (which is less than the speed of light). And a later shot shows *Voyager* traveling at sublight speeds. A light-year is the distance light travels in one (Earth) year's time. At full impulse, it would have been a long trip!

After they realize the other ship is the *Voyager*, they have a meeting. Tom recaps the action by saying they were investigating a distress call. However, they didn't receive the transmission until after hitting the singularity. They weren't investigating, but just stumbled onto it.

Equipment Malfunctions

Tuvok tells Chakotay that B'Elanna was confined to her quarters. Chakotay rings her doorbell, and the door opens without her asking him in. Does confinement to quarters not allow you any privacy?

Memory Failures

Chief Seska, the Bajoran Maquis woman seen here and in several other shows, is seen wearing a blue outfit. Blue outfits are worn by science officers. In her other appearances, she has worn yellow. Yellow outfits are worn by engineering and security officers.

When the bridge crew decides to search for "a hole in the ice," Tom Paris is instrumental in locating the fracture. Why is the navigator conducting this search? Shouldn't Mr. Kim, who is assigned to ops, be doing

complete bioneural energy drainage, multiphasic bandwidth, magneton scanner, magneton flash scan, parity trace scan, sensor matrix, trianic-based energy beings, Metreon Cascade, a high concentration of metreon isotopes, metremia, regenerative fusion, bond cohesion, animated suspension of disintegrated biomatter, magnaton scanner, bio-neural gel pack infection, plasma gas, conventional isolinear circuits, a possible cascade feedback, microresonator, an inverted symmetric warp field infusing a high-energy plasma burst into the bio-neural gel packs, subspace vacuoles, a blind beamout, Natinoline, a scinitaph, differentially charged polaric ions, polaric radiation, a subspace chain reaction, polaric ion energy, temporal flux, subspace fractures, magnaton surface scan, polaric ion generator, nadion particle resistance, neutronium alloy, bioelectric rocks, KLS stabilizer, cytoplasmic stimulator, holographic lungs, dilithium matrix power, rotating phase modulated shields, neuroresonator, quantum-imaging scanners, gravimetric flux densities, singularity event horizons, frozen power grid relays, a subspace tractor beam, time-delayed quantum subspace reflections, dechyon beams, a stream of warp particles detecting a subspace gravimetric event horizon distortion fracture, coherent tetryon beams, massive mobile displacement wave made up of polarized magnetic variations this? Or perhaps Mr. Tuvok, who is on tactical? But not the pilot!

Chief Seska is obviously Bajoran. Why doesn't she wear the mandatory Bajoran earrings? Are there different factions of the Bajoran faith?

When the shuttlecraft is first shaken, the footage of the actresses is played at a reduced speed.

The captain orders full impulse speed to the fracture. The model shot shows the *Voyager* flash its nacelles. Why? Those nacelles are for the warp engines; the impulse drive has always been separate.

When Lieutenant Carey shakes B'Elanna's hand, he has his left hand behind his back. When the camera changes to the long shot, his hand is at his side.

After B'Elanna is chosen as chief engineer, her first task is to get the warp engines back on line. She complains about the amount of time she has to do this. Yet the closing model shot shows *Voyager* traveling at warp speed. Hmmm, Chakotay was right . . . she is good!

Episode 4: "Time and Again"

Production number: 104
Stardate: Supplemental
Air date: January 30, 1995
Teleplay: David Kemper and Michael Piller
Story: David Kemper
Director: Les Landau
Guest Stars: Brady Bluhm: Latika; Ryan MacDonald: Shopkeeper; Joel Polis: Teria; Jerry Spicer: Guard; Nicolas Surovy: Makull; Steve Vaught: Officer

Spoiler-free Opinion Service Rating: 7.1
Nielsen Ratings: 8.8

The writers fail to play fair with the viewing audience. They hinge the episode on a paradox, then fail to deliver a logical explanation at the end.

Voyager discovers a new planet with an apparently recently deceased civilization. Janeway beams down with an Away Team. They learn the world used a dangerous power source.

Those who opposed the power source were considered a radical fringe.

Logic falls apart when they learn that the two *Voyager* crew members who go back in time actually destroyed the civilization. The *Voyager* destroys the planet before discovering it. Janeway ultimately averts the catastrophe.

Kes reveals psychic powers.

Key Quotation
The Doctor: "Your brain is . . . not on file."

Plot Misfires
Normally I don't object to aliens looking like humans and speaking English because it rarely affects the plot. This time Janeway and Paris would have been in big trouble if they didn't walk and talk just like everyone else. If these people had had so much as a ridged nose, a lot of explanations would have been necessary.

Evidently no one briefed the guard at the power plant on the uses of the metal bars across his window. When the eco-terrorists shoot the first guard, the guard inside the booth *runs outside* before attempting to fire.

This gives the terrorists plenty of time to shoot him.

As the disaster approaches, Janeway makes a reference to how many minutes remain. The storekeeper at the beginning of the show said that these people keep time with "intervals," not minutes. Yet the terrorists seem to understand what she is saying.

As usual, the time continuum is shot to hell. There was at least one paradox here, possibly two. They cause an explosion, which leads them to investigate, but only by investigating would they have caused the explosion! Likewise, when the disaster is averted and everything just "resets," Kes somehow remembers what happened—did it or did it not occur? Like the writers, I was confused.

Equipment Malfunctions
During the first landing party investigation, everyone is strolling around, scanning with their tricorders, except for Tuvok. Evidently he is going to listen to what the others say and not explore for himself. Is that logical?

After Kes turns off the emergency medical program, there is an exceptionally long lag time, allowing the Doctor to give one last snide remark before disappearing. Does the program design call for comic timing of shutdown?

Memory Failures
When the explosion rocks *Voyager*, the camera shakes and everyone is thrown about. Then they cut to Kes in bed. Unfortunately, they stop shaking the camera before she wakes up.

When Paris first falls back in time, the window behind him is broken in the past. For the second and final visit, it is unbroken.

Episode 5: "Phage"

Production number: 105
Stardate: 48532.4
Air date: February 6, 1995
Teleplay: Skye Dent and Brannon Braga
Story: Timothy DeHaas
Director: Winrich Kolbe
Guest Stars: Cully Fredricksen: Alien #1; Martha Hackett: Ensign Seska; Stephen B. Rappaport: Alien #2
Spoiler-free Opinion Service Rating: 6.8
Nielsen Ratings: 8.5

A debilitating plague, the "phage," victimizes the Vidiians. It deforms bodies and causes organs to fail. Vidiians harvest organs from other beings to perpetuate their own lives.

They kidnap Neelix and beam his lungs out of his body. The Doctor saves the Talaxan by placing him inside a twenty-fourth-century iron lung, then Neelix and Kes commiserate until the Doctor transplants a lung from Kes. Janeway threatens to use deadly force if the Vidiians ever threaten her ship again.

Neelix opens a cafeteria.

Key Quotation
Neelix: "He's just one giant . . . hormone walking around the ship!"

Plot Misfires

Neelix demonstrates an extraordinary amount of technical knowledge during this episode. First, he sets up his barbecue, re-routing power systems, and turning off the fire detection/suppression system. Then he interprets a variety of tricorder signals. He certainly shows a lot of progress for someone who was first exposed to this technology a few weeks ago.

Phasers are ruled out as a usable weapon in a mirror chamber because they might bounce around and hit the *Voyager*. They could have used photon torpedoes. Unless the walls are rubber, they wouldn't bounce.

The captain took an incredible risk when she beamed potentially contagious aliens on board. The "phage" could have wiped out the crew in an hour!

Captain Janeway orders Type-III phasers for the second Away Team, those big rifles last seen in "Caretaker." The security guys show up with what look like standard "dustbuster" Type-II phasers.

The captain refers to Mr. Tuvok as "Lieutenant," despite his two gold pips and one black. That normally indicates the rank of lieutenant commander (like Data, Geordi, and Worf), and lieutenant commanders should be addressed as either "Lieutenant Commander" or "Commander." This also occurred in previous episodes.

Equipment Malfunctions

When Chakotay and Kim discover Neelix on the ground, they kneel down to restrain him and request emergency transport to sickbay. When they arrive, they're standing while restraining Neelix at waist level on the biobed.

Evidently the sickbay replicators run on a different system than the food replicators. The captain expressed her displeasure for having to eat MRE's at the beginning of the show.

The Doctor has to explain the holographic lungs to Paris, and he slaps him. Then the Doctor goes to a control panel to modify his solidity. Why does the program

---

Top Ten Scenes Cut from *Voyager* Premiere

10. Premission briefing in which Starfleet security places top-secret surveillance equipment inside Janeway's massive hairdo.

9. All three of Neelix's reggae numbers.

8. Kes being brought back from brink of death by audience clapping and repeating, "I do believe in fairies! I do believe in fairies!"

7. Chakotay's Indian wrestling pitted against Tuvok's Vulcan neck pinch.

6. The holographic toupee.

5. Cleverly disguised product placement in which Torres's human side likes the whole wheat goodness, while her Klingon side likes the frosting.

4. Christening of ship by Admiral Saavik.

3. Scene with Tom Paris's prison cellmate, Berlinghoff Rasmussen.

2. Humorous interlude when Horta officer gets drunk on ship's bio-neural gel packs.

1. Chakotay's *other* tattoo.

need to manipulate an external control panel in order to run itself? Isn't that like a computer program that types commands to itself on the keyboard?

Someone needs to run a check on the transporter's biofilters. They're supposed to screen out bacteria in transport or alert the transporter chief that something unknown is coming through, but these disintegrating aliens come right through without a beep.

Memory Failures

They reuse the set from "Time and Again" for the alien corridors on the rogue planetoid. Last time they were tunnels inside the power plant.

Episode 6: "The Cloud"

Production number: 106
Stardate: 48546.2
Air date: February 13, 1995
Teleplay: Tom Szollosi and Michael Piller
Story: Brannon Braga
Director: David Livingston
Guest Stars: Luigi Amodeo: the Gigolo; Angela Dohrmann: Ricky; Judy Geeson: Sandrine; Larry A. Hankin: Gaunt Gary
Spoiler-free Opinion Service Rating: 6.7
Nielsen Ratings: 7.9

The *Voyager* enters a strange cloud, then barely escapes. Then Janeway discovers they have injured a life form, and she risks her ship to heal the wound.

Chakotay teaches Janeway his people's path to inner peace by helping her contact her animal guide. Their scenes together demonstrate an increasingly strong work relationship, and they discover more similarities than differences between them, despite their dissimilar backgrounds.

The holodeck appears for the first time.

Key Quotation

Captain Janeway: "There's coffee in that nebula!"

Plot Misfires

Upon first contact with "The Cloud," Tuvok disciplines Kim for exclaiming astonishment. He says that such statements would unnecessarily concern the junior officers. Excuse me, but what is Mr. Kim? An *ensign!* You can't get much more "junior" than that!

When Tom awakens Harry to take him to the holodeck, Harry is wearing a nightmask. If he needs total darkness to fall asleep, why are there bright blue lights shining on his bed?

When the *Voyager* goes on its roller coaster ride, the inertial dampers fail. Everyone gets tossed around. This is shown by clips of chaos from the bridge and engineering. However, moments after the IDF are restored, Neelix and Kes show up on the bridge with snacks. How did they prepare so much food in such short time? The ship certainly would have made a mess out of the kitchen during its spiraling.

Equipment Malfunctions

During the aforementioned Tuvok/Kim exchange, both officers are in the same shot. Tuvok taps his communicator and says

"Tuvok to Kim," and the words simultaneously come from Kim's comm badge. How did the communicator know who to call before Tuvok said "to Kim?"

After B'Elanna and the Doctor determine "The Cloud" is alive, B'Elanna goes straight to the captain. They establish a comm link to sickbay and the senior staff discuss the problem. When Janeway wonders if they hurt "The Cloud," the Doctor gives a great line listing all the obvious harm they've done, but how did the Doctor know? He wasn't active during the investigation.

Memory Failures

When Harry expresses his concern over drinking wine, Tom dismisses him because "it's holographic wine." Previously the holodeck replicated real food and drink.

Episode 7: "Eye of the Needle"

Production number: 107
Stardate: 48579.4
Air date: February 20, 1995
Teleplay: Bill Dial and Jeri Taylor
Story: Hilary J. Bader
Director: Winrich Kolbe
Guest Stars: Vaughn Armstrong: Telek (R'Mor); Michael Cumpsty: Burleigh; Carolyn Seymour: Mrs. Templeton; Tom Virtue: Lt. Baxter
Spoiler-free Opinion Service Rating: 8.4
Nielsen Ratings: 7.7

Voyager finds a wormhole, but only a probe can fit inside. A Romulan ship with a friendly captain lies at the other end in the Alpha Quadrant. It turns out this wormhole goes through time and space, and the Romulan ship is twenty years in the past.

A subplot further humanizes the Doctor.

Plot Misfires

Janeway and Tuvok need to check their math. While discussing the probability of the wormhole's terminus being in the Alpha Quadrant, Tuvok says there is a 75 percent chance it is not. Apparently, he is assuming the wormhole's terminus must be in our galaxy. Why is this assumption valid? Aren't wormholes wacky, unpredictable things? I'd speculate the chances of the wormhole's terminus being elsewhere is incredibly high . . . say 99.999 percent. Likewise, Janeway's assertion is also invalid.

The microprobe sent into the wormhole is slowly being crushed, causing them to plan quickly, before the probe is destroyed. Yet no one tries another probe. Was it the only microprobe in stock? If so, why couldn't they replicate more?

Janeway wins over the Romulan captain by directing his thoughts to his seven-month-old daughter. She was born after he began his mission.

Romulans and Klingons are ancient enemies. Why doesn't the Romulan react to B'Elanna?

Memory Failures

Upon seeing the small size of the wormhole, why doesn't anybody ask if they can enlarge it? The wormhole at *Star Trek: Deep Space Nine* is normally closed; it opens when you get close enough to it. The

Barzan wormhole ("The Price," *Star Trek: The Next Generation*) was closed but opened regularly like Old Faithful. Who can tell what the Harry Kim wormhole could have done, given a chance?

This has got to be the most unorthodox and trusting Romulan. He is from 2351, living during the Romulan silence following the Tomed Incident. That silence is not broken until 2364 ("The Neutral Zone," *Star Trek: The Next Generation*). Yet the captain nonchalantly calls up his superiors and says, "Hey, I've got a Federation starship on line 3. Shall I put them through?" He even allows the *Voyager* to beam a container onto his ship. Lastly, he volunteers to beam onto their ship. What did he tell the rest of his crew to explain his departure?

Episode 8: "Ex Post Facto"

Production number: 108
Stardate: Supplemental
Air date: February 27, 1995
Teleplay: Evan Carlos Somers and Michael Piller
Story: Evan Carlos Somer
Director: LeVar Burton
Guest Stars: Henry Brown: Numiri Captain; Francis Guinan: Minister Kray; Aaron Lustig: Doctor; Robin McKee: Lidell (Ren); Ray Reinhardt: Tolen Ren
Spoiler-free Opinion Service Rating: 6.2
Nielsen Ratings: 8.0

On a hostile world, Tom Paris is framed for the murder of a scientist. He is sentenced to continually relive the horror of the murder through the eyes of the victim. Then Tuvok solves the crime.

The secondary storyline shows Kes and the Doctor becoming friends and Kes learning medicine from the Doctor.

Tuvok performs his first mind meld.

Plot Misfires

How could anyone know about Paris' prison record? Neither race would have access to Starfleet records! So why does Dr. Ren say, "I know you were in prison!" Of course, that line could have been edited in by the traitorous CMO, but I fail to understand how he would know about that either.

Memory Failures

A drawing used in "Angel One" (*Star Trek: The Next Generation*) reappears as the alien planet cityscape.

Episode 9: "Emanations"

Production number: 109
Stardate: 48623.5
Air date: March 13, 1995
Writer: Brannon Braga
Director: David Livingston
Guest Stars: Cecile Callan: Ptera; Jeffrey Alan Chandler: Hatil; John Cirigliano: Alien #1; Robin Groves: Hatil's Wife; Martha Hackett: Ensign Seska; Jerry Hardin: Dr. Neria
Spoiler-free Opinion Service Rating: 6.6
Nielsen Ratings: 7.1

An Away Team consisting of Chakotay, B'Elanna, and Harry Kim discover an asteroid filled with dead aliens. The Away Team beams back to the *Voyager* when a dimensional distortion threatens them. A recently deceased alien corpse appears in Harry's place, while Harry shows up in an alternate dimension. The alien Vhnori transport their dying to an afterlife they call "The Next Emanation." Harry's appearance causes them to question their sacred beliefs, even as the revived alien woman on the *Voyager*, Ptera, learns she didn't evolve into a higher state of consciousness.

Yet, after passing through from the other dimension, alien corpses release energy that merges with the beautiful radiation rings around the world. Janeway tells a returned Harry Kim that this may be the higher level of consciousness Vhnori religion promises.

Plot Misfires

Mr. Kim studied Prime Directive and first-contact situations at Starfleet Academy, yet he makes frequent references to coming from another planet and traveling on a starship—big no-no's when you don't know the status of a society's space exploration.

The other senior officers also screw up. When they accidentally beam back with the fresh alien corpse, only Chakotay objects to reviving her. The captain ignores him when B'Elanna notes that the alien can provide the only clues to rescue Harry. They have no right to tamper with the alien.

When the corpse beams aboard, a thick layer of that white stuff covers her despite brain activity. However, only a very thin layer covers her when she dies in the transporter accident.

Early in the program, an alien refers to the "thanatologist," or "one who studies death." The word comes from the combination of "thanatos" and "ology." Yet, near the end of the show, someone refers to the "thanologist." What is that? The etymology is all wrong.

What did Mr. Kim do with his clothes and equipment? He couldn't conceal them beneath the tight death shroud. Leaving them behind would violate the Prime Directive.

Equipment Malfunctions

Chakotay insists that the bodies only be inspected visually, without tricorders, but tricorders change nothing and don't leave a radioactive trace. Perhaps Chakotay overreacts? Or perhaps the writers overdo his Amerindian perspective?

Episode 10: "Prime Factors"

Production number: 110
Stardate: 48642.5
Air date: March 20, 1995
Teleplay: Michael Perricone and Greg Elliot
Story: David R. George III and Eric A. Stillwell
Director: Les Landau
Guest Stars: Josh Clark: Lt. Carey; Ronald Guttman: Gath; Martha Hackett: Ensign Seska; Andrew Hill Newman: Jaret; Yvonne Suhor: Eudana
Spoiler-free Opinion Service Rating: 7.9
Nielsen Ratings: 7.3

The *Voyager* meets the Sikarans, an advanced, but hedonistic, race. The friendly aliens refuse the *Voyager* crew only one thing, what they want most, a way home. They have a spacial trajector capable of transporting someone forty thousand light-years in an instant, but their Canon of Law forbids them from sharing advanced technology.

A few aliens secretly trade the technology with Tuvok, who acts without Captain Janeway's knowledge. When Torres acts before Tuvok wants her to, the spacial trajector proves incompatible with *Voyager* technology. Janeway learns of the conspiracy and confronts Tuvok for his betrayal of her trust, and Torres reveals her role to her captain.

This episode establishes Seska as an important character, setting things up for "State of Flux."

Memory Failures

In "Time and Again," Tom tried to convince Harry to join him on a double date with the Delaney sisters. Harry was adamant that he already had a girl back home. In the opening conversation of this show, it seems Harry has changed his mind.

Why didn't anyone object to using the trajector? In "The High Ground" (*Star Trek: The Next Generation*), terrorists folded space. It caused biological damage to the traveler. While these aliens have solved that problem, the Federation folks would be concerned.

Upon receiving the distress signal, Captain Janeway orders to slow to impulse, yet the establishing shot shows the ship already at sublight speed.

Harry is not wearing his communicator at the dinner party. Everyone else is, regardless of their other attire.

Harry and a woman watch a binary sunrise during their trip through the trajector. The light on her face intensifies very quickly. This implies that the suns move quickly through the sky, yet they aren't moving quickly at all when we see them.

When B'Elanna and Seska "theorize" about folding space, B'Elanna punches up a screen display. The women analyze the diagram before Lieutenant Carey interrupts them, but when they turn to face him, the screen suddenly reverts to its normal display, although no one pressed any buttons.

Episode 11: "State of Flux"

Production number: 111
Stardate: 48658.2
Air date: April 10, 1995
Teleplay: Chris Abbott
Story: Paul Robert Coyle
Director: Robert Scheerer
Guest Stars: Josh Clark: Lt. Carey; Anthony DeLongis: First Maje Jal Culluh; Martha Hackett: Ensign Seska
Spoiler-free Opinion Service Rating: 8.3
Nielsen Ratings: 6.5

The Kazon return. They have vowed vengeance against the *Voyager*.

The *Voyager* picks up a distress call from a Kazon ship after skirmishing with crew members on the planet's surface. Only one Kazon remains alive when they arrive. Investigation reveals the Kazon have caused a radiation leak and explosion by trying to install Federation technology on their ship. Someone on the *Voyager* gave them the technology.

Chakotay suspects Carey while Janeway looks to Seska, and she proves right. Chakotay's ex-lover turns out to be a Cardassian spy. The exposed Seska escapes to a Kazon ship at the end.

B'Elanna Torres gets a good defining character bit.

Key Quotation

"If you were working for her, and she was working for them, was there anyone on that ship working for me?" Chakotay to Tuvok, frustrated over both Tuvok's and Seska's deception.

Plot Misfires

Everyone refers to an "Ensign" Seska. The character wears one black rank mark, denoting the rank of "chief."

Equipment Malfunctions

The door to Chakotay's quarters wasn't eager to let Seska leave. As she got very close to the door, she suddenly stopped and turned to Chakotay. The door failed to open despite her proximity.

Memory Failures

In "The Cloud," B'Elanna asked why the Doctor, when activated, always began by saying "Please state the nature of the medical emergency." He said that was his program. Evidently someone changed the program. When Chakotay calls the Doctor near the end of the show, the Doc doesn't give his little speech.

Janeway has impressive visual skills. When a light burst illuminates the cloaked ship, it shows a partial silhouette for a brief second.

Janeway positively identifies the Kazon ship, something she has seen only once.

When Janeway orders Mr. Paris to let Seska and the Kazons go, she tells him to set a departure course and leave at warp 4 ASAP. Yet when Chakotay speaks to Tuvok, in the final model shot, the ship is traveling at sublight speed. Didn't Tom follow orders?

Episode 12: "Heroes and Demons"

Production number: 112
Stardate: 48693.2
Air date: April 24, 1995
Writer: Naren Shankar
Director: Les Landau
Guest Stars: Michael Keenan: Hrothgar; Marjorie Monaghan: Freya; Christopher Neame: Unferth
Spoiler-free Opinion Service Rating: 7.0
Nielsen Ratings: 6.4

After *Voyager* beams aboard samples from a proto-star, strange things begin to happen on the holodeck. It won't shut down Harry's "Beowulf" program. Chakotay and Tuvok investigate after he vanishes and find Grendel. Then they also disappear.

Life forms on the proto-star somehow control the holodeck. Captain Janeway orders the Doctor on his first "Away Mission" to investigate, since only he is immune due to his energy state. The nervous Doctor undertakes his mission after a pep talk from Kes.

The Doctor has his first romance, with Freya. The missing crew members return to the *Voyager* and Janeway issues the Doctor a commendation.

The Doctor displays genuine emotions.

Plot Misfires

Grendel takes Kim, Chakotay, Tuvok, and their equipment. A tricorder for the Doctor must be beamed to the holodeck. Yet when Grendel attacks, and he drops his tricorder, it is retrieved. How come?

While investigating the photonic life forms, one escapes and roams the ship. B'Elanna and Paris try to capture it with force fields. At one point, they trap it on three sides but report that it escaped through the fourth. Someone wasn't thinking three-dimensionally, because there are actually *six* sides.

Equipment Malfunctions

Starfleet dislikes giving up old technologies. Most things on Starfleet ships have invisible or futuristic connectors and fasteners. Doc Zimmerman's desk terminal, however, has very prominent Phillips-head sheet metal screws holding it together.

The Doctor struggles to pick up a sword during his first visit to the holodeck. This is irrational, as he is an image. He doesn't lift anything; a tractor beam would do that for him while his image pretends to lift the item.

Memory Failures

When the Doctor receives a "talisman," he is warned that he will have to remain solid to carry it. This implies he only has two states, solid or intangible, and cannot vary his degree of solidity. Yet, in "Phage," he desolidifies his head but retains solid fingers. Earlier in this program, when Unferth slices through the Doctor, he is at least partially solid, but his tricorder is still in its holographic holder!

What could swords and spears do to the Doctor? He has no internal organs to rupture, no bones to break, and no nerves to feel pain. If you prick him, he does not bleed.

Episode 13: "Cathexis"

Production number: 113
Stardate: 48734.2
Air date: May 1, 1995
Teleplay: Brannon Braga
Story: Brannon Braga and Joe Menosky
Director: Kim Friedman
Guest Stars: Michael Cumpsty: Burleigh; Brian Markinson: Lt. Durst; Carolyn Seymour: Mrs. Templeton
Spoiler-free Opinion Service Rating: 6.2
Nielsen Ratings: 6.4

An alien attacks Chakotay's shuttle, renders him comatose, and possesses Tuvok. Another entity is loose on the ship. The second entity turns out to be Chakotay's disembodied spirit, protecting the ship from the alien.

Kes again displays psychic powers. Janeway works as a nanny in a nineteen-century home in a holodeck program.

Plot Misfires

When the Doctor realizes another brainwave is being superimposed over the crew's, he says it is something completely alien to him, but it is Chakotay, roaming the ship. Shouldn't it resemble his patterns?

Why didn't Chakotay try to identify himself? He apparently couldn't use his hosts for speech, but couldn't he pick up a PADD and type a short note?

After B'Elanna/Chakotay ejects the warp core, Janeway reacts with surprise, because B'Elanna doesn't have the authority to do that on her own. Why not? Isn't she the chief engineer? Isn't ejecting the warp core something done in emergencies, when command level officers might not be available? Apparently it's not a big deal either as the core can be picked up and reinstalled with little difficulty.

Memory Failures

Carolyn Seymour plays a woman in the opening holonovel. She previously appeared in three *Star Trek: The Next Generation* episodes: "Contagion," "First Contact," and "Face of the Enemy."

Tuvok finally wears correct rank insignia, but the pips change several times during the episode. When Tuvok checks with Mr. Kim on the sudden course change, his uniform has three pips; two gold and one black, which incorrectly marks him as a lieutenant commander. In his next scene, in sickbay, he has ditched the black pip and is a lieutenant. Unfortunately, when he returns to the bridge to plan a course inside the nebula, the black pip reappears. After B'Elanna/Chakotay shuts down the warp core, he rushes to engineering, apparently having discarded the black pip for the rest of the episode.

After B'Elanna/Chakotay shuts down the warp core, main power goes out. Lights all over the ship go dark. Oddly, during Neelix's paranoid conversation with the Doctor, the lights are at full strength.

Episode 14: "Faces"

Production number: 114
Stardate: 48784.2
Air date: May 8, 1995
Teleplay: Kenneth Biller
Story: Jonathan Glassner and Kenneth Biller
Director: Winrich Kolbe
Guest Stars: Rob Labelle: Talaxan prisoner; Brian Markinson: Lt. Durst; Brian Markinson: Sulan; Barton Tinapp: Guard #1
Spoiler-free Opinion Service Rating: 6.5
Nielsen Ratings: 6.1

The Vidiians return to kidnap a *Voyager* Away Team on a planetoid. They use a Genotron to divide half-breed B'Elanna into two people, one weak, timid, and fully human, the other strong, brutal, and entirely Klingon.

The Klingon ultimately sacrifices her life protecting the human, but the Doctor says he has to rejoin her two sides or B'Elanna will die. She never reconciles her two inheritances and predicts that she will always suffer internal conflict.

This time the monstrous aliens kill a *Voyager* crew member, but Captain Janeway still takes no revenge despite earlier threats.

Plot Misfires

The story depends on all Klingons being brave, stupid, and murderous and all humans being smart, cowardly, and cringing.

Thus, personality is entirely determined by DNA.

Kim says that "quantum microfissures" in Vidiian force fields close quickly. Why, then, did they take their time beaming Chakotay through them?

Why do they send the ship's second-in-command on a suicide mission?

Equipment Malfunctions

How can the human B'Elanna log in to the Vidiian security net and understand it in a matter of seconds?

Memory Failures

Voyager is short on supplies and in a hurry to get home. Why do they drop people off at planets and leave them there for days for no apparent reason?

Episode 15: "Jetrel"

Production number: 115
Stardate: 48832.1
Air date: May 15, 1995
Teleplay: Jack Klein, Karen Klein, and Kenneth Biller
Story: James Thomton and Scott Nimerfro
Director: Kim Friedman
Guest Stars: Larry Hankin: Gaunt Gary; James Sloyan: Jetrel
Spoiler-free Opinion Service Rating: 6.3
Nielsen Ratings: 5.8

Neelix meets the man who created the device that killed three hundred thousand Talaxans, including his own family. Jetrel invented the Metreon Cascade the Haakonians used to conquer the Talaxans.

Top Ten Starfleet General Orders Other than the Prime Directive

10. Order 13: No flag officer shall be required to perform a fan dance.

9. Order 101: No transmissions on an open channel may contain the term "gnarly."

8. Order 4: Pony tails are only allowed for personnel who have whacked a guy with a bat'leth.

7. Order 21: Phaser rifles may no longer be used to warm cheeseburgers.

6. Order 993: During first contact situations, senior officers are discouraged from telling alien races that they "smell like old socks."

5. Medical Regulation 702-B: All cheese products must report for annual physical.

4. Order 218: Unused bridge stations may be used for "Mortal Kombat" tournaments only in dry dock.

3. Order 8: When the Prime Directive is violated, the nearest starbase shall convene a court martial to determine if it was a dramatic necessity.

2. Order 66: When in a parking orbit over a non-Federation world, "The Club" should be locked in position over Conn and Ops stations.

1. Order 231: If bridge officers wish to chew gum, they must bring enough for entire bridge crew.

Radiation poisoning, an aftereffect of the Cascade, is still slowly killing survivors. A repentant Jetrel wants to find a cure before he dies in hopes of making small restitution.

This story focuses on Neelix. Neelix reveals more about his past. A touch of tragedy is added to this previously comic character.

Plot Misfires

Genetic patterns cannot be found at a subatomic level. All subatomic particles—protons, electrons, and so on—are exactly alike other particles of the same type.

Neelix was a draft dodger, a crime that carries a heavy penalty on Talax. How did he get chosen for the team that went back to Rinax so soon after the attack?

Jetrel is allowed transporter access. Tuvok should know better.

Equipment Malfunctions

The doctor now has exclusive control over turning himself off. Then how did a total stranger with no security clearance deactivate him?

Episode 16: "Learning Curve"

Production number: 116
Stardate: 48846.5
Air date: May 22, 1995
Writer: Ronald Wilkerson and Jean Louise Matthias
Director: David Livingston

Guest Stars: Thomas Alexander Dekker: Henry Burleigh; Lindsey Haun: Beatrice Burleigh; Catherine MacNeal: Crewman Henley; Derek McGrath: Crewman Chell; Kenny Morrison: Crewman Geron; Armand Schultz: Crewman Dalby
Spoiler-free Opinion Service Rating: 6.8
Nielsen Ratings: 6.1

Captain Janeway returns to her gothic holodeck as the governess of two small children whose mother has recently died. The little girl claims her mother isn't dead but the boy insists that she is.

The main story focuses on Tuvok.

When Tuvok questions crew member Dolby about his repair of a conduit, Dolby stalks off. Other Maquis misfits cause problems, lack discipline, and refuse to respect command structure. They are not professionals who graduated Starfleet Academy but ordinary, untrained people who joined the Maquis to protect their homes and families.

Janeway wants Tuvok, a former Starfleet Academy instructor for sixteen years, to set up a training course aboard the *Voyager*. Tuvok fails as an instructor because he is used to teaching dedicated cadets, not ragtag rebels. The rigid Vulcan alienates his students, and they refuse to come to class. Neelix advises Tuvok to become more flexible.

Meanwhile Chakotay confronts the students. When Dolby says he wants to do things the Maquis way, Chakotay agrees and decks him with one punch, reminding the junior officer that that is also the Maquis way. The four Maquis students decide to return to class. To their happy surprise, they find a changed instructor.

Plot Misfires

Tuvok was a Federation spy aboard the Maquis ship before the crews merged. The average Maquis crew member remembers him as a traitor who helped lead to the demise of their ship. Why choose him to tutor the Maquis?

Season Two: August 1995 Through May 1996

Episode 17: "37's"

Production number: 120
Stardate: 48975.1
Air date: production week beginning August 28, 1995
Writer: Jeri Taylor and Brannon Braga
Director: James L. Conway
Guest Stars: John Rubinstein: John Evansville; David Graf: Fred Noonan; Mel Winkler: Jack Hayes; James Saito: Japanese Soldier; Sharon Lawrence: Amelia Earhart
Spoiler-free Opinion Service Rating: 6.0
Nielsen Ratings: 8.8

After atmospheric disturbances force the crew to land *Voyager* on a mysterious planet, Captain Janeway leads an Away Team in search of the source of an SOS, only to discover an old Earth aircraft. Upon further in-vestigation, the team finds a massive chamber containing eight Terrans in cryogenic units, one of whom is Amelia Earhart. After releasing them from suspended animation, the *Voyager* crew comes under attack when a group of the planet's inhabitants mistake them for Briori, an alien race that abducted more than three hundred people from Earth in 1937 and brought them to this planet as slaves. The slaves later revolted and killed the aliens. Since then, the descendants of the original three hundred have cultivated the planet and created a home much like Earth. The crew of *Voyager* is invited to stay.

Plot Misfires

Tuvok orders "all security personnel" to leave the *Voyager*. That would leave the ship vulnerable in a potentially hostile neighborhood.

How did Earhart's copilot take Janeway and crew hostage with a primitive pistol when *Voyager* crew members already had phasers drawn?

Why did aliens with the technology to rapidly fly back and forth between the Delta Quadrant and the Alpha Quadrant, clearly more advanced than the UFP in the twenty-fourth century, fly all the way to Earth to grab twentieth-century human slaves? Had Amelia Earhart's aviation fame really spread that far?

Equipment Malfunctions

The tricorders fail to detect concealed guns, but they must have simple metal detectors.

The primitive little radio in the pickup somehow broadcasts a distress signal across space and through *Voyager*'s thick hull.

Memory Failures

Janeway's PADD moves on its own. In one scene, in the wide shot, it is behind her chair as she sits with her arms crossed, yet, in the close-up, she holds it in front of her chair.

Janeway's hair also moves on its own. A thermal atmospheric rocks the ship as it begins to land. Janeway's hair bounces out of place, but the strand bounces right back into place all by itself.

Janeway orders that only human crew members be present for unfreezing the twentieth-century humans. Then Kes joins the group. Has she switched species?

Episode 18: "Initiations"

Production number: 121
Stardate: 49005.3
Air date: September 4, 1995
Writer: Kenneth Biller
Director: Winrich Kolbe
Guest Stars: Aron Eisenberg: Kar; Patrick Kilpatrick: Razik; Tim deZarn: Haliz
Spoiler-free Opinion Service Rating: 7.0

When First Officer Chakotay borrows a shuttlecraft to perform the Pakra, a solitary Indian ritual commemorating his father's death, he inadvertently drifts into Kazon-Ogla territory and becomes the target of a Kazon youth attempting to earn his Ogla warrior name by killing the Federation enemy. Chakotay disarms and destroys the Kazon ship, but not before rescuing the young boy, Kar, by transporting him aboard the shuttlecraft. Soon a tractor beam pulls the shuttlecraft to a larger Kazon vessel. Led by Razik and Haliz, the Kazon-Ogla hold Chakotay prisoner. Kar has failed in his first mission, doesn't earn his name, and is sentenced to die. Meanwhile, fearing their missing comrade is in danger, the *Voyager* crew sets out to find Chakotay, but Chakotay and Kar escape on their own. The young boy ultimately kills the Kazon leader, redeeming himself.

Equipment Malfunctions

When Kar attacks Chakotay's shuttle, the *Voyager* crew's long-range sensors don't reveal it. Then they can't find him, following an ion trail instead.

Computer-generated evasive maneuvers fail when Chakotay attempts to escape from the main Kazon ship. His shuttle slowly banks then makes a beeline for his destination. Very relaxing, but not much of an "evasive maneuver."

Memory Failures

The Kazon force-field booby trap catches the Away Team. Then they're free, but we never learn how.

Chakotay had his medical kit on the shuttle. The shuttle was destroyed. He didn't have the kit with him on the moon. Then, at the end of the program, he did. Huh?

Why did the Doctor analyze the wreckage to find human remains? What are tricorders for?

Chakotay seems to forget he abandoned his Starfleet uniform upon joining the Maquis when he brags to Kar about how he earned it. He wears it now by direct order from Captain Janeway.

B'Elanna couldn't establish a dampening field to communicate with the planet. Then, suddenly Janeway's comm badge beeps: Paris calling. We never get to see how.

Episode 19: "Projections"

Production number: 117
Stardate: 48892.1
Air date: September 11, 1995
Writer: Brannon Braga
Director: Jonathan Frakes
Guest Stars: Dwight Schultz: Barclay
Spoiler-free Opinion Service Rating: 7.8

The Doctor receives information that *Voyager* has suffered a massive Kazon attack and that the crew has abandoned ship. Then the Doctor must determine what is and what is not reality, his life as Dr. Lewis Zimmerman or his existence as a hologram.

Plot Misfires

There is a danger that the Doctor's files could be lost. Don't they backup their drive?

Equipment Malfunctions

Why does the Doctor have the computer download information to a terminal. He's a program in the same computer. Sort of like deciding you have to write something down before thinking it.

Memory Failures

Torres tells the Doctor that she couldn't risk moving an injured Janeway. Then she pushes Janeway onto her feet, risking serious back damage.

Janeway tells the Doctor it would take her thirty minutes to get to the mess hall from sickbay without turbolifts. Later she tells Neelix she will come and arrives minutes later. Janeway, Torres, Neelix, and the captured Kazon immediately appear in sickbay.

Barclay says that radiation prevents them from beaming the Doctor off the holodeck. This implies that they could otherwise, yet *TNG* maintained that they couldn't.

Episode 20: "Elogium"

Production number: 118
Stardate: 48921.3
Air date: production week beginning September 18, 1995
Story: Jimmy Diggs and Steve J. Kay
Director: Winrich Kolbe
Guest Stars: Nancy Hower: Ensign Clarke
Spoiler-free Opinion Service Rating: 5.0

Aggressive space-dwelling lifeforms attach themselves to the *Voyager*, creating an electrophoretic field. The lifeforms want to mate with the ship, until an aggressive male appears. The electrophoretic field forces Kes to prematurely enter elogium, the time of life when Ocampan females become fertile. The elogium occurs only once, so if Kes is ever to have a child, it must be immediately. Before making his decision whether or not he will father Kes' child, Neelix consults Tuvok, while Kes speaks with the Doctor.

Key Quotation

Tuvok: "It appears that *Voyager* has lost its sex appeal."

Plot Misfires

If Ocampan females only give birth once and to only one child, the race must eventually die out. At best ten Ocampa can only have nine children, as at least one of the ten must be male. Then the nine can only give birth to eight, and so on. If a male could impregnate both mother and daughter, it would only slow the process, not end it. At some point a male must be born, and no female can do more than replace herself. Of course, if more than one male is born to a generation, it accelerates the process. Females impregnated by non-Ocampa do not count, as their offspring are half-breeds with the Ocampa genes diluted.

Memory Failures

Neelix picks up Kes to carry her to sickbay. She has leaves in her hands. The shot changes, and she then holds leaves and apples.

Episode 21: "Non Sequitur"

Production number: 122
Stardate: 49011
Air date: production week beginning September 25, 1995
Writer: Brannon Braga
Director: David Livingston
Guest Stars: Louis Giambalvo: Cosimo; Jennifer Gatti: Libby; Jack Shearer: Admiral Strickler; Mark Kiely: Lieutenant Lasca
Spoiler-free Opinion Service Rating: 6.6

Ensign Harry Kim awakens to find himself on Earth in San Francisco, working as an engineer at Starfleet Engineering and engaged to be married to Libby. When he accesses his service records, they mysteriously indicate that he was never a crew member aboard *Voyager*. Although he wants to be home, he decides to return to the reality he knows, especially after he encounters a Tom Paris whose life remains in tatters without

---

Top Ten Yet-to-Be-Revealed Attributes of *U.S.S. Voyager*

10. Secret compartment for curing hams.
9. Side-impact airbags.
8. Bio-neural gel packs that come in strawberry, lime, and grape.
7. In addition to doctor, ship comes equipped with holographic waiter, carpenter, and insurance claims adjuster.
6. Button on captain's chair that activates emergency isolinear plot device.

5. Curb feelers.
4. Like all starships, supply of rocks hidden in bulkheads to make explosions more dramatic.
3. Life-sized statue of Carrie Fisher in all crew quarters.
2. Sonic showers set to pleasing Motown beat.
1. Disco lights in officer's mess allow it to pull double duty as dancehall.

Janeway's intervention. Soon Kim meets Cosimo, an alien disguised as a local shop owner, who explains that a temporal anomaly in the space-time continuum has shifted him to a different reality.

Plot Misfires

When Harry Kim tampers with the ankle transponder the Federation security personnel put on him, why don't they beam him directly into a holding cell? When they chase him instead, why does Starfleet send a Nebula-class ship after a runaway? And how does a runaway escape through Earth's defensive net?

Memory Failures

The footage of the shuttle flying by the San Francisco Bridge came from *Star Trek: The Motion Picture*.

Starfleet Headquarters still has the old Federation logo.

The actress who played Libby was Worf's girlfriend in *TNG*'s "Birthright, Part 2."

The shot of the Bay Bridge at night comes from *Star Trek VI*.

Episode 22: "Twisted"

Production number: 119
Stardate: Supplemental
Air date: production week beginning October 1, 1995
Teleplay: Kenneth Biller
Story: Arnold Rudnick and Rich Hosek
Director: Kim Friedman
Guest Stars: Judy Geeson: Sandrine; Larry A. Hankin: Gaunt Gary; Tom Virtue: Baxter
Spoiler-free Opinion Service Rating: 5.6

A spatial phenomenon distorts and disables *Voyager* and alters everyone on it. The crew must return things to normal.

Key Quotation

The Doctor: "I'm a doctor, not a bartender."

Plot Misfires

Paris reports that the distortions have formed a "ring" around the ship. So why not fly up or down?

Equipment Malfunctions

Chakotay says he will use his tricorder to leave a "photo-plasmic" trail, then there's no trail.

Memory Failures

Chakotay and Neelix meet a lieutenant. In the first shot, Neelix is facing the lieutenant. In the next shot, Neelix is facing Chakotay.

Episode 23: "Parturition"

Production number: 123
Stardate: Supplemental
Air date: production week beginning October 9, 1995
Writer: Tom Szollosi
Director: Jonathan Frakes
Spoiler-free Opinion Service Rating: 5.9
Nielsen Ratings: 5.9

Kes spends free time with a smitten Tom Paris, filling Neelix with jealousy. The captain then sends Paris and Neelix on a shuttle mission to an M-class planet to replenish food supplies. When their craft encounters an interference pattern, they crash on the planet. Paris and Neelix seal themselves inside a cave, then discover they have company, an embryonic pod that hatches an alien baby. They must work together to save the newborn, and save themselves after its angry mother appears. Paris and Neelix become friends after Paris reassures Neelix of Kes's love for the Talaxan.

Plot Misfires

Why do Paris and Neelix leave the shuttle without wearing protective clothing on a world with a corrosive atmosphere?

They lose Paris and Neelix's shuttle, endangering both crew members. What does Janeway do? She heads for her ready room. Nothing to concern her, right?

They go to the world looking for food. Did they ever get it?

Equipment Malfunctions

Neelix heats the rocks in the cave with his phaser. They glow from the bottom up instead of radiating from the point of phaser impact.

Episode 24: "Persistence of Vision"

Production number: 124
Stardate: Supplemental
Air date: October 30, 1995
Writer: Jeri Taylor
Director: James L. Conway
Guest Stars: Michael Cumpsty: Lord Burleigh; Carolyn Seymour: Mrs. Templeton; Stan Ivar: Mark; Warren Munson: Admiral Paris; Lindsey Haun: Beatrice; Thomas Dekker: Henry; Patrick Kerr: the Bothan; Marva Hicks: T'Pel

Spoiler-free Opinion Service Rating: 6.8
Nielsen Ratings: 6.1

As *Voyager* heads for a first encounter with the Bothan, a strange psionic field puts the crew into a delusional state, which unearths buried fears. Characters in Janeway's holonovel program come to life and her fiancé, Mark, appears; Paris is confronted by his overbearing father; Tuvok meets his wife; Kim encounters Libby; and Torres is seduced by Chakotay. The crew is disabled and only an unaffected Kes and the Doctor can end the mysterious field.

Plot Misfires

Chakotay orders "evasive maneuvers," but the ship flies straight forward.

Memory Failures

One Botha ship attacking *Voyager* is footage of a Kazon ship from "The Caretaker."

The musical instrument that appears on Tuvok's station is called a lute, but it's a lyre or harp.

Episode 25: "Tattoo"

Production number: 125
Stardate: Supplemental
Air date: November 6, 1995
Teleplay: Michael Piller
Story: Larry Brody
Director: Alexander Singer
Guest Stars: Henry Darrow: Kolopak; Richard Fancy: an alien; Douglas Spain: Young Chakotay; Nancy Hower: Ensign Wildman; Richard Chaves: the chief

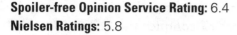

Spoiler-free Opinion Service Rating: 6.4
Nielsen Ratings: 5.8

When Chakotay leads an Away Team to drill for minerals on a moon, they accidentally disturb a village. A regretful Chakotay experiences flashbacks of himself as a defiant fifteen-year-old who disappoints his father by not embracing the traditions of his tribe. The natives disable *Voyager* and the endangered Away Team transports out, leaving Chakotay behind. The aliens recognize his tattoo. Chakotay assures the natives of Starfleet's peaceful intentions. They turn out to be the "Sky Spirits" that guided his people to civilization long ago. He reconciles his conflicts with his now-deceased father and the traditions of his tribe. Meanwhile Kes challenges the Doctor to show more compassion for his patients. So, he programs himself with a simulated flu virus to experience the discomforts suffered by living beings.

Key Quotation

The Doctor: "I don't have a life, I have a program."

Plot Misfires

Chakotay says that he received a recommendation from a Captain Sulu when he applied to Starfleet Academy. Is this good, old Hikaru? One hundred years later, and still only a captain? Shame.

Prime Directive Violation: Torres, Tuvok, and Chakotay drop their weapons to show the natives their peaceful intentions. Chakotay later removes his uniform with the tricorder still in its holder. When

Kes, Torres, and Tuvok retrieve Chakotay, they leave behind the three phasers and the tricorder.

Janeway orders a landing for *Voyager* after learning that a powerful, potentially hostile, alien race with complete control of the atmosphere lives there. Not very smart.

Equipment Malfunctions

The *Voyager* transporter beam normally moves vertically. Here it moves horizontally while transporting Neelix.

Memory Failures

Chakotay's father looks like Vulcan Admiral Savar in *TNG*'s "Conspiracy." They're both played by Henry Darrow.

Episode 26: "Cold Fire"

Production number: 126
Stardate: Supplemental
Air date: November 13, 1995
Teleplay: Brannon Braga
Story: Anthony Williams
Director: Cliff Bole
Guest Stars: Gary Graham: Tanis
Spoiler-free Opinion Service Rating: 6.9
Nielsen Ratings: 6.0

Ocampan colonists on an alien space station contact *Voyager*. Tuvok tutors Kes on her mental abilities, concluding that they have underestimated her powers. Tanis, a male Ocampan colonist, agrees to introduce Captain Janeway and her crew to Suspiria, the female mate of the Caretaker. As the *Voyager* crew hopes to return home,

Tanis begs Kes to stay with her people on the alien space station.

Memory Failures

After Kes killed all the plants in the arboretum, she is shown lying on the floor with her legs underneath her. After the camera focuses on the man coming over to help her, her legs are on her left side.

Tuvok's Vulcan blood is black instead of green.

Both B'Elanna and Tuvok had an assistant along when the Caretaker attacked. Where did they go? Neither Tuvok nor B'Elanna look for them when they land.

During the first meeting on Voyager, seven people occupy the conference room: Janeway, Chakotay, Kes, Tuvok, and three Ocampa. The Ocampa leader wants to speak to Kes alone, so Janeway, Tuvok, and one Ocampa leave. What happened to Chakotay and the third Ocampa?

Episode 27: "Maneuvers"

Production number: 127
Stardate: 49208.5
Air date: November 20, 1995
Writer: Kenneth Biller
Director: David Livingston
Guest Stars: Martha Hackett: Seska; Anthony DeLongis: Culluh; Terry Lester: Haron; John Gegenhuber: Kelat
Spoiler-free Opinion Service Rating: 7.6
Nielsen Ratings: 5.4

Kazon intruders board *Voyager* and steal a transporter control module. Their leader,

Culluh, then persuades rival sects to join together to conquer the Federation ship. Seska, Chakotay's Cardassian ex-lover, masterminds the plot. When Chakotay learns of Seska's involvement, he sets out alone to thwart her, but the Kazon capture him. *Voyager* prepares for a showdown, but Seska has yet another trick.

Plot Misfires

Why weren't the access codes changed when Seska first fled from *Voyager*?

Why did *Voyager* go into a fight against six other ships without phasers set at maximum?

When they had the drop on the Kazon, why didn't they ask for Seska's return?

If they could kidnap the leaders of the Kazon, why didn't they transport Seska?

Chakotay flies to the Kazon-Nistrim ship to destroy the transporter module and keep Federation technology out of their hands. Then he gives Seska his phaser, another piece of Federation technology!

Memory Failures

When Tuvok leaves the bridge to go to the cargo bay, the bridge is filled with smoke. When the scene cuts back there a few minutes later, all the smoke is gone.

Episode 28: "Resistance"

Production number: 128S
Stardate: Supplemental
Air date: November 27, 1995
Teleplay: Lisa Klink
Story: Michael Jan Friedman and Kevin J. Ryan

Director: Winrich Kolbe
Guest Stars: Alan Scarfe: Augris; Tom Todoroff: Darod; Glenn Morshower: the guard; Joel Grey: Caylem
Spoiler-free Opinion Service Rating: 7.5
Nielsen Ratings: 5.9

A search for tellerium to power *Voyager* brings Janeway, Tuvok, Torres, and Neelix to an Alsaurian city occupied by hostile Mokra. Mokra soldiers capture Tuvok and Torres, while Janeway escapes with Caylem, a local eccentric who thinks she's his long lost daughter. Neelix transports back to *Voyager* with the tellerium and the bad news. As *Voyager* searches for its kidnapped crew, Janeway goes undercover, relying only on herself and Caylem to break into the prison and rescue Tuvok and Torres.

Plot Misfires

When *Voyager* is under attack, why doesn't Chakotay take evasive measures and/or counterattack?

Janeway, Tuvok, Torres, and Neelix go to an Alsaurian city to buy tellerium. What do they intend to use for money?

Equipment Malfunctions

Why don't *Voyager*'s sensors spot Janeway? She repeatedly returns to the place last seen by Neelix.

Memory Failures

Janeway's universal translator is contained in her communicator pin. She quickly loses her pin. How does she communicate with the natives for the rest of the episode? Do they conveniently speak English?

When Caylem hides from the Mokra in a side corridor in the marketplace, his nose-bridge disappears. It returns when he moves into a crowd.

Episode 29: "Prototype"

Production number: 129
Stardate: Supplemental
Air date: January 15, 1996
Writer: Nicholas Corea
Director: Jonathan Frakes
Spoiler-free Opinion Service Rating: 7.2
Nielsen Ratings: 5.8

The crew finds a deactivated humanoid robot with an unfamiliar power source floating in space. Chief Engineer B'Elanna Torres repairs the robot. Automated Unit 3947 explains that its kind is near extinction and asks Torres to build a prototype for more units. After Janeway declines the request because of the Prime Directive, the robot abducts Torres to force her to construct the prototype. She does, then ultimately, and tearfully, destroys her work.

Plot Misfires

Why do they beam a potentially hostile robot aboard and then leave it unwatched in main engineering, only a few yards from the warp core?

The robot transports itself and Torres off the ship. When did the robot learn how to use *Voyager*'s transporter?

157

Equipment Malfunctions

Torres speaks while in a transporter beam after her vocal cords have begun dematerializing.

Memory Failures

Why was half-Klingon engineer Torres so emotional over terminating a mobile computer?

Episode 30: "Alliances"

Production number: 131
Stardate: Supplemental
Air date: January 22, 1996
Writer: Jeri Taylor
Director: Les Landau
Guest Stars: Charles O. Lucia: Mabus; Anthony DeLongis: Culluh; Martha Hackett: Seska; Raphael Sbarge: Michael Jonas; Larry Cedar: Tersa; John Gegenhuber: Kelat; Simon Billig: Hogan
Spoiler-free Opinion Service Rating: 7.5
Nielsen Ratings: 5.4

Kazon attack *Voyager* and kill a crew member. Chakotay appeals to Janeway to think more like the Maquis. Janeway knows she must strengthen *Voyager*'s position in the Delta Quadrant and agrees to an alliance with Kazon factions. Seeking an intermediary to begin talks with the Kazon, Neelix shuttles to Sobras, a planet with a Kazon settlement. He makes contact with an acquaintance, Jal Tersa of the Kazon-Pommar. Janeway's initial meeting with Culluh and Seska is unsuccessful, but Neelix befriends Mabus, a governor of the Trabe, an exiled sect and bitter enemy of

the Kazon. Thinking that they and the Trabe have compatible goals, Janeway forms an alliance, but is betrayed.

Plot Misfires

Janeway left Culluh and Seska with a *Voyager* access terminal and no guard.

Equipment Malfunctions

Voyager's torps do little damage to the Trabe ship or the building behind it although they score direct hits.

When *Voyager* searches for Neelix's shuttle using long-range sensors, they find nothing out to two light-years. Then they detect a large armada of Kazon ships close to *Voyager*.

Memory Failures

Kes works as a nurse aboard *Voyager* because all other medical personnel have died, but at least three crew members wear green medical uniforms in the funeral scene.

What becomes of Neelix's shuttle?

Stars aren't seen moving through the window during the meeting in the observation lounge at the end of the episode, indicating that *Voyager* is not moving, yet the exterior shot shows the ship in motion.

Where are the other fourteen Kazon sects? Only six of twenty show up for the meeting. And where are the familiar Kazon-Ogla?

Episode 31: "Threshold"

Production number: 130
Stardate: 49373.4
Air date: January 29, 1996
Teleplay: Brannon Braga

Story: Michael De Luca
Director: Alexander Singer
Guest Stars: Raphael Sbarge: Michael Jonas
Spoiler-free Opinion Service Rating: 4.4
Nielsen Ratings: 6.2

Lieutenant Paris becomes the first person to make a transwarp flight. He undergoes startling changes soon after his shuttle returns. His cell membranes degrade and he dies. Hours after his death, Paris revives, as his body mutates. The mutated Paris captures and mutates Janeway, then kidnaps her to a planet where they breed offspring together.

Plot Misfires

Why doesn't the entire crew use warp 10 to return home? They'll evolve into salamanders for a time, but they can change back. That would end the series, of course.

If Paris and Janeway can be made human, couldn't their children also be transformed? In either case, are they completely unconcerned with abandoning their kids never to meet them again?

Equipment Malfunctions

When Kim sends the sensor logs to Janeway and Torres, he says he is "downloading," instead of "uploading," them.

What happened to the force fields that keep atmosphere inside shuttle bays? Janeway tells Kim to depressurize a bay.

Why does the Doctor ask Torres to bring him information instead of downloading it? Besides, isn't he a program in the same computer?

Why doesn't the universal translator interpret the noises the salamanders make?

Memory Failures

How could Paris take a shuttle from Shuttle Bay 2? *Voyager* only has one shuttle bay.

Chakotay reports that internal sensors are off-line. Then Janeway fires a phaser and Lieutenant Kim reports that a phaser was fired on Deck 6. How did he know with internal sensors off-line?

Episode 32: "Meld"

Production number: 132
Stardate: Supplemental
Air date: February 5, 1996
Teleplay: Michael Piller
Story: Michael Sussman
Director: Cliff Bole
Guest Stars: Brad Douri: Suder; Angela Dohrmann: Ricky; Simon Billig: Hogan
Spoiler-free Opinion Service Rating: 7.3
Nielsen Ratings: 5.1

When a crew member is murdered, Tuvok's investigation leads to another crew member, Ensign Suder, who admits his crime. Tuvok attempts to understand the violent impulses by performing a mind meld. Tuvok then removes himself from duty, and the Doctor must initiate treatment that removes Tuvok's emotional suppression abilities. Meanwhile, Chakotay puts Paris on report for running an illegal gambling operation.

Key Quotation

Tuvok: "I want the truth."

Plot Misfires

Vulcan mental abilities are a learned discipline, not a physical area that can be surgically removed from the Vulcan brain.

Memory Failures

A close-up of Suder shows that he wears the Maquis rank pip for a crew member on his collar. He calls himself "Crewman Suder." So why does everyone call him "Ensign Suder"?

Episode 33: "Dreadnought"

Production number: 133
Stardate: 49447
Air date: February 12, 1996
Writer: Gary Holland
Director: LeVar Burton
Guest Stars: Raphael Sbarge: Michael Jonas; Nancy Hower: Ensign Wildman; Michael Spound: Lorrum; Dan Kern: First Minister Kellan
Spoiler-free Opinion Service Rating: 7.8
Nielsen Ratings: 6.0

Voyager spots a Cardassian-designed, self-guided missile as it travels toward Rakosan, a heavily populated planet. Previously, the Cardassians had created it to use against the Maquis. Torres had intercepted and reprogrammed it to attack Cardassians when she was a Maquis, but it later went astray. Now Torres volunteers to transport to the missile's interior and reprogram it again. Before she can detonate the warhead, the onboard computer tries to destroy her. Meanwhile, Janeway learns about the negative image her ship has in the Delta Quadrant.

Equipment Malfunctions

When the Rakosan fleet appears, the dreadnought says there are fifteen targets approaching, yet there are sixteen blips on the tactical display, not counting *Voyager*.

Memory Failures

The dreadnought computer says its programming backups were installed during stardate 46437.5. Torres, as a Maquis, accessed the dreadnought computer system on stardate 47582, yet the Maquis were created in opposition to the border provisions of the treaty unveiled on stardate 47751.2. This doesn't add up.

The computer says they are in the Delta Quadrant, 75,000 light-years from their starting point, but when they arrived in the Delta Quadrant, they were only 70,000 light-years from home. Has *Voyager* been going in the wrong direction?

Episode 34: "Death Wish"

Production number: 134
Stardate: 49301.2
Air date: February 19, 1996
Teleplay: Michael Piller
Story: Shawn Piller
Director: James L. Conway
Guest Stars: John de Lancie: Q; Jonathan Frakes: Commander William T. Riker; Gerrit Graham: rebel Q
Spoiler-free Opinion Service Rating: 8.4
Nielsen Ratings: 6.8

The nearly omnipotent Q returns to a Starfleet vessel on the heels of a suicidal rebel Q escapee, who demands asylum aboard the *Voyager*. Janeway holds a hearing to consider the request for asylum. Federation personnel preside over a trial in which Q must defend the Continuum as the ever-logical Tuvok acts as counsel for the escaped Q. Everyone from William Riker to Isaac Newton shows up.

Key Quotations

Q: "Is this a ship of the Valkyries?"

Q: "We've all been the scarecrow."

Plot Misfires

How did the comet hold the suicidal Q prisoner?

Why does the comet have a tail? There's no nearby star and thus no solar wind to blow ice and dust off its nucleus.

Memory Failures

Riker recognizes Janeway and the *Voyager*, so why is he wearing the outdated communicator with the oval and not the rectangle? Riker is wearing commander's pips.

Q2 was imprisoned for three hundred years. How does he know what a modern Starfleet uniform looks like?

The comet shot at the beginning is from *TNG*'s "Masks."

Q2 needs Q to grant him mortality, yet previously all Q's had the ability to give up their powers.

Episode 35: "Lifesigns"

Production number: 135
Stardate: 49504.3
Air date: February 26, 1996
Writer: Kenneth Biller
Director: Cliff Bole
Guest Stars: Susan Diol: Dr. Danara Pel; Raphael Sbarge: Michael Jonas; Martha Hackett: Seska; Michael Spound: Lorum; Rick Gianasi: the gigolo
Spoiler-free Opinion Service Rating: 7.3
Nielsen Ratings: 5.6

Voyager detects a distress call from a small spacecraft and beams a deathly ill Vidiian female to sickbay. The Doctor treats her for advanced stages of the phage and transfers her consciousness into a temporary, healthy holographic program. He then falls in love with the alien, a hematologist named Danara Pel. Lieutenant Paris continues to be insubordinate, and Seska instructs Jonas to damage *Voyager*'s warp coils.

Key Quotations

The Doctor on love: "Why would people seek out situations that induce such unpleasant symptoms?"

Kes: "Romance isn't a malfunction."

The Doctor: "I find myself romantically attracted to you, and I wonder if you have similar feelings for me."

Equipment Malfunctions

The Doctor says holo-Pel's patterns must quickly be returned to her physical body from the computer or they will degrade. Do all memories stored within *Voyager*'s computers quickly degrade? And doesn't it frequently back them up?

Memory Failures

Footage from "Dreadnought" appears in the preview for this episode, although not in the episode.

Riker's girlfriend was killed by the Crystalline Entity in *TNG*'s "Silicon Avatar," but she apparently returns as Pel.

When the Doctor constructs the body for Pel, the forehead has no vertical ridge. It later appears.

Episode 36: "Investigations"

Production number: 136
Stardate: 49485.2
Air date: March 13, 1996
Teleplay: Jeri Taylor
Story: Jeff Schnaufer and Ed Bond
Director: Les Landau
Guest Stars: Raphael Sbarge: Michael Jonas; Jerry Sroka: Laxeth; Simon Billig: Hogan
Spoiler-free Opinion Service Rating: 7.2
Nielsen Ratings: 4.9

Neelix begins producing a talk show. He then learns that Tom Paris plans to leave *Voyager* to become a pilot with a Talaxan convoy. The Kazon-Nistim, and the scheming Seska, attack the Talaxan fleet and abduct Paris. Meanwhile, Neelix suspects a traitor aboard *Voyager*, and sleuthing leads him to Paris. Plots dwell within plots in this episode of spies and counterspies. (Note: The person talking to Harry Kim when he meets Neelix at the beginning is played by Prince Abdullah Bin Al-Hussein of Jordan.)

Plot Misfires

Voyager disables the Kazon ship, Paris knows Seska is on the ship, but nobody tries to get her back. Huh?

How did Neelix know how to restore weapons and access to engineering?

Equipment Malfunctions

When Paris is in the Kazon shuttle fleeing the mother ship, he grabs the window frame, and his fingers wrap all the way around. No glass.

Chakotay says the job might be dangerous for Neelix, then Tuvok orders that a comm link be kept open to Neelix at all times. Why does Neelix have to tap his badge and yell for help?

Memory Failures

Data previously used the instrument Neelix hit Jonas with to carry antimatter in *TNG*'s "We'll Always Have Paris."

While Torres is in the computer core, a crew member takes a batch of PADDs, then another crew member brings her another PADD. Why don't they upload the information for Torres?

Episode 37: "Deadlock"

Production number: 137
Stardate: 49548.7
Air date: March 18, 1996
Writer: Brannon Braga
Director: David Livingston
Guest Stars: Nancy Hower: Wildman; Simon Billig: Hogan; Bob Clendenin: Vidiian Surgeon; Ray Proscia: Vidiian Commander; Keythe Farley: Vidiian; Christopher Johnston: Vidiian
Spoiler-free Opinion Service Rating: 8.4
Nielsen Ratings: 5.8

Astounding consequences occur when *Voyager* enters a plasma cloud while evading pursuing Vidiian vessels. Then their engines stall, antimatter supplies drain, and proton bursts cause heavy casualties and breach the hull. When Ensign Kim and Kes are sucked into a void in space, Captain Janeway discovers a duplicate *Voyager* with an identical crew in a parallel universe. Meanwhile, the Doctor struggles to save Ensign Wildman's newborn, half-human, half-Katarian baby. Then Janeway discovers that, although a divergence field caused every particle on the ship to duplicate, there is not enough antimatter to sustain both vessels. As the Vidiians close in, she and the other Janeway decide which of the two ships will survive.

Key Quotation

Janeway: "We're Starfleet officers. Weird is part of the job."

Plot Misfires

Janeway's signal through subspace causes the other *Voyager*'s display to read: "Emergency Transmission; Lock—12 Gigahertz." Torres then announces, "I think someone is telling us to lock onto a frequency of 12 Gigahertz." Brilliant deduction, but she's not certain. Now I know why she's a top engineer.

Janeway finds a spatial rift on *Voyager* Deck 15 and says it "might" be where the other Kes came from. Where else? Fairyland?

First Janeway says they can't evacuate the damaged *Voyager* because it would cause an imbalance and destroy both ships. Then she offers to send a security detachment through the rift.

Voyager is flying through the plasma field on impulse power when Paris tells Janeway that the warp engines have stalled. She then orders him to "Fly at impulse."

Doesn't *Voyager* have repair crews? Why waste the time of the operations officer and chief engineer patching a hull breach?

Poor Harry! They brought him back from the dead, sent him to an alternate San Francisco, and now they've killed him and replaced him with a double.

Equipment Malfunctions

Why doesn't Torres shut the Jeffries tube door after a hull breach sucks Kim into space? It's open to the bridge and there are no emergency force fields up.

Why wasn't everything sucked out into space through the hull breech? Harry holds onto a ladder while Torres stays in place.

163

Janeway instructs the computer to delete audio warnings about self-destruct. The computer then announces that the ship will self-destruct?

Memory Failures

The graphic Torres and Janeway see on the workstation is from the previous episode.

The Katarian pleasure girl Riker spent time with in *TNG*'s "The Game" had no horns.

When sickbay lost power, the Doctor wasn't affected even as systems went off-line. Previously, more minor disruptions of power supply almost shut him down.

Does Janeway have the authority to take Wildman's baby and give it to the Wildman on the other ship? She is the captain, but...

Episode 38: "Innocence"

Production number: 138
Stardate: Supplemental
Air date: April 8, 1996
Teleplay: Lisa Klink
Story: Anthony Williams
Director: James Conway
Guest Stars: Marnie McPhail: Alicia; Tiffany Taubman: Tressa; Sarah Rayne: Elani; Tahj D. Mowry: Corin; Richard Garon: Bennet
Spoiler-free Opinion Service Rating: 6.1
Nielsen Ratings: 5.1

Tuvok and Bennet's shuttle crashes on a sacred haven of the Drayan, an isolationist race. Three frightened Drayan children venture out from hiding. They tell Tuvok they were abandoned by their people to die, and they beg his help against the imminent arrival of the "morrok," the messenger of death. Then, during the night, two youngsters disappear. Meanwhile, Janeway makes contact with the Drayan's First Prelate, Alicia, and learns an amazing revelation about this mysterious race.

Plot Misfires

Prime Directive Violation: Before Tuvok learns if the children come from a people capable of space flight, he tells them he is a Vulcan.

Equipment Malfunctions

Why does the universal translator fail to translate Chakotay's Amerindian language?

Episode 39: "Thaw"

Production Number: 139
Stardate: Supplemental
Air date: April 29, 1996
Teleplay: Joe Menosky
Story: Richard Gadas and Michael Piller
Director: Marvin Rush
Guest Stars: Michael McKean: the clown; Thomas Kopache: Viorsa; Carel Struycken: Spectre; Patty Maloney: the little woman; Tony Carli: the physician; Shannon O'Hurley: the programmer
Spoiler-free Opinion Service Rating: 6.9
Nielsen Ratings: 4.7

Voyager activates an automated message from members of the Kohl settlement who survived an environmental catastrophe by entering artificial hibernation. When the crew transports the hibernation pods on board, they find sleeping humanoids with active minds and complex sensory systems controlled by a computer. Torres and Kim equip two pods with Starfleet technology and submit themselves into stasis. They enter the environment created by the computer and find that the humanoids' fears have manifested a devious, omnipotent clown and other nightmarish characters. The clown holds Torres and Kim hostage while making increasingly unreasonable demands of Janeway.

Key Quotation

The Doctor: "I have a very trustworthy face."

Plot Misfires

Why didn't Janeway send the Holodoc into the computer-generated virtual world as she did when they confronted Grendel? He is best suited for the environment.

A native dies of a massive heart attack. No one tries to revive him. Later, when the clown lets the prisoners go and they begin to regain consciousness, Kes says, "Their own hearts are taking over." Then how did the poor native already die of a heart attack?

The clown makes historical references to Earth and Vulcan, but the programmers of the computer would not have known about the Alpha Quadrant.

Equipment Malfunctions

When they scan the planet's surface, they find warp anti-matter reactors. No wonder the world had an environmental catastro-phe—normally, you find these on a starship in space.

Memory Failures

The second piece to Kim's clarinet used to look hi-tech, yet now it looks traditional.

Starfleet had some type of "mental landscape generator" for individuals involved in deep space flight, sort of an individual holodeck. This never appeared before.

Janeway is walking around the briefing room, when Neelix mentions joking with the clown. Then, inexplicably, Janeway is shown sitting down.

Episode 40: "Tuvix"

Originally titled: "Symbiogenesis"
Production Number: 140
Stardate: 49655.2-49678.4
Air date: May 6, 1996
Teleplay: Kenneth Biller
Story: Andrew Price and Mark Gaberman
Director: Cliff Bole
Guest Stars: Tom Wright: Tuvix; Simon Billig: Hogan; Bahni Turpin: Swinn
Spoiler-free Opinion Service Rating: 7.3
Nielsen Ratings: 5.1

A strange occurrence begins when Neelix and Tuvok beam back from an away mission. A new humanoid with dark speckled skin and pointy ears appears. The Doctor's bio-scanner shows that Neelix's and Tuvok's patterns have merged into Tuvix—a humor-filled, logic-defying fusion. While Tuvix starts to become a valued member of the team, the Doctor devises a method to restore Tuvok and Neelix.

Plot Misfires

How were uniforms and other physical objects merged by flower enzymes? Later, where does the extra uniform come from?

Equipment Manfunctions

If the transporter converts both Neelix and Tuvok into energy, how can they chemically interact?

When the two people became one person, where did the rest of the matter go?

Memory Failures

After Tuvix is restrained, a shot shows Chakotay facing Janeway, yet the next shot shows him facing Tuvix.

Episode 41: "Resolutions"

Production Number: 141
Stardate: 49690.1-49694.2
Air date: May 13, 1996
Writer: Jeri Taylor
Director: Alexander Singer
Guest Stars: Susan Diol: Dr. Danara Pel; Simon Billig: Hogan; Bahni Turpin: Swinn
Spoiler-free Opinion Service Rating: 7.0
Nielsen Rating: 4.5

Janeway and Chakotay are afflicted with a deadly, contagious virus and the Doctor cannot find a cure. They must confine themselves to a small planet while the rest of the crew continue the journey home under the new, permanent command of Tuvok.

The former captain and commander, alone on a strange planet, begin to explore another side of their relationship.

Equipment Malfunctions

Why can't the transporters filter out the virus?

They left Janeway and Chakotay a replicator. What will they power it with?

Memory Failures

Tuvok never put on a red Command uniform.

Tuvok's log entry says that *Voyager* left Janeway for six weeks, but he tells Kim three weeks.

In Janeway's garden scene, Chakotay comes out of their shelter and closes the door. They talk, then when they go over to the shelter, the door is open again.

Episode 42: "Basics, Part I"

Production Number: 142
Stardate: Supplemental
Air date: May 20, 1996
Writer: Michael Piller
Director: Winrich Kolbe
Guest Stars: Brad Dourif: Suder; Anthony De Longis: Culluh; John Gegunhuber: Teirna; Martha Hackett: Seska; Henry Darrow: Kolopak
Spoiler-free Opinion Service Rating: 7.4
Nielsen Rating: 4.9

Seska lures *Voyager* through the Kazon-Nistrim territory into a trap on the season finale. The Kazon seize *Voyager* and abandon the crew on a primitive planet.

Stripped of their technology, the crew must use basic skills to survive while their enemy lifts off with their ship and with two hidden Starfleet crew members on board.

Key Quotations
Chakotay: "Do you think it is a trap?"

Plot Misfires
Culluh becomes an instant expert on Federation ships, able to land on the planet with no prior experience.

Kazon repair crews understand Federation technology. How come?

Memory Failures
The Kazon board through the shuttle bays, but the ship only has one shuttle bay.

They are stripped of all technology, yet Neelix and Kes communicate with the crew without universal translators.

APPENDIX A

Trekker's Guide to the Internet

The Internet

This appendix lists a few of the many *Star Trek: Voyager* resources on the Internet. Caution: These can change quickly due to the nature of Internet. All are accurate as of May 1, 1996.

Mail

The United Federation of Players
A Star Trek role-playing game by e-mail. Send mail to joinufp@umich.edu to join the game, or use the WWW form.

Engage—The European Star Trek/Sci-Fi mailing list
To subscribe, e-mail listserv@le.ac.uk with the command "info startrek".

mailserver@cis.ksu.edu (...!rutgers!depot!mailserver)
This mailserver provides access to the alt.startrek.creative archive.

trek-info-request@scam.berkeley.edui (ncc1701e!rasi-l@uunet.uu.net)
This list contains the contents of the Usenet newsgroup rec.arts.startrek.info, a newsgroup dedicated to the dissemination of information about Star Trek.

STARGAME on LISTSERV@PCCVM.Bitnet
This mailing list is for the Star Trek Role-Playing Game by FASA. There are two main purposes for this list, either to discuss the Star Trek Role-Playing Game and the enhancements that FASA puts out for it or to play the game.

   To subscribe, send the command SUB STARGAME and your full name to LISTSERV@PCCVM.Bitnet

TREK-REVIEW-L on LISTSERV@cornell.edu
This has closed down. The material that was on this list can be found in the newsgroup: rec.arts.startrek.reviews.

STREK-L on LISTSERV@PCCVM.BITNET

A list for the discussion of the many aspects of Star Trek, ranging from discussions about the movies, series, and books; discussions about the characters and/or actors; discussions about Star Trek fan clubs; to anything else dealing with Star Trek. This list is open to anyone with an interest in Star Trek. To subscribe, send the following command to LISTSERV@PCCVM via mail or interactive message: SUB STREK-L your_full_name.

News

Your local news server might not carry some of these groups, especially the alt.* groups. Periodic posting are archived in ftp://rtfm.mit.edu and many other ftp-servers.

Global Newsgroups

These groups should be available on all news servers.

rec.arts.startrek.current   *New Star Trek shows, movies and books*
rec.arts.startrek.fandom   *Star Trek conventions and memorabilia*
rec.arts.startrek.info   *Information about the universe of Star Trek (moderated)*
rec.arts.startrek.misc   *General discussions of Star Trek*
rec.arts.startrek.reviews   *Reviews only!*
rec.arts.startrek.tech   *Star Trek's depiction of future technologies*

Alt Newsgroups

The alt hierarchy is not carried by all news servers.

alt.binaries.startrek
alt.ensign.wesley.die.die.die
alt.fan.surak
alt.french.captain.borg.borg.borg
alt.lwaxana-troi.die.die.die
alt.sex.fetish.startrek
alt.sexy.bald.captains
alt.shared-reality.startrek.klingon
alt.starfleet.rpg   *Starfleet (the Role-Playing Game) Home Page*
alt.startrek.cardassian
alt.startrek.creative   *Stories and parodies related to Star Trek. Archive available via ftp, gopher, and www.*
alt.startrek.klingon   *Discussion of all matters Klingon*

alt.startrek.romulan
alt.startrek.uss-amargosa
alt.startrek.vulcan
alt.tv.star-trek.ds9
alt.tv.star-trek.tos
alt.tv.star-trek.voyager

Local Newsgroups

These newsgroups are only available in certain geographical areas, and the main language used may not be English.

aus.sf.star-trek
de.rec.sf.startrek   *(German) Deutschsprachige Newsgroup über 'Raumschiff Enterprise'*
fj.rec.sf.startrek
uk.media.tv.sf.startrek
z-netz.freizeit.startrek.allgemein
z-netz.freizeit.startrek.daten

ftp

ftp.uu.net/usenet/rec.arts.startrek
rtfm.mit.edu/pub/usenet-by-hierarchy/rec/arts/startrek
ftp.std.com/obi/Star.Trek.Parodies and ftp.std.com/obi/Star.Trek.Stories
ftp.healer.com/pub/misc/startrek   *Archive of alt.startrek.creative*
137.229.18.65/pub/scifi-lists   *Archive of Richard S. Guses Lists*
netcom.com/pub/guides/PROMOS   *Promos*
ftp.netcom.com/al/aleph/asfs.pic   *Lots of pictures.*

Telnet

grimmy.cnidr.org:1701TrekMUSE (also has a www-gateway)
Final Frontiers II (also has a www-gateway)
TOS TrekMUSE

Gopher

chop.isca.uiowa.edu:8337/11/star-trek   *Star Trek Reviews by Timothy Lynch*
gopher.med.umich.edu:70/11/Entertainment/Sounds/Star Trek (TOS)   *Star Trek (TOS) Sounds*
wiretap.spies.com:70/11/Library/Media/Trek Star Trek Library   *Mostly Usenet Periodic Postings*

depot.cis.ksu.edu:70 +/11/Star Trek Stories   *Gopher version of the alt.startrek.*
  creative archive.
depot.cis.ksu.edu:70   *Ascii Pictures*

World Wide Web (WWW)

Star Trek: Voyager Update

  http://www.users.interport.net/~ask/vv/vvhome.html

Voyager Voyeur</A>

  http://home.cc.umanitoba.ca/~umsharif

Adventure: Star Trek Voyager

  http://www.htp.com/bill/delta.html

Delta Quadrant, The

  //www.bradley.edu/campusorg/psiphi/voy

Star Trek: Voyager [bradley.edu)

  //www.aplus.com/seth/trek/voyager.html

U.S.S. Voyager

  http://www.eeng.dcu.ie/~stdcu/voyager/voyager.html

Voyager News

  http://underground.net/~koganuts/Galleries/stvoy.html

Star Trek: Voyager Central

  http://www.xmission.com/~jlwright/voyindex.html

Star Trek: Voyager Episode Reviews

  http://www.users.interport.net/~ask/vv/vv18.html

Paramounts OFFICIAL Star Trek: Voyager

  http://voyager.paramount.com/VoyagerIntro.html

Star Trek: Voyager

  http://www.eeng.edu.ie/~stdcu/startrek/voyager.html

Star Trek: Voyager at A Beginner's Guide to Star Trek
peterson/trek/voyager.html

Asimov's St: Voyager Page
http://mo.net/~asimov/voy

Star Trek: Voyager at ASTRA
http://www.gu.edu.au/others/astra/VOY

The Franchise: Voyager
http://curay.cudenver.edu/~mwzecca/trek/vger.html

Voyager at the Spoiler-Free Opinion Summary
http://hci.ise.vt.edu/~jreiss/sos/sos.cgi/voy

STAR TREK: Voyager Reviews
http://www.xmission.com/~jlwright/voyindex.html

Star Trek: WWW
http://www-iwi.unisg.ch/~sambucci/scifi/startrek/index.html

WWW Star Trek
http://www.chem.ed.ac.uk/adamstar.html

Star Trek : Voyager at The Ultimate TV List
http://tvnet.com/cgi-bin/utl?card+1086

Kasey's Star Trek Nexus
http://userwww.sfsu.edu/~kschang/startrek.htm#TrekVoyager

Star Trek: Voyager Central
http://underground.net/~koganuts/Galleries/stvoy.html

Star Trek: Voyager Rescource Page
http://soho.ios.com/~capjanwy/voy.html

Star Trek ASCII Art Home
http://www.ucalgary.ca/~jsbell/sta.html

Star Trek Voyager Files

http://www.indirect.com/www/gransee/voyager.html

Vaguely Red Dwarf at The Trekker Reviews </A>

http://ringo.psy.flinders.edu.au:80/trekker/voy

Trek Reviews Archive

http://www.mcs.net/~forbes/trek-reviews/archive.html

Nitpicker Central Home Page (Voyager section)

http://www.woodtech.com/~nitcentral/voyager/voyager.html

Admiral Wombat's Nitpicker Page

http://www.cif.rochester.edu/users/wombat/nit.html

Star Trek Conventions

http://www.wwod.com/shows/strekconv.html

Mikael Rechtsman's Star Trek Page

http://www.interlog.com/~mcr/trek.html

The Particles of Star Trek

http://www.hyperion.com/~koreth/particles

Admiral Jarok's Star Trek Page, with the Star Trek Top Ten Lists

http://www2.netdoor.com/~lainh/STtopten.html

The #ReadyRoom Home Page

http://soho.ios.com/~capjanwy/capt.html

Federation Frontiers

http://ccc-shop.wpi.edu/rogue/trek/default.html

The Roxanne-Biggs Dawson Online Fan Club

http://www.ualberta.ca/~tgee/rbdfc

Books

Here are some brief comments by John Ordover, the Star Trek novels editor. Following that is a list of those books.

On Plots

All the novels are consistent with the shows—up until the moment they are put into production, that is, until we can't make any more changes.

We have a lead time of around nine months to a year for a novel. The TV show has a lead time of around six weeks for an episode. It's a logistical impossibility to keep the two *completely* interconnected.

As for *Voyager*, no plot point in the books will ever be a "will they get home this week" plotline. Heck, the show shouldn't do 'em either, since we all know it won't happen. But the problem is, while the Various Enterprises and *DS9* have many goals, keep the peace, protect the federation, and so on, *Voyager* has only two goals: "Survive" and "Find a Way Home." Since we know they'll survive, and we know they won't find a way home, telling *Voyager* stories is difficult. If you add in the Prime Directive, which makes it hard for them to ever get involved with another race, it becomes very difficult. But I think we've done a good job in the *Voyager* novels so far.

On Covers

We're at long last giving up the "heads in space" look for the Trek novels. Why? Because I was finally able to convince my boss that it was getting old. The *Voyager* covers were dark and poor because the art department kept making them that way, until I screamed holy heck about it: No more purple!!!

As for why Janeway was on the first few covers of *Voyager*, it's the same reason that she's always the one who pops up on the *TV Guide* cover when they do a Trek issue, because the "female Captain" was getting tons of publicity and was very recognizable. We're going to be slipping other characters onto the covers as time goes by.

Book Title Checklist

The following books are listed by title, in the order of publication. The notation in parentheses refers to the series number.

Caretaker by L.A. Graf (Paperback 01), February 1995
Caretaker Audio Book, read by Robert Picardo (Audio 01), 1995
The Escape by Dean Wesley Smith and Kristine Kathryn Rusch (Paperback 02),
   May 1995
Ragnarok by Nathan Archer (Paperback 03), June 1995
Violations by Susan Wright (Paperback 04), September 1995
The 37's by Diane Carey (unnumbered), October 1995
Incident at Arbuk by John Betancourt (Paperback 05), November 1995
The Murdered Sun by Christine Golden (Paperback 06), February 1996
Ghost of a Chance by Mark A. Garland and Charles G. McGraw (Paperback 07),
   April 1996
Cybersong by S. N. Lewitt (Paperback 08), June 1996
Final Fury ("Invasion!" IV) by Daffyd ab Hugh (Paperback 09), August 1996
Mosaic by Jeri Taylor (Hard Cover 01), October 1996
The Garden by Melissa Scott (Paperback 10), December 1996

Fan Clubs

Robert Beltran (Chakotay)

The Commander fan club is officially sanctioned by Robert Beltran, and membership includes a subscription to the newsletter.
   Membership: $12/year U.S., $14/year Canada, payable to:
The Commander
c/o Barbara O'Leary
P.O. Box 183
Reading, PA 19603

Ethan Phillips (Neelix)

EPIC stands for the Ethan Phillips International fan Club, and it is officially sanctioned by Phillips. Members receive an 8 x 10 personally autographed photo, membership card, and a year's subscription to the quarterly newsletter. Note that all moneys received by EPIC that are not used directly in the administration of the club shall be donated to charities of Ethan's choosing.

Membership: $20.00 ($25.00 outside the U.S.), payable to:
EPIC
c/o Rande Goodwin
PO Box 4818
Waterbury, CT 06704

Martha Hackett (Seska)

The Official Martha Hackett Fan Club is indeed official, as Hackett has sanctioned it. Make checks payable to Donna J. Abate

Membership: $15/year, U.S. funds only, send to:
Official Martha Hackett Fan Club
c/o Donna J. Abate
3699 Barnard Dr.
Apt. 517
Oceanside, CA 92056.

APPENDIX
B

Episode
Credits

Actors

A

Luigi Amodeo	The Gigolo (The Cloud)
Vaughn Armstrong	Telek [R'Mor] (Eye of the Needle)

B

Majel Barrett	Computer Voice (Caretaker, Phage, State of Flux, Heroes and Demons, Cathexis, Jetrel, Learning Curve, Initiations, Projections, Non Sequitur, Parturition, Persistence of Vision, Tattoo, Maneuvers, Threshold, Meld, Dreadnought, Investigations, Deadlock); Narrator (Cold Fire)
Robert Beltran	Commander Chakotay (all episodes)
Roxann Biggs-Dawson	Lieutenant B'Elanna Torres (all episodes)
Simon Billig	Hogan (Alliances, Meld, Investigations, Deadlock)
Brady Bluhm	Latika (Time and Again)
Henry Brown	Numiri Captain (Ex Post Facto)

C

Cecile Callan	Ptera (Emanations)
Larry Cedar	Tersa (Alliances)
Jefrey Alan Chandler	Hatil (Emanations)
Richard Chaves	The Chief (Tattoo)
John Cirigliano	Alien #1 (Emanations)
Josh Clark	Lieutenant Carey (Caretaker, Parallax, Prime Factors, State of Flux)
Bob Clendenin	Vidiian Surgeon (Deadlock)
Alicia Coppola	Lieutenant Stadi (Caretaker)
Terry Correll	N.D. Crew Member (Elogium); Crew member (Twisted)
Michael Cumpsty	Burleigh (Eye of the Needle, Cathexis, Persistence of Vision)

D

Henry Darrow	Kolopak (Tattoo)
Thomas [Alexander] Dekker	Henry [Burleigh] (Learning Curve, Persistence of Vision)
John de Lancie	"Q" (Death Wish)
Anthony DeLongis	First Maje Jal Culluh (State of Flux, Maneuvers, Alliances)
Peter Dennis	Sir Isaac Newton (Death Wish)
Tim deZarn	Haliz (Initiations)
Susan Diol	Dr. Danara Pel (Lifesigns)
Angela Dohrmann	Ricky (The Cloud, Meld)
Brad Dourif	Ensign Suder (Meld)

E

Aron Eisenberg	Kar (Initiations)

F

Richard Fancy	The Alien (Tattoo)
Keythe Farley	Vidiian #2 (Deadlock)
Jonathan Frakes	Commander William T. Riker (Death Wish)
Cully Fredricksen	Alien #1 (Phage)
Bruce French	Ocampan Doctor (Caretaker)

G

Richard Garon	Ensign Bennet (Innocence)
Jennifer Gatti	Libby (Non Sequitur)
Judy Geeson	Sandrine (The Cloud, Twisted)
John Gegenhuber	Jal Kelat (Maneuvers, Alliances)
Louis Giambalvo	Cosimo (Non Sequitur)
Rick Gianasi	Gigolo (Lifesigns)
Maury Ginsberg	himself (Death Wish)
David Graf	Fred Noonan (The 37's)
Gary Graham	Tanis (Cold Fire)
Gerrit Graham	Q3 (Death Wish)
Joel Grey	Caylem (Resistance)
Robin Groves	Hatil's Wife (Emanations)
Francis Guinan	Minister Kray (Ex Post Facto)
Ronald Guttman	Gath (Prime Factors)

H

Martha Hackett	Ensign Seska (Parallax, Phage, Emanations, Prime Factors, State of Flux, Maneuvers, Alliances, Lifesigns, Investigations)
Larry A. Hankin	Gaunt Gary (The Cloud, Twisted, Jetrel)
Jerry Hardin	Dr. Neria (Emanations)
Lindsey Haun	Beatrice [Burleigh] (Learning Curve, Persistence of Vision)
Marva Hicks	T'Pel (Persistence of Vision)
Hugh Hodgin	Automated Unit 6263 (Prototype); Prototype Unit 0001 (Prototype)
Nancy Hower	Ensign Clarke (Elogium); Ensign Samantha Wildman (Tattoo, Dreadnought, Deadlock)

I

Stan Ivar	Mark (Caretaker, Persistence of Vision)

J

Chris Johnson	Vidiian #1 (Deadlock)
Eric David Johnson	Daggin (Caretaker)

K

Michael Keenan	Hrothgar (Heroes and Demons)
VJ Kennedy	Crew member (Persistence of Vision) [uncredited]
Dan Kern	First Minister Kellan (Dreadnought)
Patrick Kerr	The Bothan (Persistence of Vision)
Mark Kiely	Lieutenant Lasca (Non Sequitur)
Patrick Kilpatrick	Razik (Initiations)

L

Rob Labelle	Talaxan prisoner (Faces)
Basil Langton	Banjo Man (Caretaker)
Norman Large	Ocampa (Cold Fire)

Sharon Lawrence	"Amelia Earhart" (The 37's)
Terry Lester	Jal Haron (Maneuvers)
Jennifer Lien	Kes (all episodes)
Charles O. Lucia	Mabus (Alliances)
Aaron Lustig	Doctor (Ex Post Facto)

M

Ryan MacDonald	Shopkeeper (Time and Again)
Scott MacDonald	Rollins (Caretaker)
Catherine MacNeal	Crewman Henley (Learning Curve)
Brian Markinson	Lieutenant Durst (Cathexis, Faces); Sulan (Faces)
Jeff McCarthy	Human Doctor (Caretaker)
Derek McGrath	Crewman Chell (Learning Curve)
Robin McKee	Lidell [Ren] (Ex Post Facto)
Robert Duncan McNeill	Lieutenant Tom Paris (all episodes)
Marnie McPhail	First Prelate Alicia (Innocence)
Marjorie Monaghan	Freya (Heroes and Demons)
Kenny Morrison	Crewman Geron (Learning Curve)
Glenn Morshower	Guard #1 (Resistance)
Tahj D. Mowry	Corin (Innocence)
Kate Mulgrew	Captain Kathryn Janeway (all episodes)
Warren Munson	Admiral Paris (Persistence of Vision)

N

Christopher Neame	Unferth (Heroes and Demons)
Andrew Hill Newman	Jaret (Prime Factors)

O

Gary O'Brien	Crew member (Elogium)
Gavan O'Herlihy	Jabin [Kazon] (Caretaker)

P

Joseph Palmas	Antonio (Tattoo)
Jennifer Parsons	Ocampa Nurse (Caretaker)
Angela Paton	Aunt Adah (Caretaker)
Ethan Phillips	Neelix (all episodes)

Robert Picardo	The Doctor [Dr. Lewis Zimmerman] (all episodes)
Richard Poe	Gul Evek (Caretaker)
Joel Polis	Teria (Time and Again)
Ray Proscia	Vidiian Commander (Deadlock)

R

Stephen B. Rappaport	Alien #2 (Phage)
Sarah Rayne	Elani (Innocence)
Ray Reinhardt	Tolen Ren (Ex Post Facto)
Lindsay Ridgeway	Suspiria (Cold Fire)
John Rubinstein	John Evansville (The 37's)
Tim Russ	Lieutenant Tuvok (all episodes)

S

James Saito	Japanese Soldier (The 37's)
Raphael Sbarge	Michael Jonas (Alliances, Threshold, Dreadnought, Lifesigns, Investigations)
Alan Scarfe	Augris (Resistance)
Armand Schultz	Crewman Dalby (Learning Curve)
Dwight Schultz	"Barclay" (Projections)
David Selburg	Toscat [an Ocampa official] (Caretaker)
Carolyn Seymour	Mrs. Templeton (Eye of the Needle, Cathexis, Persistence of Vision)
Jack Shearer	Admiral Strickler (Non Sequitur)
Armin Shimerman	"Quark" (Caretaker)
Keely Sims	Farmer's Daughter (Caretaker)
James Sloyan	"Jetrel" (Jetrel)
Douglas Spain	Young Chakotay (Tattoo)
Jerry Spicer	Guard (Time and Again)
Michael Spound	Lorrum (Dreadnought, Lifesigns)
Jerry Sroka	Laxeth (Investigations)
Yvonne Suhor	Eudana (Prime Factors)
Nicolas Surovy	Makull (Time and Again)

T

Tiffany Taubman	Tressa (Innocence)
Barton Tinapp	Guard #1 (Faces)
Tom Todoroff	Darod (Resistance)

V

Steve Vaught	Officer (Time and Again)
Tom Virtue	Lieutenant Baxter (Eye of the Needle, Twisted)

W

Garrett Wang	Ensign Harry Kim (all episodes)
Justin Williams	Jarvin (Parallax)
Mirron E. Willis	Rettik (Alliances, Threshold)
Mel Winkler	Jack Hayes (The 37's)
Rick Worthy	Automated Unit 3947 (Prototype); Cravic Unit 122 (Prototype)

Directors

The credits are written in production order rather than air date order.

Cliff Bole
1. Cold Fire
2. Meld
3. Lifesigns
4. Symbiogenesis
5. False Profits

LeVar Burton
1. Ex Post Facto
2. Dreadnought

James L. Conway
1. The 37's
2. Persistence of Vision
3. Death Wish
4. Innocence

Jonathan Frakes
1. Projections
2. Parturition
3. Prototype

Winrich Kolbe
1. Caretaker
2. Phage
3. Eye of the Needle
4. Faces
5. Elogium
6. Initiations
7. Resistance
8. Basics, Part I
9. Basics, Part II

Kim Friedman
1. Parallax
2. Cathexis
3. Jetrel
4. Twisted

Les Landau
1. Time and Again
2. Prime Factors
3. Heroes and Demons
4. Alliances
5. Investigations

David Livingston
1. The Cloud
2. Emanations
3. Learning Curve
4. Non Sequitur
5. Maneuvers
6. Deadlock

Robert Duncan McNeill
1. Sacred Ground

Marvin Rush
1. The Thaw

Robert Scheerer
1. State of Flux

Alexander Singer
1. Tattoo
2. Threshold
3. Resolutions

Producers

Rick Berman
First and second season: Executive Producer

Kenneth Biller
Second Season: Coproducer (from "Dreadnought" on)

Brannon Braga
First season: Producer (all except "Caretaker")
Second season: Supervising Producer

Dan Curry
   First and second season: Visual Effects Producer

Merri Howard
   First and second season: Producer

Peter Lauritson
   First season: Producer
   Second season: Supervising Producer

David Livingston
   First season: Supervising Producer

Wendy Neuss
   First season: Coproducer
   Second season: Producer

Michael Piller
   First and second season: Executive Producer

Jeri Taylor
   First and second season: Executive Producer

Writers

The credits are written in production order rather than air date order. As a result, episodes that were filmed for one season but shown in another (such as "The 37's" or "Sacred Ground") will be listed in the season during which they were filmed.

Chris Abbott	Season 1	1. State of Flux, Teleplay
Hilary J. Bader	Season 1	1. Eye of the Needle, Story
Rick Berman	Season 1	1. Caretaker, Story

Kenneth Biller	Season 1	1. Faces, Story and Teleplay
		2. Jetrel, Teleplay
		3. Elogium, Teleplay
		4. Twisted, Teleplay
	Season 2	1. Initiations, Writer
		2. Maneuvers, Writer
		3. Lifesigns, Writer
Ed Bond	Season 2	1. Investigations, Story
Brannon Braga	Season 1	1. Parallax, Teleplay
		2. Phage, Teleplay
		3. The Cloud, Story
		4. Emanations, Writer
		5. Cathexis, Story and Teleplay
		6. Projections, Writer
		7. The 37's, Writer
	Season 2	1. Non Sequitur, Writer
		2. Cold Fire, Teleplay
		3. Threshold, Teleplay
		4. Deadlock, Writer
Larry Brody	Season 2	1. Tattoo, Story
Nicholas Corea	Season 2	1. Prototype, Writer
Paul Robert Coyle	Season 1	1. State of Flux, Story
Timothy DeHaas	Season 1	1. Phage, Story
Michael De Luca	Season 2	1. Threshold, Story
Skye Dent	Season 1	1. Phage, Teleplay

Bill Dial	Season 1	1. Eye of the Needle, Teleplay
Jimmy Diggs	Season 1	1. Elogium, Story
Greg Elliot	Season 1	1. Prime Factors, Teleplay (Was to be: Story and Teleplay)
Michael Jan Friedman	Season 2	1. Resistance, Story
David R. George, III	Season 1	1. Prime Factors, Story
Jonathan Glassner	Season 1	1. Faces, Story
Gary Holland	Season 2	1. Dreadnought, Writer
Rich Hosek	Season 1	1. Twisted, Story
Steve J. Kay	Season 1	1. Elogium, Story
David Kemper	Season 1	1. Time and Again, Story and Teleplay
Jack Klein	Season 1	1. Jetrel, Teleplay
Karen Klein	Season 1	1. Jetrel, Teleplay
Lisa Klink	Season 2	1. Resistance, Teleplay 2. Innocence, Teleplay
Jean Louise Matthias	Season 1	1. Learning Curve, Writer
Joe Menosky	Season 1	1. Cathexis, Story
Scott Nimerfro	Season 1	1. Jetrel, Story
Michael Perricone	Season 1	1. Prime Factors, Teleplay (Was to be: Story and Teleplay)

Michael Piller	Season 1	1. Caretaker, Story and Teleplay
		2. Time and Again, Teleplay
		3. The Cloud, Teleplay
		4. Ex Post Facto, Teleplay
	Season 2	1. Tattoo, Teleplay
		2. Death Wish, Teleplay
		3. Meld, Teleplay
Shawn Piller	Season 2	1. Death Wish, Story
Arnold Rudnick	Season 1	1. Twisted, Story
Kevin J. Ryan	Season 2	1. Resistance, Story
Jeff Schnaufer	Season 2	1. Investigations, Story
Naren Shankar	Season 1	1. Heroes and Demons, Writer
Evan Carlos Somers	Season 1	1. Ex Post Facto, Story and Teleplay
Eric Stillwell	Season 1	1. Prime Factors, Story
Michael Sussman	Season 2	1. Meld, Story
Tom Szollosi	Season 1	1. The Cloud, Teleplay
	Season 2	1. Parturition, Writer

Jeri Taylor	Season 1	1. Caretaker, Story and Teleplay
		2. Eye of the Needle, Teleplay
		3. Prime Factors, Teleplay (Not listed in credits)
		4. Learning Curve, Writer (Not listed in credits)
		5. Elogium, Teleplay
		6. The 37's, Writer
	Season 2	1. Persistence of Vision, Writer
		2. Alliances, Writer
		3. Investigations, Teleplay
James Thomton	Season 1	1. Jetrel, Story
Jim Trombetta	Season 1	1. Parallax, Story
Ronald Wilkerson	Season 1	1. Learning Curve, Writer

Bibliography

Most of the quotes used in this book have been taken from magazine or newspaper articles or from various convention transcripts. One obvious source for information, is *The Official Star Trek: Voyager Magazine*. The other sources are listed below. If I've referenced more than one article in a single issue, or several issues of a magazine, these have been grouped under the magazine's name. All other sources follow these grouped references in chronological order.

Cinescape

January 1995: "Premiere Episode Synopsis," "Maiden Voyage"

Entertainment Weekly

January 20, 1995: "Star Trip, Space Cadets"
January 27, 1995: "Trekker Treat"
September 15, 1995: "Fall TV Preview: Monday"

The Official Star Trek: Voyager Magazine

Issue 2, June 1995: "Tim Russ," "Garrett Wang"
Issue 3, August 1995: "Ethan Philips," "Jennifer Lien"
Issue 4, October 1995: "Michael Piller"
Issue 5, February 1996: "Kate Mulgrew," "Brannon Braga"

Sci-Fi Entertainment

Vol. 2, No. 4, 1994: "In the Footsteps of Spock"
Vol. 1, No. 5, 1995: "The One and Only Katherine Janeway"

Time

January 16, 1995: "Paramount and Warner Networks"
February 27, 1995: "To Boldly Go Where Seven Movies and 300-Plus TV Shows Have Gone Before"

TV Guide

October 8–14, 1994: "*Voyager*—A 'Star Trek' Is Born," "Where No Woman Has Gone Before," "Bon *Voyager*"
April 8–14, 1995: "What's up, Doc?"
February 17, 1996: Special Star Trek issue

Other Sources

"Colors of Loyalty," *Starlog*, Issue 213, April 1995

"Interview with Jeri Taylor," *Dreamwatch*, December 1995

"Getting Inside the Vulcan Mind," *The Age*, April 25, 1996

"Mulgrew Ready for Challenge of Trek Captain," *Houston Chronicle*, January 15, 1995

"Old Problems Rear Their Heads in New Ways with the Latest Star Trek Spin-Off" *SFX Futurenet*

"On Our Cover," *Working Mother*, September, 1995

"Paramount Syndication Plans," *Broadcasting & Cable*, November 28, 1994

"Q&A on Bujold's Quitting," *Parade Magazine*, November 27, 1994

Special Star Trek Issue, *Cinefantastique*, January 1996

"Star Trek, Boldly Voyaging," *Sci-Fi Universe*, Issue 10, October 1995

"TV Doctors, Then and Now" (with section on Robert Picardo), *People*, July 17, 1995

"UPN Bows Big Behind *Voyager*," *Variety*, January 17, 1995

"UPN Beats…Everybody," *Broadcasting & Cable*, January 23, 1995

"The Voyage Continues," *Orbit*, January 1995

"*Voyager* Off to a Smart Start," *USA Today*, January 16, 1995

"Voyager's Beltran Proud to Uphold Trek Tradition," *L.A. Life*, April 8–14, 1995

Index